LOEB CLASSICAL MONOGRAPHS

❦ ❦ ❦ ❦

In Memory of
JAMES C. LOEB

STYLE AND TRADITION IN CATULLUS

David O. Ross, Jr.

❧ ❧ ❧ ❧

HARVARD UNIVERSITY PRESS

CAMBRIDGE, MASSACHUSETTS · 1969

*The Loeb Classical Monographs are
published with assistance from the
Loeb Classical Library Foundation.*

Distributed in Great Britain by Oxford University Press, London

Library of Congress Catalog Card Number 69–18043

SBN 674–85340–7

Printed in Great Britain

D M
Russell A. Edwards
si quicquam mutis gratum acceptumve sepulcris

PREFACE

The substance of this book was presented as a doctoral dissertation at Harvard University in the spring of 1966; the summary published then (*HSCP* 71 [1966] 344–46) will not be misleading. Subsequent revisions have changed the presentation and organization of many parts, and certain entirely new sections have been added. I have thought it best, however, to keep to the original format and purpose. Though I realize only too well the shortcomings of dissertation style and form, and though much of what I have to say will be lost or seem irrelevant to a reader only generally familiar with the history of Latin poetry, the addition of background material and a more complete discussion of the Neoterics and their importance would have obscured the fairly simple conclusions I offer for the consideration of scholars.

My greatest single debt is to the American Academy in Rome, where the original thesis was written; as a Fellow for two years (1964–1966), I enjoyed the luxury of leisure and the stimulation of Rome itself. Without the prospect of two uninterrupted years I could not have indulged myself in following so many blind trails, and so would not have happened upon those few which led somewhere. Among the many friends from whose advice and conversation I profitted directly or indirectly during that time, I can mention here only Miss Berthe Marti and *il professore* Warren Myers. I am happy to be able to add my name to the long list of those who have acknowledged the patient help of Mrs. Nina Longobardi, the soul and spirit of the Academy's Library, and to offer final thanks to its Director, Frank E. Brown.

Many individuals are named in my notes for help on specific problems. Extensive comments and corrections were offered by C. P. Jones; and G. P. Goold produced, with customary delight, a list of "howlers" and many precise suggestions for improvement. My thanks are due, too, to the scholarly readers of Harvard University Press, and to Mrs. Dorothy Souvaine for her careful editing. I alone, of course, assume full responsibility for whatever blunders and misconceptions remain.

Acknowledgment is hereby made to B. G. Teubner Verlag, Stuttgart, for permission to quote extensively from E. Norden, *P. Vergilius Maro Aeneis, Buch VI;* to C. W. K. Gleerup, Lund, for permission to quote from B. Axelson, *Unpoetische Wörter;* and to the Clarendon Press for permission to use the text of Catullus of R. A. B. Mynors, *C. Valerii Catulli Carmina.*

It remains to offer inadequate thanks to W. V. Clausen, who read with care the original thesis and each subsequent addition and revision, and whose friendship has meant encouragement at every stage. To his example I owe as much as to his teaching.

To my wife, who has long endured, belongs my final word of appreciation; her patience has provided more support than she can realize.

D. O. R., Jr.

New Haven, Connecticut
January 1969

CONTENTS

CONTENTS

STYLE AND TRADITION IN CATULLUS

INTRODUCTION

This study of Catullus is divided into two parts, each of which represents an attempt to restate, clarify, and answer on a new basis certain questions about his poetry which have not previously received proper attention. The first part deals with Catullus' poetic vocabulary and its distribution in the three parts of his work (the polymetric poems 1–60, the longer poems 61–68, and the epigrams 69–116), and forms the basis for the questions raised in the second part concerning the relation of each group of poems to each other and to the literary traditions in which they were written. It is hoped that the study of the poetic vocabulary will help to settle not only such problems as the split personality attributed for so long to Catullus, learned Alexandrian and subjective lyricist, *doctus poeta* and the passionate poet of love, elegant versifier and rough improvisor; but will also establish, by a re-examination of his antecedents, the proper place of his poetry in Latin literary history and will lead to some new interpretations of certain obscure aspects of this history.

Some explanation and apology must be given for a study of Catullus' poetic vocabulary: the vocabulary of his poems is one aspect which is usually considered to have received full attention. Almost half a century ago K. P. Schulze published an exhaustive survey of the vocabulary appended to a review of recent Catullan scholarship, a survey based for the most part on the work of previous editors,[1] and since then more has been done.[2] Yet, in addition to the fact that the poetic vocabulary *per se* has never been systematically treated, two important shortcomings in all studies of the vocabulary must be mentioned.

The first failure of these studies is that they have never attempted

[1] *Bursian's Jahresb.* 183 (1920) 47–72. Schulze refers to the collections of examples in the introductions to the editions of Baehrens, Riese, Schmidt, and throughout the commentaries of Friedrich and Ellis.

[2] One such study devoted entirely to a special aspect of the vocabulary may be mentioned here: H. Heusch, *Das Archaische in der Sprache Catulls* (Bonn 1954). Numerous other points have been treated in the literature to be cited throughout.

a systematic answer to one important question (perhaps the most important for an understanding and appreciation of Catullus' poetry): what is the relation of the three groups of Catullus' poems? The second is in part an explanation of the first failure: no single category of the vocabulary has as yet been isolated which would indicate, without a doubt, how and why one group of poems differs from another; therefore it had not appeared possible that there was any thorough difference in the vocabulary of the separate groups of poems which would allow valid distinctions to be made. We have been told little more than that the vocabulary of the epyllion c. 64 is epic, that the shorter poems are colloquial.

Colloquial features, for example, form one category that has received much attention, yet every list of such elements leads one to think that they belong primarily in the polymetrics and epigrams (the "shorter poems", as these two groups are together often called), though they can be found frequently enough even in the longer, "learned" poems;[3] and indeed diminutives, which are commonly taken simply as a colloquial feature, occur frequently in both the polymetrics and longer poems but rarely in the epigrams. No satisfactory conclusions can be reached simply by collecting examples of colloquialisms in Catullus: even such further refinements as separating, when possible, vulgarisms from elevated colloquialisms add little. Too often it has been forgotten that Catullus, a poet, both inherited and molded, re-worked and added to, a flexible literary language already formed by different traditions and genres, in which any element which we might coldly classify as colloquial may have had a far more valid place as a poeticism.

---

[3] See J. Svennung (*Catulls Bildersprache*, Uppsala Universitets Årsskrift 1945: 3, p. 24) for a sampling of previous scholars who made no distinction between the polymetrics and epigrams (Svennung's correction of this view is of the utmost importance). A. L. Wheeler, for instance, could write (*Catullus and the Traditions of Ancient Poetry* [Berkeley 1934], 58) ". . . the conclusion which emerges from all the evidence is that Catullus viewed all the little poems including the elegiacs as constituting one general group." Wheeler, again, is not unique in basing his view of the stylistic unity of "the shorter poems" on the colloquialisms they seem to contain (p. 50): "The most striking feature of the style of the short poems is colloquialism (often vulgarism), an element which is infrequently present in the long poems (e.g., LXI, LXVII). Now this colloquial element is not confined to one group of the little poems as against the other, but pervades them both alike—the elegiacs and the lyric group. . . . Certainly the two groups are connected by the bond of a common style."

H. Tränkle has recently performed a great service to Propertius by analyzing in detail, in the context of the poetic language, many of the "vulgarisms" previously thought to mar his poetic diction.[4] The problem is in part a semantic one, for poetic diction is thought to be an artificial process of refinement culminating in Virgil, Horace, and the Augustan elegists, into which any vulgarism had crept only while the poet nodded or had been driven to distraction by impossible metrical demands. It must be recognized, however, that there is a thread of unrefined colloquialisms running throughout Catullus' poetry, but especially that many of these colloquialisms are, in different ways, special poeticisms. The problem is to discover, where possible, what sort of poeticisms they are, and how and why they were so used by the poet.

Archaisms are another category which can prove nothing about Catullus' poetry or the relationship of one group of poems to another: archaisms can be found in any group, and can be as numerous as the investigator is inclined to stretch the heading. It is far more important to consider why any such element is so used, and even the question of whether a certain word or usage is an archaism or a current rusticity is less important than the question of its place and purpose in its poetic setting.

It is not sufficient, then, merely to list such features as colloquialisms or archaisms in Catullus, for they will be found throughout his work and may or may not be indicative of any poetic purpose. If it can be assumed that there is a difference between the three groups of Catullus' poems (an assumption always made but as yet ill-defined and with debatable results), and that the poet, for instance, wrote one poem in hendecasyllables and another, perhaps on the same theme and in much the same manner, in distichs not for mere metrical variation but because there was a genuine poetic difference between the two meters and the way in which each was regarded and treated by the poet, then we may expect to find a difference in the poetic language of the two poems. Difference in genre, as Horace notes when distinguishing his

---

[4] *Die Sprachkunst des Properz und die Tradition der Lateinischen Dichtersprache*, Hermes Einzelschriften 15 (1960).

and Lucilius' satiric hexameters from the epic hexameters of Ennius (*Sat.* 1.4.56–62), is not so much one of meter as of simple vocabulary. If Catullus' purpose in any group of poems can be ascertained, and if this group can be placed in an existing poetic tradition, then the poetic vocabulary should provide the means of doing so.

What is meant by "poetic vocabulary" will become apparent in the course of the discussion and need not be rigidly defined here. B. Axelson's important work is the source for much of what follows and his method the guiding principle for all.[5] The uniqueness of Axelson's studies lies not so much in any novelty of method,[6] but rather in that it is the first systematic attempt to outline what constituted a poetic (or unpoetic) word for the Latin poets. In so doing Axelson also demonstrates that it is possible to distinguish between genres solely on the basis of vocabulary, and that the history of any genre may be traced by studying the development of its vocabulary. The first part of this study, then, attempts to define the proper place in the development of the poetic language of certain words or types of words, to trace their origins to certain genres of poetry, and so to define the nature of the group of Catullus' poems in which they predominate. For instance, it is often possible to say without question that a certain word is "epic" by showing that it was first used (and for a particular purpose) by the early writers of epic hexameters and was subsequently used only by epic poets; it is also possible to attribute certain types of words to the neoteric poets and to be certain that such words reflect neoteric principles. It makes little difference whether these words or types of words are archaic or colloquial as long as the poetic principles which led to their introduction and use by certain poets for a certain genre can be defined and understood. It is assumed here that the study of poetic vocabulary may hold the key to an understanding of the origin and poetic nature of any of the three groups of Catullus' poems

---

[5] *Unpoetische Wörter, Ein Beitrag zur Kenntnis der Lateinischen Dichtersprache*, Skrifter Utgivna av Vetenskaps-Societeten i Lund 29 (1945). The most important review is that by Ernout (*Rev Phil* [1947] 55–70); it is remarkable that this work has never been reviewed in an English or American journal.

[6] What Axelson does has long been an essential part of literary scholarship, as he himself acknowledges when he begins his study with a citation from Lachmann's commentary on Lucretius.

and may be used to place them in the literary tradition to which they belong.

The following study of Catullus' poetic vocabulary is not intended to be exhaustive. There is no list here of all the poetic words of a certain type found in his poetry, no catalogue or index of, for example, Ennian or neoteric words. To have attempted such lists would have been as pointless as compiling lists of archaic or colloquial features. For one thing, the text of Catullus is too small to allow any reliance on the appearance of any one word in any one group of poems: a study of Wetmore's *Index Verborum Catullianus*, for instance, will produce many words instantly recognizable as epic which appear, perhaps, only in c. 64, or once or twice in the polymetrics or epigrams; no conclusions can be drawn from such random appearances. For this reason, few individual nouns, adjectives, or verbs have been discussed, even when they clearly belong to the vocabulary of a certain genre. On the other hand, certain types or formations of nouns or adjectives occur with a sufficiently high frequency to allow definite conclusions to be drawn from their distribution throughout Catullus' poetry, and the history and place of a particular type or formation can be recognized more easily and with greater certainty than that of any single word. The discussion has thus been restricted to words which are common enough (particles, conjunctions, prepositions) to provide reliable figures and whose history and development in the poetic vocabulary are well known, or to types of words which clearly indicate the purpose for which they were used in any group or groups of poems; even of the latter certain types have been omitted because their distribution provides no clear indication of the nature of any one of the three groups of poems.

It may be objected, then, that the following study presents only evidence which leads to and supports its ultimate conclusions. To a certain extent this is true, for evidence which has not delineated the character and poetic nature of any one of the three groups of poems has been carefully ignored: to have done otherwise would have led once again to meaningless lists of words whose distribution in Catullus was in no way significant. No evidence, however, which contradicts the final conclusions has been omitted; the process of selection has only limited the material to the significant, and of this everything points in the same direction.

This study of Catullus' poetic vocabulary, then, is not exhaustive but is rather intended to be suggestive. We cannot claim to be able to define the sphere and tone of more than a small fraction of his poetic vocabulary, and that only by a labored process at best; we must be satisfied if, in the process, we can suggest reasonable explanations for Catullus' use of this fraction. For this reason no exhaustive work on poetic vocabulary may ever be written, though this need not detract from the validity of the conclusions reached. Neither is this a statistical study: although figures for the occurrence of words in Catullus and other writers are a necessary part of the method, statistics by themselves may be misleading. For this reason there are few tables, even where they might have been of some help; each occurrence of a word must be controlled by the context in which it occurs and by its purpose (when it can be inferred) in that context. Furthermore, all figures are only relative: one word or form occurring six times in a group of poems or an author may be viewed as being relatively infrequent, while another form occurring three times in the same lines may have to be regarded as frequent; the standards for comparison must be set for each word or type discussed.

Finally, an obvious difficulty: when comparing the frequency of certain words in the three groups of Catullus' poems, it must be kept in mind that the groups vary greatly in length. The polymetrics 1–60 have 848 lines; the longer poems 61–68 have a total of 1120 lines (the elegiacs 65–68, 325 lines); and the epigrams 69–116, 319 lines. It will often appear that the absolute figures (unconverted to percentages) presented here are deliberately misleading: it has seemed better, however, to run this risk in order to emphasize both common sense and context—statisticians may be forced to conclude that even percentages can often give a misleading impression. There are too many factors involved (linguistic, literary—including metrical considerations—, the individual preference of any author) to allow a simple unexamined statement of the figures of the occurrence of any item to carry much weight. As an example, if the statement is made that a word occurs 9 times in the polymetrics and only 3 times in the epigrams 69–116, it is obviously wrong to gain a quick impression (*culpa nostra*) that there is a great difference between the two groups of poems in the use they make of this word; and yet it may be equally wrong to rely on the fact that, statistically, the word is equally frequent in both groups: the word may appear in only one or two of the epigrams, and those epigrams may be very different from the great majority of the others—and may in fact be recognizable, from other similarities in vocabulary and stylistic features, as experimental polymetrics in epigrammatic form. Once again, this is not a statistical study.

It is most important that the method here employed not be confused with Catullus' method as a poet. For Catullus, the language in which he wrote was a living element, to be worked and refined by his mind and ear, to which his every response was natural and immediate; the demands made upon poetic vocabulary by each genre, and the limits set by any genre, were likewise a natural part of the education and sensibility of every good poet. For us there can be no immediate response, but only a slow intellectual awareness of what must have been the tone or sphere of propriety of a certain word. Catullus never had to ask himself whether it was permissible, according to the rules of the genre in which he was writing a poem, to use *atque* in a certain way: his response was direct. Nothing which follows should be taken to imply an artificially conscious effort on the part of the poet: where the word "conscious" (or the like) is used of Catullus' selection of vocabulary, it should be taken to mean a natural, though in part intellectual, response to the traditions of earlier poetry and to all that formed the technical distinctions between existing genres, the force of which is for us hard to imagine and understand.

A point must now be raised which concerns both the first and second parts of this study. It is assumed that the three parts into which our manuscripts divide the existing poems of Catullus reflect the poet's intention, that is, that Catullus himself may have divided his work into three distinct groups of poems. A. L. Wheeler has studied this problem most fully,[7] and his conclusion is bluntly negative: "Catullus himself is not responsible for the three main groups of poems as they stand in our collection."[8] To Wheeler's summary of the external evidence nothing can be added here by way of proof or disproof, and the basic assumption of this study must contradict Wheeler only by indifference and by pragmatic, if somewhat circular, reasoning based on internal evidence. It is not entirely necessary to assume that Catullus himself arranged his poems in three groups for the purpose of an edition; but that he considered his polymetric poems or the longer poems to be of a very different nature from his epigrams seems unquestionable. Proof, however, must come from the discussion of the poetic vocabulary and other stylistic points.

Thus far, too, the word genre has been used loosely, and a strict definition and description of various genres might appear necessary. Such distinctions, however, can be pressed too far, and it is a mistake to assume that Catullus differentiated between genres in the same

---

[7] *Catullus and the Traditions*, chap. I, "The History of the Poems," 1–32; the important bibliography to the question is given throughout the notes to this chapter, but esp. 249, n. 4. See now the thorough review of the problem by I. K. Horváth, "*Catulli Veronensis Liber*," *Acta Antiqua* 14 (1966) 141–73, an interesting and valuable survey which, unfortunately, has been brought to my attention too late to be of help in this study.

[8] Wheeler sees the arrangement of our text as a later compilation: "Our collection is best explained as derived from an edition of Catullus which was put together not earlier than the second or third century" (p. 32). Though proof is not available, it might be objected that this is a strangely late date for a collected edition of so important a poet. Had Virgil read the epyllion only in a "monobiblos", or did Martial know Catullus only from a collection of the polymetric pieces? Even assuming that the entire text was too much for a single roll, surely several rolls must have contained the poems in much the same three groups as we now have them, and these must have gone back, if not to the poet himself, to some time shortly after his death. For the latest discussion of this question see H. Tränkle, *Mus Helv* 24 (1967) 100–103, who argues for an arrangement of the poems by Catullus himself. My own conclusions (which cannot be argued here) I now find agree with Horváth (p. 164 n. 74): "Nous avons la conviction que deux recueils de poésies de Catulle parurent de son vivant même: les *nugae* (contenant en gros les poésies de I à LX, telles que nous les connaissons aujourd'hui) et les *epigrammata* (comprenant les pièces de LXIX à CXVI) qui constituaient deux recueils absolument indépendant l'un de l'autre. Par la suite, ces deux recueils furent en partie complétés, en partie précédemment réunis aux pièces de la partie dite médiane—tout porte à croire que ces pièces avaient déjà été publiées précédemment, une par une—par un ami ou un admirateur du poète après la morte de ce dernier, de façon que la partie médiane constitue une transition, du point de vue métrique, entre les deux petits recueils." This position, Horváth notes, is basically Friedrich's.

manner as did previous poets, Greek or Latin,—equally a mistake to attempt to confine his poetry to the boundaries of genre established by poets of even the next generation. As Wheeler notes: "There had been ample time for genres to develop and decay. In literature definite distinctions do not persist forever. But some give way sooner than others, and new distinctions arise. At any given period there are always confusions, nebulous regions."[9] To attempt to distinguish between epithalamium, hymn, invective, lyric, elegy, and epigram is a difficult and, more often than not, pointless task, for there is absolutely no evidence that Catullus saw these distinctions as the most important: for instance, a hymn form can appear in an invective poem, and the attempt to distinguish between lyric, elegy, and epigram has led Catullan scholarship into a nearly hopeless muddle. Catullus never calls his epigrams by a collective name, nor does he ever hint at a form or genre of elegy: there is no sense in applying, by force, the distinctions (sometimes real, sometimes obviously artificial) of later poets and grammarians until we can be sure, by applying other criteria, that they were valid, and in what way they were valid, for Catullus.

The distinction between epigram and elegy, the origins of the latter, and which poems of Catullus are to be considered elegies, have been much discussed for a long time. For instance, Rothstein considered that certain poems of Catullus broke the genre restrictions, namely cc. 72, 73, 99, 107, and 109,[10] and Wheeler states emphatically, "We have from Catullus only five elegies (including the translation from Callimachus): LXV–LXVIII, and LXXVI—a total of 402 lines."[11] A solution to these difficulties will be offered in different terms in the second part of this study, but the question may be raised here whether we are justified in discussing, using terms which Catullus never mentions, distinctions of genre based on subject matter and the treatment of themes. Content provides only a hazardous basis for settling such

[9] *Catullus and the Traditions*, 33.
[10] M. Rothstein, *Die Elegien des Sextus Propertius* (Berlin 1898) xxi: "Zwar ist die Scheidewand zwischen beiden Gattungen hier und da durchbrochen worden; namentlich von einzelnen Gedichten des Catull (72.73.99.107.109) wird man nicht mit Sicherheit sagen können, ob sie ausgeführte Epigramme oder kurze Elegien sind."
[11] *Catullus and the Traditions*, 166. It is worth noting in passing that Wheeler considered c. 67 an "elegy".

questions, yet the discussion continues mostly along these lines. It is clear, for instance, that as far as content is concerned, many polymetric poems have their counterparts among the epigrams, whether invective, erotic, or otherwise. What, however, distinguished the two groups of poems? Why is one of the two poems of similar content considered a lyric, the other an epigram or even an elegy? It would seem that unrealistic definitions of genres and an unjustified reliance upon content or theme or treatment to differentiate between genres have hopelessly confused the issue. If Catullus himself tells us nothing on such points, it would seem better to assume that such distinctions were perhaps unimportant to him and to try to understand, from the internal mechanics of his verse rather than from later external and often artificial criteria, where he stood in the historical development of the forms in which he wrote.

The word genre will thus disappear as much as possible from the following discussion, and when it does appear it should be regarded as a loose convenience rather than as a technical term. Cc. 69–116 are called "epigrams" throughout this study, but (it should be remembered that Catullus had no collective name that we know of for these poems) this too is more a matter of convenience than an attempt to place them all in one rigidly defined genre: there is no greater need to see a unity of genre in this last group than there is in the "polymetrics" or "longer poems", again terms of convenience. The unifying characteristics of these three groups must be found in the developing literary traditions to which each belongs. Thus, though the term epyllion almost certainly was not used by Alexandrian Greeks or Augustan Romans, the type of poetry we designate by this label existed in a clearly definable form: we may use this term as long as it is clear that it is to be applied as a convenience (as are the others we have adopted) to a literary tradition.

This investigation will thus be concerned, particularly in the second part, with tracing the various traditions active for Catullus. K. Quinn has suggested certain lines of development:[12] after acknowledging the existence of Greek influences (both classical and Hellenistic), he describes three lines of Roman poetic tradition, the "epic-tragic," the

---

[12] *The Catullan Revolution* (Melbourne Univ. Press 1959) 7–18.

"comic-satiric," and a "third element," that of the "slighter genres, such as the epigram." Though he makes little attempt to justify the reality of these terms and does not discuss in any detail how Catullus' poetry reflects these traditions, the approach is nevertheless more accurate and realistic than that of strict reliance upon the development of specific genres.

It seems advisable, however, to be even less specific. There is no question that Catullus was a neoteric poet. Is it possible to arrive at a definition of what constituted neoteric poetry? The neoterics were, by contemporary definition, writing a new sort of verse. What was new in what they wrote, and what was old? If a study of poetic vocabulary and other stylistic features will show how their poetry was new, then the absence or disregard of recognizable neoteric features will indicate the old. It must be remembered, however, first that the *poetae novi* wrote very different kinds of verse, ranging from the epyllion (the masterwork expected of every aspiring new poet) to informal occasional poems addressed to friends or enemies—therefore, though certain elements definable as neoteric will appear in all neoteric verse, some will predominate in the more formal verse, some in the less formal— and secondly that neoteric features may be derived from more than one tradition, that is, that the new poets may have adopted certain features from the epic-tragic tradition, others from the comic-satiric, making such terms useful only for tracing the origin of any feature that should, for Catullus, more properly be called simply neoteric. *Ex nihilo nihil fit*, and by this principle what was new for the neoterics was so only by virtue of its being accepted according to the principles by which they wrote; conversely, what was old must be defined as that which they did not accept: an element which had its origin in the epic verse of Ennius, for instance, may still be properly considered a neoteric mannerism.

It is worth repeating that this study will be confined to certain technical features (the vocabulary and other stylistic elements) of Catullus' verse in the belief that only in this way can a valid under-standing of the nature and the place in the literary traditions of each group of poems be gained. The dispute has long continued over the question of which poems represent the *doctus poeta*, the Alexandrian poet of elegance and learning, and which the lyrical, passionate Catullus, but, though recently the two poetic personalities have been made to merge,[13] the whole discussion may be considered to be largely misspent effort. The related question of the nature of each group of poems has also been discussed in terms which are all too subjective and therefore invite dispute, and which often depend on vague external considerations. Ilse Schnelle writes: "Die Epigramme unterscheiden sich grundlegend von den Polymetren dadurch, dass ihnen objektive, bleibende Sachverhalte zugrunde liegen, die unabhängig vom Dichter und vom Zeitmoment bestehen, und dass Catull Objektives über sie aussagen will; er äussert über sie Gedanken, Urteile—seltener Empfindungen—, stellt Beziehungen zwischen ihnen her: er denkt, reflektiert über sie."[14] There is a great deal of truth in these observations, but they express only the surface results of a far more essential process: it can be shown that the historical development of certain literary traditions produced the situation Schnelle observes.

Furthermore, failure to define the traditions as precisely as possible can lead to a misunderstanding of the proper relation of one group of Catullus' poems to another. La Penna[15] has recently referred to Hezel's study of Catullus' epigrams[16] and Schnelle's arguments[17] to conclude that "Negli epigrammi, dunque, prevale una tradizione culturale ellenistica, nei polimetri una latina,"[18] but behind this conclusion lie

---

[13] See, for instance, E. A. Havelock, *The Lyric Genius of Catullus* (Oxford 1939); J. P. Elder, "Notes on Some Conscious and Subconscious Elements in Catullus' Poetry," *HSCP* 60 (1951) 101–36; and M. Putnam, "The Art of Catullus 64," *HSCP* 65 (1961) 165–205. Other literature pertinent to the question is cited elsewhere in this study.

[14] *Untersuchungen zu Catulls dichterischer Form, Philologus*, Supplementband 25, Heft 3 (1933) 72. The psychological approach of this study has often been criticized for its subjectivity.

[15] A. La Penna, "Problemi di Stile Catulliano," *Maia* 8 (1956) 141–60.

[16] O. Hezel, *Catull und das Griechische Epigramm, Tübinger Beiträge zur Altertumswissenschaft* 17 (1932).

[17] La Penna summarizes, "Gli epigrammi presentano rispetto ai polimetri un'arte più elaborata e più composta: maggior numero di metafore, simmetria ed equilibrio delle parti, mentre i polimetri hanno per lo più un movimento impetuoso, incomposto, assimetrico" (147). Much of this statement, however, is debatable.

[18] P. 150. This statement is cited as a convenient summary of the prevailing view of the traditions represented by these two groups of poems.

only the observations that Hellenistic epigram (as represented in Rome by Antipater of Sidon and Meleager) must have something to do with Catullus' epigrams, and that in both Laevius and Catullus' polymetrics diminutives are frequent (neither of these arguments is discussed in any detail). The conclusion reached in this study is the exact opposite of La Penna's.

It must be admitted, finally, that the difficulties and dangers in discussing the traditions of Catullus' poetry are almost overwhelming. His is the only neoteric verse we possess to any considerable extent.[19] Of pre-neoteric epigram we possess only a handful of poems, so unfertile a field in which to work that no substantial study devoted exclusively to these poems has ever been published;[20] it is hoped, however, that the study of the vocabulary and technique of Catullus' epigrams (in contrast to the polymetric and longer poems) will provide a new understanding of this obscure area. The danger of reconstructing an almost nonexistent tradition (that of pre-neoteric epigram) from Catullus and then using the reconstruction to explain Catullus is all too obvious, but the attempt may be justified on the grounds that all the evidence used in doing so comes from poetic technique, from vocabulary and elements of style, and not from external suppositions, that the final result is consistent, and that some of the contradictions and perplexities associated with the present state of Catullan scholarship disappear and other problems are resolved.

[19] That is, contemporary neoteric verse: much, however, can be learned from Virgil and others (though by Virgil's generation neoteric principles had been to a great extent transformed and restated), and the *Culex* and *Ciris* can be regarded as examples of neoteric epyllia written by retarded poets who had missed the show by a generation or two. In the course of this study I do not refer to "the neoterics" unadvisedly; when, for instance, some stylistic feature of Catullus is set down as an "innovation of the neoterics", there has always been some reason (though often little real evidence) for viewing it not simply as an individual mannerism. Calvus, for example, is so implicated in the language of c. 50 that we might easily ascribe the poem to him; and Catullus' epyllion could not, stylistically, have been very different from other neoteric epyllia.

[20] The most extensive discussion of Aedituus, Licinus, and Catulus is that of H. Bardon in *La Littérature Latine Inconnue* I (Paris 1952) 115–32, of which only part is devoted to the epigrams; the literary histories and handbooks grant only passing notice to these epigrams. Our only other examples of pre-neoteric epigrams (*CIL* 4.4966–73) have been virtually ignored.

I· THE POETIC VOCABULARY

THE POETIC VOCABULARY

COMPOUNDS AND DIMINUTIVES

At the end of the first chapter of *Catulls Bildersprache*,[1] J. Svennung introduces the subject of diminutives, compound adjectives, and *hapax legomena* to point out an important and long neglected aspect of the corpus of Catullus: when these types of words are considered, the three groups into which the poems have found themselves divided show a marked correspondence between the first (the polymetric poems 1–60) and second (the longer poems 61–68); the third (the epigrams 69–116) stands by itself.[2] As a basis for further investigation, compounds and diminutives in Catullus may be briefly considered.

[1] Uppsala Universitets Årsskrift 1945: 3, pp. 31–33.

[2] "Aus den obigen Ausführungen dürfte hervorgegangen sein, dass Catulls Epigramme nicht nur durch das Metrum, sondern oft auch durch bewusste formale und stilistische Ausgestaltung von den Polymetra und grösseren Gedichten des Dichters geschieden worden sind," Svennung, p. 34. These remarks have not gone unnoticed: see J. P. Elder, "Notes on Some Conscious and Subconscious Elements in Catullus' Poetry," *HSCP* 60 (1951) 111–12, who, however, seems to misinterpret the evidence by noting only the marked difference between the polymetrics and the epigrams and overlooking the important connection between the polymetrics and the longer poems: "This whole matter needs further study. But certain conclusions seem obvious even now. The chief one is that Catullus was highly conscious of the traditional elements in the epigram, and, in certain respects in his epigrams, is closer to his usage in the longer poems, whereas in his polymetrics he was far more easygoing and informal" (p. 112).

It is worth noting here a case history of the evolution of scholarly credulity. Svennung had obviously used Seitz' very incomplete list of compounds in Catullus (see below, n. 3) and Teufel's list of *hapax legomena* (below, n. 39): the vast majority of the latter are either diminutives or compounds, and thus are meaningless when used as a further independent support to the indicative distribution of compounds and diminutives in Catullus. Elder picked up Svennung's borrowed figures and important inferences, but somehow misinterpreted Svennung's words to link the longer poems and epigrams. Recently, J. Ferguson, in a review of the progress of Catullan scholarship since Wheeler's Sather Lectures ("Some Catullan Problems," *Proceedings of the African Classical Association* 8 (1965) 30), cited yet again Svennung's figures (including the irrelevant figures for *hapax legomena*), omitted conveniently all mention of the number of compounds and diminutives in the longer poems, and in conclusion echoed Elder's slip, "In fact stylistically the epigrams are closer to the longer poems than they are to the polymetrics." It will be interesting to watch for further progress in this not unimportant aspect of Catullan scholarship.

Catullus has 14 compound adjectives used 15 times in the polymetrics, 29 used 35 times in the longer poems, but only *sesquipedalis*
(97.5) in the epigrams.[3] *Sesquipedalis* can be dismissed immediately as a
prose word:[4] it can be safely said that there are no poetic compounds
in the epigrams.

The history of compounds in Latin poetry requires here only a
brief outline, as it is well known.[5] Livius Andronicus had made no
attempt (as far as we can see) to introduce Greek compounds to a
language natively hostile, and Naevius did little more.[6] It was Ennius

---

In a little over twenty years (since Svennung wrote) we have accepted (working all the
while with unchecked figures and one irrelevant set of statistics) what may be represented
as follows: if there are 25 examples of a particular phenomenon in group A, 50 in B, and
3 in C, then B and C are closely related, to the exclusion of A.

[3] For purposes of comparison and completeness, this count includes some which should
not be considered as proper poetic compounds (see discussion below and n. 21). However,
I have omitted *mirifice* (53.2, 71.4, 84.3) from this count; it is doubtful whether, as a prose
word, it should be included in a list of what were essentially poetic compounds. (See
Fordyce on 53.2, "The colloquially emphatic variation on *mire* is common in Cicero's
letters;" Kroll on 84.3, "*mirifice* gehört der Umgangssprache an und ist daher in Poesie
und höherer Prosa selten;" Axelson, p. 61, who finds it elsewhere in the poets only in
Ovid *Pont.* 4.13.5; and Hofmann, *Lat. Umgangssprache*[3], 78.) Svennung's list of compounds is in a sad state of disrepair. He omits three compounds in the polymetrics, and
his list of compounds in c. 64 (which he does not call a selection) omits 11 of the 17; he
claims none for c. 66, which actually has three. Perhaps his source is at fault ("Wir besitzen
über diese Wörter eine Materialsammlung von Fr. Seitz," *De adiectivis poetarum Latinorum
compositis*, Diss. Bonn 1878).

[4] See Lewis and Short. The word seems to appear in verse only twice elsewhere, Hor.
Ars P. 97 in a mock technical sense; and Mart. 7.14.10, *mentula cui nondum sesquipedalis
erat*, a Catullan echo.

[5] Cooper, *Word Formation in the Roman Sermo Plebeius* (New York 1895) 298–300,
notes the poverty of the language in this respect, but would connect the introduction of
compounds, especially by the dramatists, with "the greater freedom afforded by the
popular speech" in coining compounds. For compounds in early Latin poetry (with a good
list) see C. C. Coulter, "Compound Adjectives in Early Latin Poetry," *TAPA* 47 (1916)
153–72; for the Augustan poets (with an Index of compounds in elegy, Ovid *Met.*,
Virg. *Aen.*, which unfortunately includes many words which would never have been
considered compounds by the poets), J. C. Glenn, "Compounds in Augustan Elegy and
Epic", *CW* 29 (1936) 65–69, 73–77, a fine specimen of the statistical method run wild
(*fumum ex fulgore*); on Virgil's compounds and their development see Norden, *Aen. VI*[4],
esp. pp. 176–77 and 325 (*ex fumo lucem*). For a fine discussion of compounds in *-fer* and
-ger, see the study by J. C. Arens, *Mnemos.* 3 (1950) 241–62.

[6] For example, Livius renders πολύτροπον by *versutum*, and omits the epithet in translating *Od.* 6.142 (ἦ γούνων λίσσοιτο λαβὼν εὐώπιδα κούρην) *utrum genua amploctens
virginem oraret* (Morel, *FPL* 17). Naevius has, among others *arquitenens* (Morel, *FPL* 30)
=τοξοφόρος and *suavisonus* (*Trag.* 20 Ribbeck) = ἡδυβόης.

who, with the introduction of the hexameter, made a place for compounds in epic and led the dramatists to increase their number. Plautus uses compounds mostly *tragice*, and Terence has very few, limiting them largely to the prologues—an interesting indication of how they were viewed by a purist. Their later history in poetry is summed up succinctly by Norden: "Mit der freien Wortkomposition sind die augusteischen Dichter, da die sprachschöpferischen Versuche früherer Dichter (zuletzt der Neoteriker), die lateinische Sprache nach dem Muster der griechischen zu bereichern, durch das Verdikt der Analogisten, speziell Caesars, gebrandmarkt waren, äusserst zurückhaltend; erst die zweite neoterische Schule, seit Hadrian, wird wieder freier."[7] Tibullus, for example, has only two compound adjectives,[8] Horace only a few in the *Odes*.[9] It can be assumed that compounds belong generally to tragedy and epic. The fact that there are none in the fragments of epigram of Aedituus, Licinus, and Catulus is reinforced by their virtual absence from the epigrams of Catullus.

In this setting, then, it is not surprising to find so many compounds in the longer poems of Catullus. All those in c. 64 are of a well defined type. There are three each in *-sonus*[10] and *-gena*,[11] two each in *-ficus*[12]

---

[7] *Aen. VI* pp. 176–77.

[8] In Tibullus, I have found only *imbrifer* (1.4.44) and *magnificus* (2.6.11), which is perhaps not a poetic compound (see above, n. 3, on *mirifice*) or is used *tragice* for comic effect: *magna loquor, sed magnifice mihi magna locuto / excutiunt clausae fortia verba fores*. Lygdamus adds *aurifer* (3.3.29), *mortifer* (3.5.9), *quadrupes* (3.7.128), and *tergeminus* (3.4.88).

[9] On Horace's unique Greek coinage from two noun stems, see Norden, *Aen. VI* p. 325: "So hat auch Horaz, wie bemerkt [p. 177], eine für ihn singuläre Art der Komposition nach griechischen Muster (*tauriformis*) nur gewagt in dem enkomiastischen Dithyrambus pindarischen Stils 4, 14, 25 (vgl. 4, 2, 9f. von Pindar: *per audacis nova dithyrambos verba devolvit*)." On *pomifer* (also *Odes* 4.7.11) see Kiessling-Heinze on *Odes* 3.23.8, "*pomifer* das einzige Adj. dieser Bildung bei H., der die bei Virgil und Ovid so beliebten Komposita mit *-fer* und *-ger* sonst gänzlich meidet." Horace seems to have coined the compounds *bimaris, centiceps, centimanus, triformis* (see A. Waltz, *Des Variations de la langue et de la métrique d'Horace* (Paris 1881) 69–70).

[10] *Fluenti-* 52, *clari-* 125, *rauci-* 263; on the early type (Naev., Enn., Lucr., Cic.) see Norden, p. 281.

[11] *Troiu-* 355, *Nysi-* 252, *uni-* 300; see Norden, p. 177.

[12] *Ampli-* 265, *iusti-* 406; Coulter (158) notes that this is the most numerous class in early Latin poetry.

and -*animus*,[13] and one each in -*ger*, -*fer*, and -*potens*.[14] *caelicola* (386) first appears in Ennius and is the reserved property of epic.[15] *primaevus* (401) translates πρωθήβης,[16] and *veridicus* (306, 326) and *multiplex* (250, 304) were acceptable poetic compounds, perhaps archaic.[17] Of the six compounds in c. 63, three are of standard formation (*hederiger* 23, *properipes* 34, *sonipes* 41[18]), but *nemorivagus* (72), *silvicultrix* (72), and *erifuga* (51), though not without later parallels,[19] are bolder coinages allowed by the neoteric foreignness of both meter and matter. C. 66 has *magnanimus* (26), *unigena* (53) and *unanimus* (80); it should be noted that *unigena* translates Callimachus' γνωτός, in this sense a Homeric word.[20] In c. 68 four compounds are found: *omnivolus* (140) and *multivolus* (128), though unique, are formations of the common type in *omni*- and *multi*-, perhaps more colloquial than poetic; *falsiparens* (112) is another translation from Callimachus (ψευδοπάτωρ, *Hymn* 6.98), fittingly used in the pentameter whose second half contains the Greek patronymic (*audit falsiparens Amphytryoniades*); and the lofty *caelicola* appears again (138). The longer poems, then, containing

---

[13] *Magn*- 85, first in Plaut. *Amph.* 213, but see Norden, p. 223, who notes Ennian contexts for it in Virg. (it translates the Homeric μεγάθυμος); *flex*- 330 (Pac. *Trag.* 177, 422 Ribbeck).

[14] *Coniger* 106, *letifer* 394, *omnipotens* 171. On -*ger* and -*fer*, see Norden, pp. 177 and 281: Virgil has many original compounds in these forms but was very sparing in coining other compounds, from which Norden assumes that these terminations had become a mere suffix. On the great freedom of the older poets in compositions in -*potens*, see Norden, p. 177.

[15] Enn. *Ann.* 491 V². ThLL sums up, "vitatur in sermone pedestri ante APUL.," which does not give a fair impression of the grandeur of the word: in the poets it is not found in Lucr., Hor., Tib., Prop.; in Virgil it is found only in *Aen.* (8 times), in Ovid only in *Met.* (2 times), in Lucan 4 times.

[16] Norden, p. 177, finds Virgil's apparent coinage *longaevus* (μακραίων) often in Ennian settings, and compares it with Catullus' *primaevus* ("vielleicht ebenfalls aus archaischer Poesie").

[17] *Veridicus* in Lucr. 6.6, 24, and *multiplex* in Lucr. 2.163, 4.207; such words occurring in both Cat. and Lucr. might suppose a common earlier source. *Multi*- is a common element for compounds, and *multiplex* occurs later twice in the *Aeneid* (4.189, 5.264) and Ovid *Met.* once.

[18] On compounds in -*pes*, see Norden, pp. 283–84 and 325; the -*pes* element is archaic, but he calls Virgil's invention *aeripes* (χαλκόπους) "eine Bildung im Stil Catulls."

[19] See Kroll *ad loc.*: *erifuga* is after *transfuga*; Virgil has *silvicola* (*Aen.* 10.551), Petr. (55.6) *pietaticultrix*, and Lucr. (2.597) *montivagus*.

[20] See L. & S., s.v. γνωτός, Pfeiffer (*Callimachus*) *ad loc.*, and E. Fraenkel, *Gnomon* 5 (1929) 267.

compounds are all those in which one might have expected to find them: neoteric and Alexandrian compositions.[21]

The correspondence between these longer poems and the polymetric poems is not surprising when the types of compounds and their contexts in the polymetrics are considered. There are four in -*fer*, all of them Catullan coinages: *Cytore buxifer* (4.13), *lasarpiciferis Cyrenis* (7.4), *sagittiferos Parthos* (11.6), and *amnis aurifer Tagus* (29.19) all occur in mannered geographical descriptions. The three compounds in -*pes* are likewise neoteric: *tardipedi deo* (36.7) is another coinage,[22] a clever circumlocution in a clever poem whose subject is neoteric poetry; both *pinnipes Perseus* (58^b.3) and *plumipedas* (58^b.5) are invented for the mythological conceit on the impossibility of finding Camerius. C. 11 also contains *septemgeminus Nilus* (11.7).[23] The effect of the heroic *magnanimi Remi nepotes* in the context of 58.5 is well known. *Unanimus* occurs twice in poems addressed to members of Catullus' circle (9.4, 30.1), in one of which the tone is sustained by *caelicolis* (30.4). Of the force of these words and the poet's intention in using them there is no question. Their contexts are as markedly neoteric as those of any of the compounds found in the longer poems; they are employed freely where the tone of the passage requires. There is, however, some question about the three other compounds in the polymetric poems, those in *semi*-. *Semimortuus* (50.15) occurs in the poem to Calvus dealing with their composition of *nugae* the night before, and in such a context a neoteric play on an elevated compound (such as *semianimis*), yet still preserving a tone of informality, would have its place; the word, though, does not occur again till Apuleius. Cc. 54 and 59 are poems of vulgar invective, but the epithet of the cremator (*semiraso . . . ustore*)

---

21 *Semihiante* (61.213) and *Noctifer* (62.7) are included in my count but are not taken account of in the discussion here. *Semihians* was probably not felt by Catullus as a poetic compound (see the discussion of *semi*- compounds below, pp. 21–22); and *Noctifer* is a proper name corresponding to the common *Lucifer*, also probably not regarded by the poet as a poetic formation. There are no other compounds in these two poems.

22 *Tardigradus* in Pac. *Trag.* 2 (Ribbeck).

23 Perhaps (see Kroll and Fordyce *ad loc.*) an adaptation of the epithets of the Nile employed by Aeschylus (ἑπτάρους, frg. 300 N.) and Moschus (ἑπτάπορος, 2.51; ἑπτάρροος was conjectured by Merkel at Ap. Rhod. 4.269 ("improbable", according to Fraenkel, *Gnomon* 34 [1962] 259). Norden (p. 325) is less specific, "ein dürftiger Versuch einer Übersetzung von ἑπτάρρος, ἑπτάστομος."

2

in the last line of c. 59 may be taken as identical in force to the *magnanimi* of the last line of c. 58 (this word also does not occur again until Apuleius); it is unlikely, however, that a similar case could be made out for *semilauta crura* (54.2). Svennung notes that these compounds are all "aus der Alltagssprache,"[24] and one might agree with him were it not for the fact that compounds with *semi-* are frequent in epic.[25] It is possible that two of these cases, at any rate, should be considered as mock elevated compounds which, though not poetic compounds themselves, have been formed as informal or colloquial analogies to poetic compounds: often in the polymetrics the colloquial forms only a facade over a careful and learned structure and vocabulary.

Catullus' use of compounds reveals the close relationship between the polymetrics and certain of the longer poems in tone and purpose and emphasizes the isolation of the epigrams, which in this appear to belong to a tradition of their own. It is certain, at least, that Catullus enjoyed a freedom in the polymetrics and longer poems which he did not allow himself in epigram.

While compounds are essentially a feature of poetic diction, diminutives are essentially a feature of colloquial Latin: that both types, so different in origin, appear with much the same frequency in the same two groups of Catullus' poems, is a good indication of the purposeful stylistic freedom of the neoterics.

The connection of diminutives with colloquial language has long been established, but at the same time their connection with poetry has been overstressed.[26] This view has been corrected by Axelson, who

---

[24] P. 32, but he gives no reference which supports this.

[25] Lucretius has *-animus, -fer, -marinus*; Virgil *-animis, -fer, -homo, -nex, -ustus*, all in the *Aeneid* and nowhere else; Luc. *-animis, -fer, -deus, -rutus, -vir, -ustus*; Ovid was particularly fond of these compounds, which occur in all his poems (*-adapertus, -animis, -bos, -caper, -crematus, -cremus, -deus, -fer, -homo, -lacer, -mas, -necis, -ramis, -ramius, -reductus, -refectus, -sepultus, -supinus, -ustus, -vir.*).

[26] See Löfstedt, *Synt.* II 336–38: they are "besonders in der Umgangs- und Volkssprache zu Hause . . .; sie sind gefühlsbetont, persönlich und daher nicht nur von der Volkssprache, sondern auch von den Dichtern beliebt." This is followed and expanded by Schmalz-Hofmann, 834–36 (with brief bibliography): "Der Unterschied zwischen der Volks- und Kunstsprache liegt darin, dass erstere die Diminutiv infolge ihrer häufigen Verwendung vielfach wahllos und in abgeschwächter Bedeutung verwendet, während die letztere sie mit Bedacht und zur feinen Charakterisierung gebraucht." See also Hofmann, *Lat. Umgangssprache*, 139–41.

finds diminutives used sparingly by the elegiac poets and rarely in epic, though they are of course more common in satire.[27] Catullus (with Horace in his *Satires* and *Epistles*) is the one poet always cited to illustrate the role of diminutives in poetry, and this too is corrected by Axelson, who says that Catullus' fondness for these forms is in part personal, in part due to the neoteric *Programm*;[28] he is correct in not crediting it to a colloquial tendency, because diminutives are common in the elevated longer poems (27 used 36 times). They are also very common in the polymetric poems (45 used 65 times) but uncommon in the epigrams (7 used 9 times).[29] These facts have always been recognized, but their interpretation, when not neglected, can be disputed.[30]

It is not necessary to discuss the use of single diminutives, for a glance at the list and at the context of each one will show how carefully

---

[27] Pp. 38–45, a long and valuable discussion, the details of which need not be repeated here. He concludes by noting that diminutive forms should have been useful metrically for the poets ("man vergleiche nur z.B. kretische—d.h. im Hexameter und Pentameter unmögliche—Formen wie *filios litterae pallidis* mit den unbequemen Choriamben *filiolos litterulae pallidulis*") but "ihr die Hände hier durch eine Stilregel besonderer Strenge gebunden waren" (p. 44).

[28] P. 39: "Auf Catull, dessen sattsam bekannte Vorliebe für Deminutiva am ehesten als eine persönliche, z.T. wohl auch dem Programm der Neoteriker entsprechende, Stilmanier zu betrachten ist (sogar in dem strenger stilisierten Epyllion sind sie ziemlich häufig, in den tändelnden nugae allerdings noch viel häufiger), brauchen wir nicht näher einzugehen." Here he is content to cite the list in Riese's edition, pp. XXV–VI, which concludes with the assertion, "Auch Catull wendet also das Diminutiv häufig, in der Umgangssprache aber doch noch häufiger als in den Gedichten und Einzelstellen höheren Stils."

[29] These figures correspond with the list given by S. P. Platner, "Diminutives in Catullus," *AJP* 16 (1895) 186–202. P. de Labriolle, "L'Emploi du Diminutif chez Catulle," *Rev Phil* 29 (1905) 277–88, would add *tremulus* and *mentula*, and Svennung, p. 31, seems to include also *auricula* (? at any rate, his total is one more than I have been able to find) in his figure for the epigrams. The question of whether certain diminutive formations (i.e., nouns or adjectives, like *mentula* or *tremulus*, which are formed from a positive not existing) should actually be considered diminutives is often hard to decide.

[30] Though the distribution of diminutives in Catullus has always been known, the very small number in the epigrams is often overlooked in a general statement about the shorter poems (cf. Kroll on 64.60, "Die Häufigkeit der Deminutiva in den kleinen Gedichten ist bekannt," or the statement by A. S. F. Gow, *CQ* 26 (1932) 155, cited below, n. 37). As an example of the neglect given the interpretation of this distribution see the remark of de Labriolle, p. 279: "Il n'y a rien d'important à remarquer sur la répartition des diminutifs dans les diverses pièces de Catulle. Il les emploie aussi volontiers dans les *nugae* que dans les longs poèmes où il donne tout son soin et toute sa mesure. . . . A partir de la pièce 70 jusqu'à la fin du recueil, nous n'en trouvons qu'un petit nombre: c'est sans doute l'effet d'un pur hasard."

they are used.[31] They have an obvious place in the work of a poet who prides himself on being *delicatus*[32] and are often used to convey the idea of effeminacy (cf. c. 25, where 6 are used in 13 lines about *cinaede Thalle, mollior . . .*, or the 4 in the 10 lines of c. 57, addressed to Caesar and Mamurra). It is not surprising, then, to find 4 used 5 times in c. 99, addressed to *mellite Iuventi*,[33] without which poem the number in the epigrams would be reduced to 4 used 4 times.[34] Such a tone of delicacy, however, has its proper place in the polymetrics and longer poems: the epigrams obviously, except for an occasional experiment like c. 99, belong to a sterner tradition. An interesting example of this is provided by *oculus* and *ocellus*: the latter diminutive form is found 6 times in the polymetrics, once in 64.60, but never in the epigrams, in which *oculus* only is used (6 times).[35]

A. S. F. Gow characterizes Catullus' use as follows: "The general impression left by his practice is that their use depends, much as the choice of meter depends, on the mood and the subject, but that there was nothing in a diminutive *per se* which should exclude it from high

[31] Platner has discussed the majority of them singly. Löfstedt, *Philologischen Kommentar zur Peregrinatio Aetheriae*, Uppsala 1936 (hereafter *PA*) 312, notes how well they fit their contexts in Catullus: they do not denote mere size and are not used only for metrical reasons or because they provide a convenient colloquialism (as, he notes, they often are used in later epigraphical distichs). Schmalz-Hofmann repeats this observation: "Von den Dichtern ist Catull besonders reich an Deminutiven, doch sind dieselben nirgends entwertet, sondern stets dem Zusammenhang wohl angepasst" (p. 835). Löfstedt calls this a good touchstone for literary criticism.

[32] The tone of "delicacy" they lend c. 61 (where 10 are used 12 times) provides a sufficient example of this: *aureolos pedes* (160, of the bride), *Torquatus parvulus* (209, with the *semihiante labello*, 213), *ore floridulo* (186, of the bride), *brachiolum teres . . . puellulae* (174–75), *puellulam* of the bride again at 181 and of any bride at 57, *hortulo* (88), *tuis teneris papillis* (101), *floridis ramulis* (22), *zonula* (53).

[33] *Suaviolum*, 2, 14; *tantillum*, 6; *labella*, 7; *articulis*, 8. Cf. 24.1, *o qui flosculus es Iuventiorum. . . .*

[34] The special use made of the remaining diminutives in the epigrams should be noted: *Victoris rupta miselli ilia* (80.7, homosexuality) and *rosea ista labella* in the first line of the same poem; *perluciduli deliciis lapidis* (69.4); *furcillis* (105.2, a proverbial expression, probably therefore a simple colloquialism).

[35] *Oculus* is found also in the polymetrics (4 times) and in the longer poems (3 in c. 63, 1 each in cc. 64 and 65). Axelson cites figures for Propertius (p. 41): in Bk. I, *ocellus* 10, *oculus* 0; in II, 8 and 5 respectively; but in III and IV Prop. uses only *oculus* (see also H. Tränkle, *Die Sprachkunst des Properz*, Hermes Einzelschriften 15 (1960) 28–30); and for Ovid: *Am.*, *ocellus* 11, *oculus* 25; *Ars Am.*, 3 and 14; *Her.*, 2 and 48, "was auf eine strengere—der Würde der Heroinen entsprechende—Stilisierung dieses Textes hinweist" (p. 43).

and serious poetry."[36] It is true that diminutives, as a part of the neoteric *Programm*, belonged as much in their serious verse as in their *nugae*; this, however, only emphasizes the small part they play in the epigrams of Catullus, where there was indeed something in a diminutive *per se* to exclude it. This something can only be the tradition, which Gow, in referring to the restrictions placed on the use of diminutives by the Augustan elegists, recognizes clearly, if hesitantly: "It seems likely that the speed with which the reform was affected may have been due in part to the fact that the Augustans were returning to the usage of older poets; or, in other words, that the surprising innovation was not the restricted use of diminutives in the second half of the century but the freedom of their use in the first."[37] The *poetae novi* experimented with diminutives, using them not as a colloquial element in their short *nugae* alone, but as a conscious poeticism even in their serious work. This license was extended, however, only to work which belonged to them alone. Where a Roman poetical tradition already existed, a tradition which allowed little or no use of diminutives,[38] the line was drawn: Catullus felt and followed this tradition in granting himself so little freedom in his epigrams.[39]

---

[36] "Diminutives in Augustan Poetry," *CQ* 26 (1932) 155.

[37] P. 156. Gow's next remarks are worth quoting in full: "The evidence is perhaps insufficient to decide, but in favour of this view it may be said that in the serious Latin poetry of earlier date diminutives are not common. Ennius provides one or two, the tragedians about a dozen; and, among the fragments of Latin poetry, it is in the scanty remains of such poets as Laevius, Bibaculus, and Cinna that one first seems to discern something like the attitude to diminutives shown by Catullus. It might also be said that such an attitude would not be surprising in poets whose Greek models were largely Alexandrian, and that Cicero, in whose poetry diminutives are noticeably scarce, is less likely to have been a precursor of Virgil than a belated follower of the older poets as against the *cantores Euphorionis*, by whom, on this hypothesis, we must suppose Lucretius to have been influenced. But however this may be, the change was almost complete in a generation. . . . It may just be worth adding that of the longer poems in the Virgilian appendix the *Ciris* seems in this matter to follow the principles of Catullus; the others it would be possible to consider intermediate between Catullus and Virgil." Lucretius need not have been so influenced: his diminutives, like so much else in his poem, need only be prosaic. The *Ciris*, as a belated neoteric production, is interesting in this respect.

[38] For what it is worth, we may note that in the epigrams of Aedituus, Licinus, and Catulus, only *faculam* is found (Aed. 2.1; also in Prop. 2.29.5).

[39] Svennung, p. 33, also mentions the figures (cited from F. Teufel, *De Catulli Tibulli Propertii vocibus singularibus*, Diss. Freib. Br. 1872) for *hapax legomena* (50 in the polymetrics, 40 in the longer poems, only 5 in the epigrams): while these figures seem to

In the case of compounds, then, the *poetae novi* adapted what had been a feature of higher poetic vocabulary to their shorter *nugae*, retaining it as well in their more serious verse; in the case of diminutives, they turned a colloquial feature into a poetic one, using it again in both groups of their work. In both cases, however, the tradition in epigram denied them (or at least Catullus) this freedom of invention.

AC/ATQUE

Catullus' use of *ac/atque* deserves an extensive discussion. The frequency of this common connective leaves no possibility that chance can have misrepresented the figures of its distribution—an important consideration in the study of the poetic vocabulary of an opus so small as that of Catullus—and also assures that the poet's intention may be deduced from a comparison of the contexts in which the word is used. At the same time, the history of the word as used by other poets is sufficiently clear to allow conclusions to be drawn about Catullus' place in the literary tradition. The form *ac* will be discussed first, since certain positive observations can be made from its distribution and use. The study of *atque*, on the other hand, leads to a negative conclusion, but one which will be useful in correcting a misconception about the word which might otherwise misrepresent the relationship of the three parts of Catullus' work. It will be seen, however, that both forms have the same tone and are used by the poet for the same effect and with the same purpose.

Axelson, in an important discussion of the connective, concludes that neither form is especially poetic; it is somewhat stiff and formal. This is an observation based on its frequency compared with *et* and *-que*, and is therefore misleading because the role of *et* and *-que* is naturally far greater.[40] One cannot argue that a word is unpoetic,

---

reinforce the present discussion, the vast majority of *hapax legomena* are compounds or diminutives (that is, conscious neoteric poeticisms); study of the remaining ones (colloquial curiosities) reveals nothing of Catullus' purpose.

[40] On *ac* and *atque* see Axelson, pp. 82–85. He cites Wetmore's *Index* for the figures in Virgil (4168 *-que*, 3159 *et*, 457 *atque*, and 156 *ac*) and Schulte's *Index* for Valerius Flaccus

or stiff and formal, simply because it is not as frequent as its more common synonyms. In addition, it is not always safe to argue without further examination or evidence that what was true for the poets of even a generation later was true also for Catullus.

Axelson argues that of the two forms *ac* is the less useful for the poets because it is metrically equivalent to *et* (an argument of doubtful usefulness) and is forbidden before vowels and gutturals. He notes that Virgil uses *ac* only twice in the *Eclogues* (*fovet ac*, 3.4, and *desinet ac*, 4.9, in each case apparently to avoid a cacophony of *-et et*). The distribution in the *Odes* of Horace shows it falling out of favor (8 in I, 1 in II, 2 in III, 0 in IV, though in the *Epodes* it had been used only twice). Tibullus has it four times, where some readings are disputed, and Propertius only once (apart from the phrases *ac primum* and *ac veluti*).[41] Phaedrus and Martial have no safe examples. From these facts Axelson concludes that the word did not belong in the vocabularies of elegy, lyric, bucolic, fable, or epigram. Axelson's negative discussion of unpoetic words has enormous value, but the positive aspects of the use of *ac* must be gathered largely from his silence, and without further explanation it is difficult to understand why, for example, *ac* is increasingly infrequent in the *Odes* but does appear frequently in the *Georgics* and *Aeneid* (in each of the latter works, a glance at Wetmore's *Index* shows, it occurs on a rough average of more than half a dozen times in each book).

From Virgil's use one can gather that *ac* belongs to didactic and epic poetry, and this theory is supported by its high frequency in Lucretius, Horace's *Ars Poetica* (six times, four as a proper connective), Ovid's *Metamorphoses* (32) and *Fasti* (4)—it does not occur in any of Ovid's

---

(1916 *-que*, 1086 *et*, 176 *atque*, and 94 *ac*), and says, "Einen sonderlich hohen poetischen Stilwert besass *atque, ac* demnach gar nicht; vielmehr dürfte diese Partikel ein etwas steifes und papierenes Gepräge gehabt haben . . ." (p. 83). An indication of its frequency in comparison with *et* and *-que* in Republican Latin is given by H. C. Elmer, "*Que, et, atque* in the Inscriptions of the Republic, in Terence, and in Cato," *AJP* 8 (1887) 292–328: "In the inscriptions under consideration [i.e. *CIL* I] *atque* (*ac*) is comparatively rare [n. 1: "*Atque* 13 times, 9 times with copulative force; *ac* 7 times, 6 times with copulative force."], though it occurs on earliest and latest monuments alike. . . . The contracted form *ac* is not found earlier than the Lex Antonia (B.C. 71)" (p. 293).

41 3.6.13, in which case it serves as the introductory *ac* to the second of two clauses.

elegies (with the possible exceptions of *ac ne* at *Am.* 3.2.75 and *Rem. Am.* 465) except once in the *Epistulae ex Ponto* and three times in the *Tristia*, significantly in the later elegies. On the other hand, it is equally frequent in satire: Horace has it about 45 times (25 times as a proper connective) in the *Epistles*, and it occurs often in Juvenal. One does not expect epic and didactic poetry to associate with satire in this way.

The distribution of *ac* in Catullus provides a focus for this situation and also a likely explanation. The particle is used a total of 27 times by the poet,[42] but of these 18 occur in the polymetric poems and 6 in c. 64 (with one each in c. 61 and c. 66); only one occurs in the epigrams (77.1). The distribution shows the agreement of the polymetrics and longer poems in the use of this connective; the epigrams, however, in their almost total exclusion of *ac*, stand in marked contrast to the first two groups of poems. What significance this may have must be found in the way the connective was used by Catullus.

It is necessary to look first at the structure and tone of the six lines in c. 64.

> linquunt Pthiotica Tempe
> Crannonisque domos ac moenia Larisaea (64.35–36)

This is a distinctly formal neoteric line: it is spondaic, and two substantives with two attributes make up the verse, but the word order is determined by the placing of the proper names, one at the beginning, one at the end of the verse. *Ac* occurs in the central position, not only between the two substantives, but metrically after the main caesura.

> Atque ita nave levi nitens ac lenibus auris (64.84)

Here too are two substantives and attributes, separated by *nitens ac*.

> clarisonas imo fudisse e pectore voces
> ac tum praeruptos tristem conscendere montes (64.125–26)

Norden refers a similar line, 64.198 *quae quoniam verae nascuntur pectore ab imo*, to Ennius,[43] and, with Kroll, one can see Ennius behind the

---

[42] Excluding *aeque ac*, 22.16; *non minus ac*, 61.169; *simul ac*, 64.12, 86, 147, 233, 366.

[43] See on *Aen.* 6.55. The phrase *pectore ab imo* is also Lucretian (3.57), but Ennius must be the common source. In 64.125 the MSS are divided (*e* X, *ex* O), and the correct reading is to be ascertained from Lucretius, who has only *e* with *pectore* (3.908; see Friedrichs' comment on Catullus *ad loc.*).

phrase *fudisse voces* (*Ann.* 540 V.² *effudit voces*). *Clarisonas* is an epic compound and frames the verse with its substantive;[44] the verse itself is almost a "golden line", a further formality. The whole passage depends on the Alexandrian *perhibent* (124):[45] there can be no mistaking the tone of the context of *ac* here, a blend of archaic Ennius and neoteric formality.

The other three uses of *ac* in c. 64 connect nouns of epic dignity in equally formal passages: 64.218 *fortuna mea ac tua fervida virtus*, 64.229 *nostrum genus ac sedes . . . Erecthei*, and 64.289 *fagos ac recto proceras stipite laurus*. Likewise the *ac* in 61.31 occurs amid the elegance of learned geographical names (*perge linquere Thespiae | rupis Aonios specus, | nympha quos super irrigat | frigerans Aganippe*, 27–30) and wordplay of Alexandrian playfulness (*ac domum dominam voca*, 31); and in c. 66, where the *primus inventor* of iron is formally and playfully cursed (*et qui principio sub terras quaerere venas | institit ac ferri stringere duritiem*, 49–50), *ac* seems to lend a tone of mock elevation. In all these uses *ac* may be safely assumed to be a connective of archaic formality, fitting epic solemnity and useful to a neoteric poet in lending dignity to contexts either learned or of mock loftiness.

But what of the great majority of the uses of *ac*, the 18 in poems 1–60? To certain of these the same formality of tone can be attributed without hesitation. In the following two cases the subject matter is itself indicative of traditional elevation.

> num te leaena montibus Libystinis
> aut Scylla latrans infima inguinum parte
> tam mente dura procreavit ac taetra . . . (60.1–3)

It is no coincidence that Ariadne repeats the same idea (64.154–6), for these lines could very well fit into a neoteric epyllion. As the commentators note,[46] the Greek *leaena* appears to be used first here (instead of *leo femina* or *lea*), and the learned *Libystinis* is perhaps Hellenistic in origin (Fordyce)—though it does not appear in Greek until after this time—or is Latin (as Kroll cautiously suggests). The subject, which is

---

44 See Norden, p. 391–92.
45 See Fordyce on 64.1 and Norden on *Aen.* 6.14.
46 See Ellis, Kroll, Fordyce.

as old as Homer (*Iliad* 16.33f.), seems here to be a direct echo of Euripides' *Medea* (1342–3 and 1358–9), a play well known to Catullus from Ennius' translation of it.[47] The short invective ends with the address *a nimis fero corde* (5), where *a* is the pathetic neoteric exclamation, an elevated colloquialism (as discussed elsewhere). *Ac*, then, is appropriate here, as it also is in 30.9–10:

> idem nunc retrahis te ac tua dicta omnia factaque
> ventos irrita ferre ac nebulas aereas sinis.

Here too the subject is traditional and had been employed by Theocritus and Apollonius.[48] Moreover Catullus uses the figure again in c. 64 (*irrita ventosae linquens promissa procellae*, 59; *quae cuncta aerii discerpunt irrita venti*, 142). Virgil considered it epic (*sed aurae / omnia discerpunt et nubibus irrita donant*, *Aen.* 9.312–13), and it was stock enough in epyllion to be used by the author of the *Culex* (380 and 383).

From other contexts in the polymetric poems, however, *ac* would appear to be purely colloquial, and its frequent occurrence in both comedy and satire would seem at first glance to justify this assumption; but there are other factors which complicate such an assumption and which make it impossible to label *ac/atque* simply as colloquial. Martial, as Axelson notes, has no safe example of *ac*. Löfstedt, in a very interesting comment,[49] after citing the article in the *Thesaurus Linguae Latinae* with its summary "altioris generis dicendi potius quam vulgaris propria", goes on to point out that Petronius never has the particle in prose, but in his verse it occurs 30 times, and similarly it never occurs in Pompeian inscriptions,[50] facts which perhaps help to explain its absence in Martial. Yet, though the word never took firm enough root in colloquial Latin to last on into Neronian popular usage, its occurrence in Plautus and Terence must be recognized as similar to Catullus' usage. In four of the 18 occurrences in the polymetric poems *ac* joins two adverbs (*bene ac beate*, 14.10 and 23.15; *bene ac diu*, 28.9; *mimice ac*

---

[47] Cf. the opening of Ennius' *Medea* and of Cat. 64.
[48] Fordyce, *ad loc.*: "the cliché in various forms has a long history in Greek: cf. Homer, *Od.* viii. 408, Eur. *Tro.* 419, Apoll. i. 1334, Theoc. 22.168, 29.35."
[49] *PA* 85–87.
[50] The same is true, in both Petronius and Pompeian inscriptions, for *-que*.

moleste, 42.8), a common function in the two writers of comedy.[51]
A further important external indication of some colloquial quality in
the repeated phrase *bene ac beate* is supplied by a comparison with
Cicero, who uses the phrase, if I am not mistaken, ten times,[52] but
always either *bene et beate* or *bene beateque*, never with *ac* as the conjunction: this would, perhaps, imply that, though this particular phrase was
useful and proper for Cicero in his formal writings, the use of *ac* in it
would have lent it a tone too informal for his purposes (though *ac* is
otherwise used by Cicero frequently to join two adverbs, often super-
lative or elevated, in his philosophic writings and speeches—a further
indication of its use "altioris generis dicendi" dealt with above).[53]

Though the particle, on the one hand, belongs to the formal and
elevated diction of Cicero and epic and later (at any rate) was not a
part of colloquial usage, and though on the other hand it occurs very
often and in any context in comedy,[54] the contexts in which it occurs
in Catullus may furnish an explanation. C. 6 begins with the warning,
*Flavi, delicias tuas Catullo, / ni sint illepidae atque inelegantes, / velles
dicere nec tacere posses* (1–3), and concludes with a summation of the

---

[51] See G. Lodge, *Lexicon Plautinum* and P. McGlynn, *Lexicon Terentianum*; we may
cite here as parallel examples only Plautus, *serio ac vero*, *Amph.* 964; *blande ac benedice*,
Asin. 206; *lepide ac nitide*, *Cist.* 10; *bene ac pudice*, *Cist.* 173; and Terence, *parce ac duriter*,
Ad. 45 and *An.* 74; *bene ac [et?] pudice*, *Haut.* 226; *modeste ac raro*, *Hec.* 552.

[52] See ThLL s.v. *beo* (*beatus*), vol. II, coll. 1920–21: *bene et beate*, *Parad.* 15; *bene beateque*,
Brut. 4, *Fin.* 1.5, 14, *Tusc.* 4.84, 5.19, *Sen.* 4, *Off.* 1.19, 2.6, *Epist.* 6.1.3. Other phrases with
beate are handled similarly, e.g. *fortunate beateque*, *Brut.* 9; *beate et honeste*, *Rep.* 4.3; *honeste
beateque*, *Leg.* 2.11. For *ac* joining other adverbs, see Merguet's lexica to Cicero.

[53] This suggestion is far from certain. G. P. Goold has written to me, "The natural
conclusion is that Cicero considered *bene ac beate* a little *too* formal, and preferred *bene
beateque*; possibly he considered *ac* too weighty to be the natural link joining these light-
weight adverbs," and this may well have been the case. If, however, as is argued here, *ac*
was on the one hand epic and archaic and on the other the urbane colloquialism of a
sophisticated set (particularly in certain phrases), it would seem likely, from Catullus'
usage and the indications offered by comedy, that the phrase *bene ac beate* should be heard
as an urbane cliché, and the conjunction changed by Cicero to avoid the cliché: *ac*, when
joining two superlatives, would not have had the same tone for Cicero, but would have
been appropriate in elevated rhetoric.

[54] In Terence, it should be noted, the usage of the two forms has been made regular.
Elmer (above, n. 40), 293–94, states that Terence with only seven exceptions, has *atque*
(210 times) before vowels and *h* only, *ac* (66 times) only before consonants; whereas Cato,
whose fascination for *atque* is well known, "uses *ac* only three times . . . while he uses
atque (91 times in all) indiscriminately before any letter (vowel or consonant) except *u*.',

tone of the poem itself, *volo te ac tuos amores | ad caelum lepido vocare versu* (16–17). The poem is clearly *lepidum et elegans* and, as will be discussed later, composed brilliantly *lepido versu*. *Ac* is used in a central position in the central lines, *(cubile) sertis ac Syrio fragrans olivo* (8), and it is tempting to regard the *atque* of the second line, the *ac* of the next to last line (especially in its context describing the tone of the poem), and the *ac* of the middle as a typically subtle, structural pattern. In another poem (14) concerned entirely with poetry and addressed to Calvus, *ac* occurs three times: . . . *hoc novum ac repertum | munus dat tibi Sulla litterator* (8–9); *non est mi male, sed bene ac beate* (10), a "collo-quial" line;[55] and *omnia collegam venena | ac te his suppliciis remunerabor* (19–20). In c. 16 *versiculi* are again the subject:

> nam castum esse decet pium poetam
> ipsum, versiculos nihil necesse est;
> qui tum denique habent salem ac leporem,
> si sunt molliculi ac parum pudici . . . (5–8)[56]

Here, in lines concerned with the nature of his polymetric poems and written in language instantly recognizable as belonging to them, Catullus uses *ac* twice, once to join the two key words *salem* and *leporem*. Identical emphasis is obtained in c. 12: *est enim leporum | differtus puer ac facetiarum* (8–9). *Ac* occurs again in c. 22, which deals neatly with Varus, who in private life is *venustus, dicax, urbanus* (2) and *bellus* (9), but who, as soon as he reaches for his tablets, *idem infaceto est infacetior rure*, a transformation described by Catullus in the central and focal line of the poem with the words, *tantum abhorret ac mutat* (11).

From these contexts it is clear that the connective *ac* is associated with the elegance, charm, and wit of the *versiculi* of Catullus and his circle and belongs prominently to the language of this set.[57] *Ac* was

---

[55] *Non est mi male*, "colloquial" as Fordyce notes *ad loc.*; cf. Plaut. *Mostell.* 52, *Truc.* 745, and Mart. 10.13.10.

[56] Pliny, in quoting these four lines (*Ep.* 4.14.5), has *tunc* for *tum* in line 7 and *et* for *ac* in both lines 7 and 8. It may be suggested without hesitation that he was quoting from memory rather than copying from a manuscript of Catullus, and thus substituted *et* as if he were writing the lines himself, an interesting indication of the use of *ac* (or rather of its disuse) in his own day.

[57] The other uses of *ac* in the polymetric poems, not mentioned above, are: 15.1, *Commendo tibi me ac meos amores, | Aureli*; 30.5 addressed to Alfenus and containing *ac*

never vulgar and probably not strictly colloquial: its occurrence in Plautus and Terence and later in satire (Horace and Juvenal) must be regarded in the same light as the majority of the polymetric uses in Catullus—an urbane colloquialism (a feeling Martial no longer shared). Distinct from this, though, was its association with elevated prose and epic poetry; it must be this association which Catullus wants when he uses the connective in the longer poems and in the few traditionally poetic passages in the polymetric poems. Neither association, though, would fit epigram, which in this respect could be neither urbanely colloquial nor epic.[58]

Catullus' use of *atque* presents certain difficulties which, at first sight, appear to contradict our conclusions about the use and distribution of *ac*. It might be expected that *atque* was more useful to the poets than *ac*, for, as Axelson points out, *ac* is the metrical equivalent of *et*; but *atque* can supply a long syllable (when followed by an initial vowel) or a useful trochee (when followed by a single initial consonant). It is somewhat surprising, then, to find that the poets did not take advantage of the metrical possibilities of *atque*: by the time of the Augustan poets, a restriction had been placed on the use of *atque* which allowed its use regularly only before a vowel. Axelson supplies the following figures (the first figure is the total number of times *atque* occurs, the second the number of times it is found before a consonant, i.e. unelided):[59] Lucr. I–II, 90–22; Cat. 50–13;[60] Virg. *Ecl.* 19–5, *G.* 98–9, *Aen.* 294–35 (of these 35, 27 occur in VII–XII); Hor. lyrics 31–26, *Sat.* 101–51, *Epist.* 31–28; Tib. 11–3; Prop. 45–3; Ovid elegies 145–12, *Met.* 100–7; Luc. 90–8; Val. Fl. I–IV, 64–4; Sil. I–III, 80–3; Mart. 61–28; Juv. 150–54.[61] Certain observations can be made

---

twice again in the more formal lines (9–10) discussed above; and 31.8. It is not necessary to discuss the tone of every passage fully (as, for instance, that of 42.8, where one sees the *putida moecha . . . turpe incedere, mimice ac moleste / ridentem catuli ore Gallicani*).

[58] In the exception to prove the rule, 77.1, *Rufe, mihi frustra ac nequicquam credite amice*, Catullus perhaps allowed himself the connective to address an intimate.

[59] P. 84: but G. P. Goold warns me that practically all the alleged examples of unelided *atque* in Tib., Prop., Ovid are corrupt.

[60] Axelson's figure for Catullus should be corrected to 50–12.

[61] M. Platnauer, "Elision of *Atque* in Roman Poetry," *CQ* 42 (1948) 91–93, gives percentages of elided and unelided *atque* in a similar list of poets, which differ somewhat from Axelson's figures but do not affect the general picture. See also the figures given by

from these figures. We may regard as normal that anywhere from a quarter to over a third of the uses of *atque* may occur before a consonant (as Virg. *Ecl.*, Lucr., Cat., Mart., Juv.); but a far smaller fraction was allowed by those poets who wrote in a higher genre or were stylistically more self-conscious (as Virg. *G.* and *Aen.*, Tib., Prop., Ovid, Luc., etc.). *Atque* before a consonant does not play as great a role in higher poetry as its metrical utility would suggest, and in this the Augustans seem to have placed another technical restriction on their verse.

The distribution of elided and unelided *atque* in Catullus is as follows: in the polymetrics *atque* occurs 16 times, 8 of which precede a consonant; in the longer poems only one of the 20 comes before a consonant (68.48, in the formula *magis atque magis*); and in the epigrams only 3 of the 14 (77.2, 88.1, 101.10, this last in the formula *ave atque vale*). Catullus thus appears to anticipate the Augustan rule in the longer poems and in the epigrams, but in the polymetrics to take no notice of it. This implies a contradiction that cannot be ignored, because in all other aspects of his poetic vocabulary the longer poems and the polymetrics show similar usage, while it is the epigrams which ignore poetic practice. Further investigation, however, shows that the situation in regard to unelided *atque* is not as clear cut or as simple as the above figures and the rule derived from them imply: it cannot be said with any certainty that unelided *atque* came to be regarded even by the Augustans as unpoetic or conversely that the restriction of *atque* to the elided position was a purely poetic innovation.

We may begin by noting more carefully the surprising situation Horace's use of *atque* presents. Richmond notes that in the *Epodes* there are 9 instances of unelided *atque* to only 3 of elided *atque*,[62] a proportion even more striking in the *Odes* (17 unelided, 2 elided) and *Epistles* (including the *Ars P.*, 28 and 3): these proportions are the exact opposite of the Augustan rule. Horace's *Satires* have 50 elided and 51 unelided.[63]

J. A. Richmond, "A Note on the Elision of final ĕ in certain Particles used by Latin Poets," *Glotta* 43 (1965) 78–103.

[62] *Glotta* 43 (1965) 95.

[63] It is worth noting that Platnauer (*CQ* 1948) observes that in exactly half of Horace's hexameters *atque* is at the end of the line (a position found elsewhere only in Juvenal, and rarely there).

Surely it is impossible to argue that Horace willfully ignored poetic practice in the *Odes* and *Epistles*, and impossible to assume that unelided *atque* was unpoetic. Richmond suggests a plausible explanation for Horace's usage: "The *Epodes* and *Odes* were written in difficult metres; the *Epistles* aim at a much smoother metre than the rough and casual *Satires*. Consequently the former works all show free use of the unelided position to secure metrical fluency." Horace used the unelided *atque* to gain metrical fluency, and did so in just those works which are the most polished in both meter and language: it may be assumed that Catullus, in his polymetrics, did so for the same reason. In any case, it cannot be said, judging from Horace, that the high number of unelided *atque* in the polymetrics implies any sort of unpoetic roughness.

The argument of metrical utility, however, is one to be avoided when possible. It is far more important to attempt to see what reason may lie behind the general formulation that in the more elevated genres the more careful poets (though the warning of Horace must be kept always in mind) avoided unelided *atque*, and whether this reason was a poetic one or had its origin in other criteria. Though the matter is still without absolute certainty, a general understanding can be reached. Platnauer was the first to risk any sort of explanation for the fact long observed: "The only reason that suggests itself is something like this: *atque*, which despite its five letters is of no more semantic use than the three-letter -*que* and of less than the two-letter *et*, may have been felt by at any rate careful Latin poets to arrogate to itself more room than it was really worth. By means of elision they could (and so did) reduce the word to a size more in keeping with its semantic value."[64] Such an explanation (based on the size of the written word) seems rather artificial. Richmond, whose long and extremely useful article is the most recent word on the subject, begins with a valid linguistic assumption: "The alternative theory here to be defended is that unelided *atque* was avoided because in normal spoken Latin *atque* was closely pronounced with the following word and the final *e* was regularly lost before a following consonant, whereupon the word was reduced to

64 *CQ* 42 (1948) 93.

ac.[65] The basic rule, then, is that *ac* is the normal preconsonantal form, *atque* the normal prevocalic. Plautus has elided *atque* 1069 times, unelided only 110 times,[66] which must, to a great extent, represent normal speech. It has been noted above that Terence made this usage regular: with only 7 exceptions, he has *atque* (210 times) only before vowels and *h*, *ac* (66 times) only before consonants; Cato's indiscriminate use of *atque* before any vowel or consonant must therefore represent rhetorical practice, archaic and artificial rather than normal.[67] It cannot therefore be argued that the use of *atque* before a consonant is a colloquial tendency which the Augustan poets shunned, any more than it can be argued that the restriction of *atque* to the elided position is a conscious poeticism.

Richmond later concludes with a discussion of *atque* as used by the poets,[68] a summary of which may be given here. "Propertius and Ovid . . . observed the avoidance [of *atque* before a consonant] with particular strictness, but the practice of the poets in general was much more careful after the Augustan age. It is hard to resist the conclusion that a conscious rule had been evolved by the time Propertius began to write. I don't think this rule was imposed on poetry by a literary coterie. . . ." This last observation, as we have suggested in the above discussion, is an important one. Richmond's reasons for such an opinion are these: that Cicero avoids unelided *atque* save in the *clausulae*,[69] and therefore in his prose was obviously aware of the rule; that Livy has only about 78 examples of unelided *atque*, "of which

---

[65] *Glotta* 43 (1965) 80. This explanation is, of course, not new as a linguistic phenomenon: see, for instance, F. Sommer, *Handbuch der Lat. Laut- und Formenlehre* (Heidelberg 1914) 292 ("*neque*, *atque* sind (wie *quīndecim* aus *quīnque decem, etc.) bei engem Zusammenhang mit dem folgenden Wort vor Konsonanten (zugleich mit regelrechtem Untergang des labialen Elements von *qu* S. 187) zu *nec*, *ac* geworden . . .") and Stolz-Leumann, p. 88. A difficulty, however, arises from our ignorance of what the actual pronunciation was: see M. W. Lindsay, *The Latin Language* (Oxford 1894) 599 ("But in the MSS. of Plautus *atque* is sometimes used before a consonant, where the metre requires the pronunciation *ac* (e.g. *Epid.* 522), and in the MSS. of Cato *atque* is the prevailing spelling (whatever Cato's pronunciation may have been) before initial consonants and vowels alike.").

[66] The figures are those given by Richmond, p. 81.
[67] See above, n. 54.   [68] Pp. 93–94.
[69] This was observed by J. Wolff, "De Clausulis Ciceronianis," *Jahrb. f. Phil. Suppl.* 26 (1901) 637–40.

nearly half occur in the first decade where an archaic colouring of style was especially suitable"; and that Phaedrus, "who cannot be accused of any especial desire for an exaggerated refinement of style," elides all of his 13 uses of *atque*. "I think the reason is rather to be sought in the tendency to regularize the use of alternate forms which became noticeable in the Augustan age. . . . This reasoning[70] impels me accordingly to see in the treatment of *atque* the result of a rule formulated by the grammarians and adopted generally for polite speech."[71]

Finally, we need only consider the contexts of the 8 examples of unelided *atque* in the polymetrics of Catullus to see that there can be no question of unpoetical usage, and, moreover, that there is more behind this usage than metrical utility. C. 26 is a short poem on Furius' villa and the winds of debt it faces; the conceit of the winds is neoteric, and both of the names in the third line are Greek (*nec saevi Boreae aut Apheliotae*); the final line of the poem continues the tone of mock elevation (*o ventum horribilem atque pestilentem*, 5), in which *atque* must contribute some tone of solemnity and perhaps an archaic colouring. Two proper names are connected by *atque* in the poem to Sirmio (*vix mi ipse credens Thuniam atque Bithunos / liquisse campos*, 31.5–6), where again there is a certain solemnity and neoteric tone in addition to a play on words involving the two proper names. The effect of the list of Italian peoples in the Egnatius poem 39.10–13 is discussed elsewhere: that it is meant to be a comic catalogue according to neoteric principles is certain, and the two epithets joined by *atque* (*aut Lanuvinus ater atque dentatus*, 12) are certainly used for their mock loftiness of tone. In these three passages *atque* must be considered to have a definite poetic purpose. In three other instances the contexts suggest a more colloquial and informal tone, but one that is definitely neoteric in that the colloquial language is that of urbanity and wit, not of the mass: 12.2 *in ioco atque*

---

[70] Richmond is referring to "the account Axelson gives of the rules gradually adopted in elegant speech whereby *a* and *e* were used before consonants (p. 118 sq.). The vulgar language accepted *a*, but clung to preconsonantal *ex*."

[71] He admits, however, that it is strange that "no tradition about the rule was handed down by the later Latin grammarians."

vino (of Marrucinus Asinius,[72] the napkin thief who is *invenustus* and who lacks *lepores* and *facetiae*) may be compared with the similar phrase in 50.6 *per iocum atque vinum*, the poem addressed to Calvus and a perfect example of the elegant language of the neoteric *nugae*; c. 13, the invitation to Fabullus for dinner (*si tecum attuleris bonam atque magnam / cenam*, 3–4) is another example of urbanity of language.[73]

It is clear, then, that the 8 instances of unelided *atque* in the polymetrics cannot be suspected of being lapses from poetic diction: on the contrary, the contexts make it obvious that unelided *atque* had, on the one hand, an archaic and solemn tone (as we might easily assume from Cato's fondness for the connective, elided or unelided) and, on the other, may have been a conspicuous part of the urbane speech of Catullus' circle (which would, no doubt, show certain departures from standard speech for the purpose of elegance and wit). Even if we assume with Richmond that the rule against unelided *atque* had its origin in the grammarians' attempt to regularize what had become (perhaps fairly recently) the practice of normal speech, we need see nothing unusual in Catullus' use of unelided *atque* in his polymetrics (any more than we need assume anything unusual in Horace's careful preference for this form or in Cicero's recourse to it in his *clausulae*): the later restriction of the Augustan poets obviously was unrelated to any judgment that this usage was unpoetic but rather was a simple conformation to accepted speech and perhaps to a recent grammatical rule, one whose origin lay outside poetic usage. The value of this discussion for the relationship of the three parts of Catullus' poetry is a negative one, but one that is important for removing a possible

---

[72] There is still no certainty about *Marrucinus*—cognomen or not? (T. R. S. Broughton, *The Magistrates of the Roman Republic* II, 411, cautiously prints "*Asinius (Marrucinus?)*"—I owe this reference to G. W. Bowersock, who adds that even if it were a cognomen, it would be so rare as to retain its original local force.) It may be worth adding, though, a new argument against its being a cognomen: as discussed later, a mock-epic geographical epithet in this poem would be perfectly Catullan in the polymetrics, "Lordly Marrucinian, Asinius . . ." (to be taken, of course, ironically; cf. the heroic epithets of Egnatius [37.18–19], *cuniculosae Celtiberiae fili, / Egnati*).

[73] One of the other two instances of unelided *atque* in the polymetrics occurs in the same Egnatius poem, perhaps for the same effect (*dentem atque russam . . . gingivam*, 39.19); the other (*plus quam se atque suos amavit omnes*, 58.3) may be simply a matter of metrical convenience.

misconception: the fact that Catullus avoids unelided *atque* in the longer poems and the epigrams almost entirely (and thus conforms to Augustan practice) but does not do so in his polymetrics has no particular relevance for establishing any connection between the poetic usage of the longer poems and that of the epigrams.

NEC/NEQUE

Catullus' use of *nec/neque* must be considered in close connection with *ac/atque*. Again it will be apparent that previous studies of the connective are in some important aspects inadequate; further investigation is necessary in the hope that its development may be better understood and that its use and distribution in Catullus' poetry, when considered in this new light, may reveal an important and valid distinction between the three groups of his poems.

A brief initial review of the literary development of *nec* and *neque* is necessary here. Lucian Müller was the first to point out the fact that *nec* is the preferred form for Tibullus and later poets, *neque* appearing rarely or not at all.[74] Löfstedt, remarking that *nec* is the source of all the Romance forms, traces this victory of *nec* over *neque* in later prose.[75] Axelson shows that Tibullus was not alone in his preference for *nec* and gives an interesting picture of this development in poetry:[76] Virgil and Horace (in his *Odes* and *Satires*) follow the practice of the older poets by using *neque* ordinarily before vowels, *nec* and *neque*

[74] *De Re Metrica* (Lipsiae 1861) 395–97: ". . . ab Augusti inde aevo apud poetas permultos, cum nec innumeris prostet exemplis, neque aut raro invenitur aut numquam" (p. 395); he refers to Phaedrus, Manilius, Juvenal, Claudian, and others.
[75] *Synt.* I², 331–38, with a short bibliography. "Die Sache liegt so, dass *nec* in der späteren Volkssprache wenigstens im grössten Teil des Römischen Reichs den Sieg über *neque* davongetragen hat" (p. 332). His interesting sketch need not be repeated here. In comparison with *atque*, however, it may be mentioned that Apuleius, "in der oratorisch gehaltenen, teilweise an die ältere Prosa (Cicero) anknüpfenden Apologie," uses both forms equally (in the first 50 pp. of Helm's text [1912], 33 *neque*, 30 *nec*), but in the *Met. nec* predominates (in Bk. V, *nec* 47 times, *neque* only twice) (pp. 334–35). In Petr. *nec* is used more than 160 times, *neque* only 27 times (among which *neque enim* 7 times); but in the colloquial parts of the novel *neque* does not appear, and is likewise absent from Pompeian inscriptions (p. 336).
[76] Pp. 115–18. Cf. also E. B. Lease, *CR* 16 (1902) 212–14, and *CP* 3 (1908) 304–05.

alike before consonants; Propertius still prefers *neque* before vowels (17 *neque*, 5 *nec*), but begins the process of refinement by using *nec* alone before consonants (*neque* before a consonant, with the exception of 2.28.5, occurs only in the first foot of the hexameter, 5 times). Ovid continues this practice before consonants, but, like Tibullus, uses *nec*, to the almost total exclusion of *neque*, also before vowels (*neque* only in the phrase *neque enim*).[77] Tibullus, as has been observed, has *neque* only at 1.2.77, in the first foot (the reading of 1.1.64 is disputed). Horace in his *Epistles* was part of this refinement; he avoids *neque* before vowels, and before consonants has *nec* 65 times, *neque* (11 times) only in the first or fifth foot to give the required dactyl. The rule, then, came to be: *nec* is the normal form, *neque* the exceptional (only before vowels in the phrase *neque enim*, only before consonants in the first foot).[78]

The results of Axelson's study may be accepted, but his uncritical acceptance of Wagner's findings for Virgil and the older poets needs modification.[79] It is true that *neque* was the accepted form, almost without exception, before vowels; but it is misleading to consider *nec* and *neque* identical alternatives before consonants. Lucretius, I have found, in the first three books has *nec* before consonants 108 times, *neque* 49 times,[80] and Horace in the *Satires* has *nec* 46 times, *neque* 34

---

[77] P. 117: in his total elegiac production Ovid used *neque* before a vowel hardly more than 20 times (excluding *neque enim*), in the *Met.* 40 times (epic tolerates the antiquated *neque* and allows elision more often than elegy).

[78] This rule can be applied, for instance, to the question of authorship of the *Culex* and *Ciris*. Axelson notes that the *Culex* has *nec* 16 times, never *neque*; and W. Clausen, *CP* 59 (1964) 99–100, that the *Ciris* has *nec* in 23 places (3 before vowels) but *neque* in only four places (in the first foot of 62 and 116, *neque enim* in 227, and in the third foot of 116, a recall of Cat. 64.68): "Scholars who wish to see in the *Ciris* a work of Virgil's prentice hand will have to explain how it was possible for a youthful poet to anticipate, not indeed the practice of his own maturity, but the practice of a succeeding generation of poets."

[79] "Was Vergil angeht, kann ich mich allerdings mit einem Hinweis auf Wagners Quaestiones XXXI begnügen, denen zu entnehmen ist, dass V. (wie die Älteren) vor Vokalen am liebsten *neque*, vor Konsonanten sowohl *nec* als auch *neque* gebraucht" (p. 116). He makes a similar statement on Horace's usage in the *Odes* and *Satires* ("vor Konsonanten bald die eine, bald die andere Form").

[80] It is curious that none of these 49 are used to obtain the dactyl in the fifth foot (21 occur in the first foot, 20 in the second, 15 in the third, and 13 in the fourth). In regard to another Lucretian curiosity in the use of *nec* and *neque*, Lachmann's observation on 3.853 is worth citing here: "nam in primo et secundo pede tanta est codicum Lucretianorum constantia, ut ne ante vocales quidem scriptum sit *nec*, nisi in IV, 357 *Plaga nec ad nostras* et ter *nec opinanti* III, 959 V, 1320 VI, 408, in V, 777 autem *neque opinantis*. contra in tertio

times before consonants. In the *Odes*, however, his usage begins to show a decided preference for *nec* (c. 138 times, *neque* 33 times), as had been the case even more decidedly in the *Epodes* (*nec* 23 times before consonants, *neque* only 3 times): this preference might be set down to the fact that *nec* is more useful in meters where the dactyl is not much required. Virgil, however, has an even greater preference for *nec*: in the *Eclogues nec* is found 47 times before consonants, *neque* only 4 times; in the first six books of the *Aeneid*, *nec* is used before a consonant over 150 times, *neque* only 12 times. It appears, then, that in the hexameters of the older poets (if Lucretius may be taken as an example) *nec* was somewhat preferred before consonants;[81] that Horace prefers *nec* in the *Odes* (but made little distinction in the technically unrefined *Satires*), a preference definitely shared by Virgil and strengthened by Horace himself in the *Epistles*.

In Catullus' poetry *neque* is used before a vowel 17 times, *nec* 6 times.[82] This seems in accord with the practice of Virgil, Horace (*Odes* and *Satires*), and Propertius, but there is an indication that Catullus may have anticipated the later rule. In the polymetrics the figures for the prevocalic position are 15 *neque*, 3 *nec*; in the longer poems 2 and 2; but in the epigrams *neque* does not appear before a vowel, and *nec* once. It might be inferred that the polymetrics follow older practice, while the epigrams (and longer poems) show an anticipation of Tibullus' practice (and Horace's in the *Epistles*); and from this that Tibullus himself followed a refinement already a part of epigram, and that Horace in this respect placed his *Epistles* half way between the *Satires* (in which his usage was more free from technical niceties) and *Odes* (where *neque* before vowels was acceptable as an older poeticism,

---

et quarto pede is liber e quo nostri ducti sunt tam mire variat, ut ne quaeri quidem possit utrum poeta quibus condicionibus praetulerit."

81 In Cicero's verse (Baehren's edition) I have found *nec* before consonants 14 times, *neque* 6 times.

82 It may avoid ambiguity and be otherwise useful to tabulate here the complete figures for Catullus' usage of *nec* and *neque* in both positions.

| | NEC | | NEQUE | |
	+ cons.	+ vowel	+ cons.	+ vowel
1–60	36	3	3	15
61–68	34	2	4	2
69–116	16	1	3	0

as in Virgil). In support of this view it might be argued that epigram would be the one genre practised in Catullus' time which would make use of *nec* (as the common form then current in speech) and begin to exclude *neque* (as a poetic or formal archaism). But the single use of *nec* and the absence of *neque* before a vowel in the epigrams does not permit such conclusions to be drawn comfortably, and the matter may be viewed in an entirely different way.

Since *neque* was subject to the same linguistic shortening as was *atque* and by apocope became *nec* before a consonant, just as *atque* became *ac*, it would seem wiser to investigate the uses of elided and unelided *neque* in Catullus, comparing his practice with that of the other poets, just as has been done in the case of elided and unelided *atque*. Richmond again supplies figures for the poets and offers an interesting analysis of their practice: Plautus has elided *neque* 268 times, unelided 406 times; Lucr. (of his first 50 uses of *neque*) has 18 elided, 32 unelided;[83] Cat. 19 elided, 10 unelided;[84] Virg. 81, and 38;[85] Prop. 20, and 6; Ovid 86, and 18. Horace again requires special analysis. In his *Epodes* there are 11 elided *neque* and 3 unelided (the normal poetic practice of the time) but in the *Odes* 19 elided and 33 unelided, in the *Satires* 15 elided and 34 unelided, and in the *Epistles* no example of elided *neque* but 11 examples of unelided. Richmond concludes: "What is obviously the right explanation of this surprising result is given by Axelson (p. 117): Horace in his *Epistles* deliberately avoided *neque*, because it already was avoided in colloquial speech, having

---

[83] Richmond (*Glotta* 1965) 97–99, suggests his own explanation, after disposing of several others, for the preponderance of the unelided form (contrary to later usage) in Plautus and Lucretius: according to metrical theory, *nec me* took as much time to pronounce as *neque me*, but *ac me* took a mora less than *atque me*. "As I accept the theory of F. Skutsch that the short forms are 'Schnellsprechformen' [*Plautinisches und Romanisches* (Forsch. z. lat. Gramm. u. Metrik, I), Leipzig 1892, 47] as used in any utterance faster than the most deliberate and emphatic speech, I suggest that in Plautus and Lucretius *nec* often fails to supplant *neque* as it did not accelerate the delivery in the way *ac* did when substituted for *atque*." This explanation is based on the artificial and unrealistic theories of the ancient grammarians and metricians about morae, and is therefore open to serious question. An alternate explanation will be proposed here.

[84] In Catullus, I find only 17 elided.

[85] Richmond, 100–102, argues that Virgil may definitely be said to have avoided unelided *neque*: his analysis of the 38 examples of unelided *neque* shows that most of these are used for obvious metrical reasons.

42

been replaced by *nec*, and used it only in cases where the two short syllables of unelided *neque* enabled him to secure a first or fifth foot dactyl, or some other metrical advantage. This curious compromise results in Horace actually seeming to prefer the unelided position, which we have seen other poets avoided."[86]

The distribution of elided and unelided *neque* in Catullus presents some striking evidence for the difference between the three parts of his poetry. In the polymetrics elided *neque* occurs 15 times, unelided only 3 times; the proportion is similar to that found in Virgil and the later elegists, and it is clear as well that the 3 instances of elided *neque* are all due to meter (all three occur in identically worded contexts, . . . *neque servus* . . ., 23.1, 24.5, 8). In the longer poems 2 are elided, but 4 unelided (61.191, obviously for metrical reasons; 64.68, 68.5, both in the first foot; 64.68, in the third foot). In the epigrams there are no examples of elided *neque*, but 3 of unelided (91.5, in the first foot; 69.7, 112.1, both in the third foot). It may be argued, then, that Catullus is closer to the standard practice of the later poets not in his epigrams but in his polymetrics, with the longer poems (as far as the indication provided by the low frequency of *neque* is reliable) halfway between. Is there further evidence from the use of unelided *neque* which would indicate that Catullus' use of *neque* before a consonant in the epigrams is not a matter of chance (or, to put the matter another way, evidence which would satisfactorily explain the fact that *neque* occurs 17 times before a vowel (elided) in the polymetrics and longer poems, but never in the epigrams)?

Such evidence can only come from an investigation of the linguistic development of the alternate forms *neque* and *nec* and from a comparison with the forms *atque* and *ac*.[87] Though it is agreed that *nec* and *ac* are the result of the same process of shortening, as noted above, the two connectives nevertheless show considerable differences in the way they were used in both prose and poetry. These differences have all been mentioned previously, but it will be helpful here to summarize certain pertinent distinctions. 1) *Ac* is seldom found in elegy, lyric, bucolic,

---

[86] Idem, 95.

[87] I would like to acknowledge here the help and criticism received from Ernst Pulgram, with whom I have discussed the results of this study.

fable, or epigram; *nec* is common in these genres. 2) *Ac* is rare or non-existent in later colloquial prose (Petronius, Pompeian inscriptions); *nec* is very common. 3) *Ac/atque* are "altioris generis dicendi;" *nec/neque* are not. 4) Plautus prefers elided *atque* (1069–110), but unelided *neque* (268–406). 5) *Ac* is never used before vowels; *nec*, which could be used before vowels by writers of every period (though Caesar does not do so, and Cicero only on rare occasions[88]), came to be the usual prose form and to be used regularly in poetry before vowels by Tibullus and Horace in the *Epistles*.

To help explain these five observations we may cite the figures given by E. B. Lease for the frequency of the two forms of both connectives in prose:[89]

	Atque	*Ac*	*Neque*	*Nec*
Cato[90]	97	4	54	5
Sallust[91]	227	110	206	2
Nepos	69	42	155	1
Caesar	433	189	405	39
Livy (1st two books of each decade)	1011	1747	159	398
Tacitus	312	893	445	506

It will be observed from these figures that Cato avoids both shortened forms, most likely because *ac* and *nec* were recent and perhaps colloquial shortenings which he felt to lack dignity (compared with the original

[88] See E. B. Lease, *CR* 16 (1902) 213.   [89] *CP* 3 (1908) 304.

[90] S. V. F. Waite, who is compiling a computer index to all of Cato, has kindly provided me with these figures. They may be broken down (for the following works given in this order, *Agr.*, Orations [including those in the *Origines*], *Origines*, other fragments): *atque*, 6, 74, 13, 4 (=97); *ac*, 1, 3, 0, 0 (=4); *neque*, 30, 22, 2, 0 (=54); *nec*, 4, 1, 0, 0 (=5). The high frequency of *atque* in the Orations (74), compared with the *Agr.* (6), is worth noting. (H. C. Elmer gives similar figures for *atque/ac* in all of Cato, *AJP* 8 [1887] 293; and Lease, [above, n. 89] for *neque/nec*, but only for *Agr.*)

[91] It may be significant that in Sallust *ac* increases from 2.5 occurrences per 1000 words in the *Cat.* to 4.2 in the *Jug.*, while *atque* decreases from 14.0 per 1000 words (*Cat.*) to 6.6 (*Jug.*); *neque* and *nec* remain fairly constant. D. W. Packard has kindly provided me with these figures, obtained by computer; he has also supplied me with full figures for all of Livy, which generally support Lease's ratios and hence are not repeated. However, it is certainly worth noting that, surprisingly, *ac* decreases in Livy (4.0 occurrences per 1000 words in I–X; 5.5 in XXI–XXX; 3.1 in XXXI–XXXV; 1.6 in XXXVI–XL; 2.0 in XLI–XLV), as does *nec* (5.3 in I–X, 3.0 in XXXVI–XLV).

longer forms) for his literary prose. Beginning with Sallust, however, there is no scarcity of *ac*; but by comparison *nec* occurs remarkably seldom in Sallust, Nepos, and Caesar. (We may note, however, that Varro, in the *Ling.* and *Rust.*, has 205 *neque*, 77 *nec*, a high percentage for the latter form which Lease calls an exception. It need not be regarded as an exception, however, if it is remembered that Varro often writes prosaically (particularly in the *Rust.*); therefore this percentage may provide an indication of the progress made up to that time by *nec* in the colloquial, but not literary, language.)

Three general conclusions may therefore be made to explain the five characteristic differences listed above between the development of the two connectives. First, it may be that *atque* > *ac* before a consonant was the rule first, perhaps because of the more difficult consonant cluster presented by *atqu(e)* + consonant (*nequ(e)* + consonant would present no such difficulty); this is indicated by the early acceptance of *ac* in literary prose, while *neque* before a consonant is still perfectly admissible and the use of *nec* still a rarity. Second, since *nec* and *nequ(e)* are phonetically similar (the only difference being the labial element of the latter), *nec* could easily come to be used before vowels and eventually becomes the only prevocalic form, whereas the phonetic difference between *ac* and *atqu(e)* would tend to maintain the distinction in their usage. Third, since *ac/atque* was lexically unessential (having the more common synonyms *et* and *-que*—of which the latter also disappeared eventually), they were retained for a time only in the literary language which could afford to observe the rule established earlier for the use of the two forms; *nec/neque*, on the other hand, was essential in the vocabulary and thus subject to the force of colloquial usage, usage necessarily reflected in the literary language. We may summarize these conclusions, then, by noting what the historical sequence of linguistic events must have been. *Atque* belonged to elevated diction from the beginning (its common synonyms being *et* and *-que*);[92]

[92] The beginning, that is, of what we can comfortably observe with any certainty: we may note again that Elmer (*AJP* [1887] 293) finds *ac/atque* "comparatively rare" (*atque* 13 times, *ac* 7 times) in the inscriptions of *CIL* I—a good indication of its standing in the "normal" language—whereas Cato, writing a dignified literary Latin, has *atque* 91 times.

neque, however, was a necessary and common part of normal Latin. *Atque* was then shortened before consonants, by normal linguistic change, to *ac*, a change recognized and regularized by a grammarians' rule (Plautus for the most part, and Terence regularly, observe this change, though the archaizing Cato does not). Subsequently, *neque* underwent the same change, though only by analogy and never consistently, with the result that the two forms *neque* and *nec* show in various respects a diversity of usage. Finally, *nec* became the common form, and *ac/atque* disappeared entirely from the language.

To return now to Catullus' usage and the fact that elided *neque* occurs 17 times in the polymetrics (15) and longer poems (2) but never in the epigrams, it would seem that metrical utility is not the sole, or even the primary, explanation. The polymetrics quite clearly represent a literary usage, analogous to the convention which limited *atque* to the prevocalic position; the epigrams, however, by their use of *neque* only before a consonant (unelided), would seem to reflect the same situation which we have observed in the case of Plautus and Lucretius (both of whom prefer unelided *neque*), and the early prose writers (Cato, Sallust, Nepos). Accordingly the epigrams are far more traditional and conservative in their use of the connective than the polymetrics. The freedom and need to experiment which Catullus felt in his polymetrics is once again evident. The facts of the case and their interpretation seem clear: it is only when a false standard of usage, inferred unhistorically from later poets (i.e. that Tibullus' use of *nec* and avoidance of *neque* represents poetic usage and is a poetic innovation), is applied to Catullus' practice that confusion and misunderstanding result. The development of the use of *neque/nec* and the reasons behind this development must be charted and calculated as clearly as the evidence allows at every stage.

E, EX

Löfstedt was the first to formulate the distinction between *e* and *ex* used before consonants: "Das Wesentliche der Sache, das man, wie es scheint, bisher nicht erkannt hat, ist indessen nach meiner Meinung so auszudrücken, dass *ex* im Gegensatz zu *e* die von der Volkssprache bevorzugte Form war."[93] The use of *e* and *ex* before consonants in late prose confirms this, but at the time of Cicero the situation was still fluid. *ThLL* (s.v. *ex*, 1083–4) reports on Cicero, "in *rep*. ante cons. 45ies *ex*, 16ies *e* numeravi; eadem fere proportio in aliis scriptis, nisi quod in *Att*. et *epist*. forma *e* etiam rarius exstat" (which supports Löfstedt's distinction), and continues to note that the *Bellum Africum* always has *ex* except in the phrase *e regione*, that Sallust has *e* not more than 7 times, and that "Liv. Vitr. Val. Max. Sen. Curt. Colum. Plin. *nat*. Suet. Apul. haud ita raro habent formam *e*." Tacitus has *e* and *ex* equally (with no observable development), but Petronius has *e* only 5 times (and always in speeches), according to Löfstedt.

In poetry an even clearer distinction can be drawn. Löfstedt (citing F. Harder, *Fleckeis. Jahrb*. 141 [1890] 771–77) says that in early poetry and drama *ex* is much preferred, but that Lucilius has both equally; Varro (*Sat*., 11 *e*, 3 *ex*) and Cicero (22 *e*, 2 *ex*) both prefer *e* (an interesting contrast to Cicero's prose usage), and "auch bei Lucrez ist es [*e*] auffallend häufig." Cicero's verse can serve as a general date for the new preference for *e* before consonants, on which *ThLL* remarks, "formam leviorem praeferunt dactylici (item Sen. trag.), maxime elegantissimus quisque": this change, naturally enough, was established in poetry before its adoption in formal prose.[94] Virgil clearly prefers *e* before a consonant: there are only 8 cases of *ex* which cannot be explained by the normal exceptions (*ThLL* notes that the monosyllabic forms of the personal pronouns are normally preceded by *ex*, as is *quo*, and Axelson adds that adjectives used as substantives also normally have *ex*[95]). Horace, a surprising exception among the poets, in the *Odes* and

[93] *PA* 89.

[94] As J. Rolfe (*ALL* 10 [1898] 470) remarks on the similar restriction of *a* instead of *ab* before consonants in both poetry and prose, "Vielleicht also ist die historische Prosa konservativer und mehr archaisch gefärbt; jedenfalls ist die Prosa überhaupt in der Scheidung beider Formen nachlässiger als die Poesie. . . ."

[95] Pp. 119–20, some of Virgil's exceptions are perhaps to be explained in other ways. The following figures for *e*, *ex* in the poets are those given by *ThLL*, which Axelson cites (except that in the case of Ovid—for which Löwe, *Die Praep. a, de, ex bei Ovid*, Progr. Strehlen 1889, cited by *ThLL*, was not available to him—the figures on the elegies are his own). The figures for Virgil are mine.

Epodes never has *e*, though *ex* occurs only 4 times (as Axelson says, "eine rein persönliche Antipathie gegen diese Form"). Tibullus has *ex* only once (2.1.24, where Bürger would read *e*), Lygdamus and Propertius never, and Ovid in elegy has *ex* only with *me, quo, magna parte*, and substantive adjectives. Later epic usage is similar: Valerius Flaccus has *ex* only once; it is also rare in Silius, Lucan, and Statius. Satire, however, uses *ex* colloquially: Horace has *ex* before a consonant 25 times in his *Satires* and *Epistles*, *e* 5 times; Martial has *e* only 3 times, Juvenal only 5.[96] It is clear, then, that *e* is the accepted poetic form before consonants from the time of Cicero on and that *ex*, previously common in poetry, is used only with certain allowed exceptions and remained chiefly colloquial (as in satire).

In the polymetrics Catullus has *ex* before a consonant 4 times: 16.3, *ex versiculis*; 17.5, *ex tua*; 17.18, *ex sua*; 50.17, *ex quo*. *Ex quo* is normal, and *ex tua* and *ex sua* may be regarded as analogous to the normal *ex te* and *ex se*, leaving only *ex versiculis*. In the longer poems there are also 4, all explicable: 62.62, *ex parte* (cf. Ovid's *ex parte*); 64.69, *ex te* (normal); 64.73, *ex tempore* (no doubt an older formula, as Virg., *Aen.* 1.171, *ex numero*, or 5.244 and 8.186, *ex more*); 68.36, *ex multis* (substantive adjective). In both groups, then, there is only one use of *ex* before a consonant which cannot be paralleled by later poetic usage,[97] whereas *e* occurs 3 times in the polymetrics and 16 times in the longer poems (10 of which are in c. 64). In the neoteric poems Catullus' usage conforms to what had become (or was becoming) the poetic practice. The epigrams, however, show just the opposite correlation. *E* occurs only once: 80.4, *quiete e molli*, in a Gellius poem containing other neoteric elements, perhaps in order to emphasize the effeminancy of Gellius, e.g., *rosea ista labella*, 1 (in as much as *rosea* is the only adjective in *-eus* found in the epigrams, and the use of the

---

[96] W. Clausen has pointed out to me that Juv. used *e* only in the stereotyped phrases *e caelo* (2.40, 11.27) and *e medio* (9.106); *et e medio . . . acervo* (13.10) and *et e pleno . . . acervo* (6.364) may be explained by sound (*et ex* would be harsh) or by analogy with *e medio*. (See U. Knoche, *Handschriftliche Grundlagen des Juvenaltextes*, Philologus Suppl. 33 [1940].) Therefore Housman's conjecture at Juv. 3.205 (*sub eodem e marmore*) is wrong.

[97] *Ex* may have been allowed before *v*: cf. Tib. 2.1.24, *ex virgis*, and Virg. *Ecl.* 6.19, *ipsis ex vincula sertis*, and 10.35, *ex vobis* (or explicable by analogy with the monosyllabic pers. pron. ?); *Aen.* 11.533, *ex virginibus*.

diminutive *labella*—as again *Victoris miselli*, 7—is also pointed). *Ex*, on the other hand, occurs 5 times, of which only one is explicable: 87.4, *ex parte* (normal); 90.1, *ex Gelli matrisque nefando coniugio*; 90.3, *ex matre*; 111.2, *ex laudibus* (*est* V, *e* Scaliger); 111.4, *ex patruo*. In the epigrams Catullus' usage follows that of earlier poetry, indicating again a separate tradition of Roman epigram which was immune to poetic change or innovation.[98]

O! and A!

The most convenient way to outline the development of the inter-jection *o*! in Latin poetry is to divide its uses into three headings: a) with the vocative, b) with the accusative of exclamation, c) with exclamatory sentences.[99] By far the greatest number of the uses of *o* in Plautus and Terence fall under the first category.[100] Lucretius has *o* only five times, three with the vocative (*o Graiae decus*, 3.3; *o bone*, 3.206; *o genus infelix humanum*, 5.1194; perhaps also 3.1, *o* O, omitted by Q) and twice with the accusative (*o miseras hominum mentis*, *o pectora caeca*, 2.14): in spite of the impassioned quality of these utter-ances, he did not make additional use of *o* and never used it to emphasize an exclamatory sentence. In Virgil, however, *o* is used without hesita-tion and begins a sentence almost as frequently as it is used with the vocative.[101] Tibullus goes one step further and completely restricts the use of *o* to the third category (10 times in I–II).

98 It may be noted here that the similar change that took place with the preposition *a* and *ab* is observed throughout the poems of Catullus, who has *ab* before a consonant only at 59.5, *ab semiraso ustore*; 64.275, *ab luce*; and 81.3, *moribunda ab sede Pisauri* (on the "mock-heroic ring" of this whole phrase, see now E. Fraenkel, *Gnomon* 34 [1962] 258). Virgil has *ab* before *s* only in the formula *ab sede* (*sedibus*); and *ab luce* is a formula of the same type (see J. Rolfe [above n. 94] 469, who notes that *ab* is retained in "Formeln, welche der Orts- und Zeitbestimmung dienen"). Catullus' three exceptions may perhaps be regarded as archaic and epic, an interesting support for the interpretation of the compound *semiraso* as a play on epic compounds. (See also Axelson, pp. 118–19, for other exceptions in the poets, which together appear archaic-epic, and *ThLL* I, cols. 2–3, s.v.*a*.)

99 So G. Lodge, *Lexicon Plautinum* (Leipzig 1904–1933) s.v.

100 Plautus has *o* with an exclamatory sentence only 9 times, Terence 10. See the lexica of Lodge and P. McGlynn (*Lexicon Terentianum* I, London 1963).

101 See Merguet's *Lexicon zu Vergilius* (Leipzig 1912).

It has been pointed out that *o* in Latin is very different from the common *ὦ* in Greek, that it always has a definite emotional quality.[102] This is true, but is in part an overstatement, in part a misrepresentation. The common use of *o* with vocatives in comedy (and therefore, we can assume, generally in colloquial Latin) is by no means always emotional to such a degree, and perhaps it was Lucretius' need for greater emotional content which led him to restrict its use to the four passages cited above so that it would gain particular emphasis by reason of its rarity in his poem. Virgil gives it emphasis in a different way: although *o* is common in all his poems, it is used to make an entire sentence exclamatory as often as a single vocative, and this usage became, for Tibullus, the proper—and only—poetic function of the interjection. It is safe to assume that *o* in itself was not always poetic, but had to be made so by the poets in various ways.[103]

It is necessary to examine the situation in Catullus in this light. O occurs 22 times in the polymetric poems, 12 times in the longer poems 61–68 (excluding the 24 times it is used in the refrains of 61 and 62), and only four times in the epigrams (twice in c. 76, *o di*, where it is a

---

[102] For instance, Kroll on 88.5: "Der Zusatz von *o* zum Vokativ der angeredeten Person ist nie ohne Emphase." Fordyce goes further (on 46.9): "*o* is not the normal accompaniment of a vocative, as *ὦ* is in classical Greek usage, but both in colloquial and in literary Latin has an emotional content, and marks sentimental (as here), pathetic, or impassioned address. It is significant that, as K. F. Smith (on Tib. i.4.9) points out, *o* is never used with a vocative by the unimpassioned Tibullus, often by the passionate Propertius." This note is unfortunate on three counts: a) K. F. Smith points out nothing of the kind, but merely cites the passages where *o* is found in Tibullus; b) far from being "unimpassioned" in his use of *o*, Tibullus, as Smith *does* point out, uses the exclamation because it is "the passionate and pathetic *o*"; and c) it is the very restriction of *o* to its function of introducing a sentence that makes it impassioned—the "passionate" Propertius' indiscriminate use with the vocative serves only to make it less so.

[103] Horace's use of *o* is notable. In the *Odes*, *o* is a self-consciously poetic element: it begins the entire collection (in the second line of the first ode, in just the same position it occupies in the self-conscious *Carmen Saeculare*); of its 37 occurrences in the *Odes*, 11 occur in first or second lines. On the other hand, in the *Satires* it is a conversational element: it occurs 23 times, of which at least 17 are clearly in conversational, direct quotations, and others are to be understood as such. But the *Epistles*, significantly, can be neither so poetic as the *Odes* nor so colloquial as the *Satires*; in them, therefore, *o* is encountered only twice. (It may also be noted that in the *Odes*, 34 of its 37 occurrences are with a vocative of some sort: Horace found an entirely different way of making *o* poetic than did Virgil and Tibullus.)

standard sacral element). In only two instances is it used to give an
exclamatory force to a sentence,[104] and in three cases it occurs with the
accusative of exclamation.[105] The hesitation with which Catullus uses
it in the epigrams is no doubt due to the same factors which led
Lucretius to restrict it so severely: it did not as yet have a poetic
function defined in existing Roman poetry. Catullus, though, felt
himself less restricted in the two genres for which he helped to create
the standards; in the longer neoteric poems and in the polymetric
poems the function of *o* can be best understood by a comparison with
the use made of another exclamatory particle, *a*.

The *Thesaurus Linguae Latinae* summarizes *a* with the words, "vox
est poetarum propria; in prosa oratione non legi nisi apud VARR.
Men. 361 (*ab* codd.) et CIC. *rep.* 1.59 *de orat.* 2.285."[106] The two prose
instances in Cicero may be quickly disregarded, for both occur in
direct quotations and may be regarded as colloquial (the first is a remark
of Archytas of Tarentum). The words "vox poetarum propria" may be
further modified by noting the absence of *a* in Ennius and Lucretius, in
the *Aeneid*, and in satire.[107] Its occurrence in comedy leads to the assumption that it was a colloquial exclamation despite the fact that it was
ignored by the satirists, and with good reason. This reason could only
have been that after Plautus and Terence, and by the time of Horace,
a had become the exclusive property of a certain type of poetic emotion.

A fragment of Calvus' *Io* survives to document the neoteric adoption
of the exclamation:

> a virgo infelix, herbis pasceris amaris. (frg. 9)

When Virgil came to deal with Pasiphaë in what is perhaps the neoteric
section of a catalogue of poetic development in *Eclogue* 6,[108] he

---

[104] *o quantum est hominum beatiorum,* / *quid me laetius est beatiusve?*, 9.10–11, where it may
easily be taken as accompanying the implied vocative; but it may also give force to
quid . . ., as it does in *o quid solutis est beatius curis,* 31.7.

[105] 107.6, *o lucem candidiore nota*; and with urbane wit in 26.5, *o ventum horribilem atque
pestilentem,* and 56.1, *o rem ridiculam, Cato, et iocosam.*

[106] *ThLL* I, col. 1441, 41–42.

[107] Except Juv. 14.45, the formulaic *procul a procul*; and Pers. 1.8 and 3.16.

[108] The lines on the popular neoteric theme of Scylla also contain this exclamation
(6.77).

emphasized the similar situations of Io and Pasiphaë by echoing Calvus' line twice:

> a virgo infelix, quae te dementia cepit? (47)
> a virgo infelix, tu nunc in montibus erras (52)

The Corydon of *Eclogue* 2 ends his lament by twice using the exclamation *a*, by which Virgil suggests that this frustrated love is a commonplace of neoteric poetry, and reinforces this suggestion by adding *dementia*:

> quem fugis, a, demens? (60)
> a Corydon Corydon, quae te dementia cepit? (69)[109]

Finally, the lines of *Eclogue* 10 which Servius notes were taken directly from Gallus' poems[110] contain *a* in three successive lines, a definite indication of the use that poet must have made of it. It should also be noted in this connection that Propertius makes much of *a* in the first three books,[111] but abandons it completely in the fourth. The pathetic *a* was introduced to Latin poetry by the neoteric poets and continued to be a trademark of their poetry.[112]

Catullus uses the exclamation 5 times in the longer poems: once in 61.132 (*miser a miser / concubine, nuces da*), again in 63.61 (*miser a miser . . . anime*), twice in c. 64 (notably once of Ariadne, *a misera*, 71, and once by Ariadne of Theseus, *immemor a!*, 135) and finally in 66.85.[113] It occurs in two other unquestioned passages in the polymetric poems,[114] but nowhere in the epigrams. The situation is like that of *o*, and the explanation too must be similar. Catullus was not free to initiate novelty in the structure or vocabulary of the epigrams, and certainly

---

[109] W. Clausen has pointed out to me that Theocritus has ὦ (ὦ Κύκλωψ, Κύκλωψ, πᾷ τὰς φρένας ἐκπεπότασαι, 11.72), which Virgil changed, in his characteristic way, for a good reason.

[110] *Ecl.* 10.47–49. See Servius on 10.46.

[111] 9 times in I, 10 times in II, and 5 times in III.

[112] Virgil has it twice in the *Georgics*, one of which occurs in the epyllion, *a miseram Eurydicen* (4.526), with the triple anaphora of *Eurydicen*.

[113] Perhaps again in 64.178: *at* Muretus, *ah* B. Guarinus: *a* V. But the usual spelling of the interjection by the MSS. seems to be *ha* O, *ah* X. Mynors rightly reads *at* (Friedrich and Kroll both read *a*).

[114] Again with *miser* at 15.17, *a tum te miserum malique fati*; and in a traditional (and neoteric) context at 60.5. Scaliger read *a me me* at 21.11, and it has even been found lurking in the *avelte* of the MSS. at 55.9.

declined to introduce so marked a neotericism as *a* into this group of poems. In the longer poems, though, *a* definitely belonged, and there was no Roman literary tradition to hinder Catullus in using the polymetric forms as he wished. Thus *o* and *a* are both found in the first two groups of poems, but only hesitatingly or not at all in the epigrams.

ADJECTIVES IN *-OSUS*

The question of the nature of adjectives terminating in *-osus* has been answered in two ways: they may be seen either as offering the poets another means to approach Greek poetic vocabulary, or as characteristic of the *sermo plebeius* (or more particularly the *sermo rusticus*) and therefore basically foreign to poetic diction. Leumann remarks: "Ohne Zusammenhang mit metrischen Bedürfnissen, vielmehr als Wiedergabe griechischer epischer Adjektiva auf *-όεις* und Komposita mit *πολυ-* sind im Latein der Dichtersprache in der Funktion von Epitheta ornantia die Adjektive auf *-ōsus* stark vermehrt worden, die an sich keineswegs poetisch sind (*nebulosus* Cato): *frondosus* (vgl. hom. *ἀκριτό-φυλλος*). . . ."[115] In observing that they are in themselves in no way poetic, he recognizes the other side of the question, elaborately discussed by F. T. Cooper: "These adjectives form one of the most numerous classes in Latin, but in proportion to their number are used sparingly by the best writers. . . . They are regularly derived from substantives and in general only such have the sanction of classic usage. On the other hand these adjectives abound in plebeian Latin, being especially prevalent in the rustic and the African writers, and are formed alike from subs. and adjs., and occasionally even from verbs, the sonorous suffix being well adapted to satisfy the plebeian craving for lengthened and intensified formations."[116] These two views are, of course, not mutually exclusive, and the role of these adjectives in

115 M. Leumann, "Die Lateinische Dichtersprache," *Mus Helv* 4 (1947) 130 [=*Kl. Schr.* 148].

116 *Word Formation in the Roman Sermo Plebeius* (New York 1895) 122–32. Cooper cites Guericke (*De linguae vulgaris reliquiis apud Petronium et in inscriptt. pariet. Pompeianis,*

poetry of different genres is well illustrated by the use Catullus made of them, from which certain unifying conclusions can be drawn. In the polymetric poems there are 16 adjectives in *-osus* used 25 times; in the longer poems 7 used 8 times; and in the epigrams only 3, used 5 times. These groups are clearly defined; only one adjective is found in two (*verbosus*, 55.20 and 98.2). The statistics for the distribution of these adjectives in Catullus, however, are misleading, because it would appear that they are relatively as common in the epigrams as in the longer poems. Two factors must be taken into account: that some adjectives in *-osus* are (to put it simply) "poetic", others "colloquial"; and that context and usage must determine the nature and poetic purpose of any word.

Leumann's remarks may be taken as a start for discussion of the longer poems. In c. 64 four adjectives in *-osus* are found, and though it is impossible to show in each case that Catullus had in mind specific Greek originals which he was translating, it is not absolutely necessary to do so: the contexts indicate his intention. *Ventosus* is the obvious equivalent of the Homeric ἠνεμόεις, used once with *aequor* (64.12), and again, all too obviously in the function of *epitheta ornantia*, with *procellae* (64.59).[117] For *spinosus* (64.72, with *curas*) it is difficult to find a Greek parallel: Baehrens (*ad loc.*) seems to conjure up his comment ("cf. graecum ἀκανθώδεις μέριμναι") from thin air.[118] *Frondosus*,

---

[Gumbinnen 1875] 32), who "first connected them with the *sermo plebeius*, observing their frequency in Cato and the early dramatists, and citing the admonition in Prob. App., '*rabidus non rabiosus*';" and Stuenkel (*De Varroniana verborum formatione*, [Strassburg 1875] 50), who "subsequently called attention to their special frequency in the Scriptt. R.R., and regarded them as characteristic of the *sermo rusticus*, an opinion which a casual glance at those writers will confirm."

[117] On the intricate verbal pattern of this passage (64.58–60), see Putnam, *HSCP* 65 (1961) 168 and 202 n. 16.

[118] I have been unable to locate Baehrens' Greek, but the context in Catullus is typically neoteric: *a misera* addressed to Ariadne, 71; *spinosas* at the beginning of the line and its substantive *curas* at the end, with the learned cult title *Erycina* between; and the Greek rhythm of the beginning of the following line, *illa tempestate*, $--|----˘|$. (On this type see M. Zicàri, "Some Metrical and Prosodical Features of Catullus' Poetry," *Phoenix* 18 [1964] 198, who notes that it is common in Homer, not unfamiliar in the Alexandrian poets, but is rare in Latin after Ennius *Ann.* 44 and 235 V.² and Cat. 64.73, 115 and 66.11. It should be noted that Virgil, in imitating 64.115 *tecti frustraretur inobservabilis error*, removed this Grecism of meter: *frangeret indeprensus et inremeabilis error*, *Aen.* 5.591, and *hic labor ille domus et inextricabilis error*, 6.27.)

according to Leumann, represents the Homeric compound ἀκριτόφυλλός, but its use with *Idalium* in 64.96 (which the commentators all refer to Theoc. 15.100) suggests that a mist of poetic association may cloud the issue. Virgil uses *frondosus* once of Mt. Ida (*Aen.* 5.252), and it is not impossible that he was representing by *frondosus* the Homeric epithets (῎Ιδην . . . πολυπίδακα, μητέρα θηρῶν, or ῎Ιδης . . . πιδηέσσης); Catullus may have been attracted earlier by the similarity of the names Ida and Idalium and may have done the same. *Spumosus* (64.121, . . . *spumosa ad litora Diae*) may represent πολύφλοισβος—both Catullus' line and Virgil's . . . *spumosa immerserat unda* (*Aen.* 6.174) may suggest the rhythm of πολυφλοίσβοιο θαλάσσης. Though such parallels are far from obvious and these four adjectives in -*osus* may not have occurred to Catullus as representing the Homeric epithets in -όεις or πολυ- suggested here, it is nevertheless clear that in c. 64 they bring to their lines a poetic color, if nothing else, and a shading from the Greek.

Furthermore, these particular four adjectives were felt by the later poets to belong to elevated diction. Three of the four occur in Virgil, and *ventosus* and *frondosus* are his two most frequently used adjectives in -*osus*.[119] These four, too, were generally avoided by the Augustan elegists and Horace.[120] This is an unmistakable indication of their epic quality and of a propriety of diction observed by Catullus in his epyllion. Three other adjectives in -*osus* are used in the longer poems: *torosus* (63.83) and *nervosus* (67.27) occur only in Ovid *Metamorphoses* (7.429 and 6.256 respectively), though, understandably, not in Virgil's epic; and *muscosus* (68.58) occurs once in the *Eclogues* (7.45) and three times in Propertius (2.19.30, 2.30.26, 3.3.26).

Axelson, although noting the colloquial nature of these adjectives,

---

[119] *ventosus* (5 times in the *Aeneid*) and *frondosus* (3 times in the *Aeneid*) are each used 7 times by Virgil (*aquosus* and *umbrosus* are next, 5 times each); *spumosus* occurs at *Aen.* 6.174 and 12.524. For a list of Virgil's adjectives in -*osus*, see A. Ernout, *Rev Phil* 21 (1947) 64–67.

[120] *ventosus*: Hor. *Epist.* 1.19.37, 2.1.177, 1.8.12, *Odes* 3.4.46; Prop. 2.12.5; not in Tib.; Ovid 8 times. *spumosus*: not in Hor., Prop., Tib.; Ovid *Met.* 1.570. *spinosus*: not in Hor., Tib.; Prop. 4.4.48; Ovid *Met.* 2.810. *frondosus*: not in Hor., Prop., Tib.; Ovid *Met.* 8.410, *Rem. Am.* 202.

failed to appreciate their poetic potentiality sufficiently,[121] which led Ernout in his review to a longer discussion of the problem.[122] He noted the proliferation of this type of adjective in the archaic period and drew an important distinction on their formation:[123] "Virgile se garde bien d'employer de ces formations incorrectes [i.e., from adjective or verb stems instead of from noun stems] mais les types normaux en -*ōsus* sont si loin de lui répugner qu'il en use volontiers dans toutes ses oeuvres."[124] Virgil has 26 adjectives in -*osus* used 80 times,[125] all formed properly from noun stems: there is no better indication of the place of certain adjectives in -*osus* in high poetry.

The polymetric poems present a far greater number (16 used 25 times) of adjectives of this type,[126] but it is immediately apparent that their nature is quite different. None of these is found in Virgil; however, 12 of the 16 contain a cretic, which not only fits them well for the hendecasyllabic and iambic meters in which they are found but also can explain their absence from later hexameter and elegiac poetry. Thus, although Virgil has the adjective *tenebrosus* (*Aen.* 5.839 and 6.107), he cannot use *tenebricosus*, which form, in turn, Catullus may have

---

[121] P. 61, discussing *formosus* and *pulcher*: "Wie so manche andere Bildung auf -*osus* hatte *formosus* zweifellos ein etwas triviales Gepräge, das es für die hohe Distanzsprache als weniger geeignet denn *pulcher* erscheinen liess."

[122] *Rev Phil* 21 (1947) 64–67.

[123] "Ce qui est vrai c'est que, à l'époque archaïque, ces formations en -*osus* ont été multipliées à l'excès . . ." (p. 64). This remark may be interpreted to apply both to colloquial Latin (cf. the remarks of Cooper cited above on "the plebeian craving for lengthened and intensified formations") and to the language of drama and satire; but no adjective in -*osus* appears in the scant remains of epigram and, as discussed below, there is no reason for supposing that they played as large a part in the vocabulary of early epigram as this early proliferation might suggest.

[124] It may be noted here that Ernout corrects Axelson's statement on *formosus* (used 16 times by Virgil in the *Eclogues*, only once in the *Georgics*, and never in the *Aeneid*, and therefore, according to Axelson, belonging only to the lesser genres, the observation that perhaps led to his generalization on adjectives in -*osus*): *formosus* ". . . a sans doute été fait sur le grec μορφήεις qu'on trouve notamment dans Pindare avec le sens de εὔμορφος" (p. 65); *formosus* refers to physical beauty (more fitting in the *Bucolics* than the *Aeneid*), *pulcher* to a moral or ethical sphere of beauty.

[125] See Ernout's list (above, n. 119).

[126] The complete list is: *aestuosus*, 7.5, 46.5; *araneosus*, 25.3; *cuniculosus*, 37.18; *curiosus*, 7.11; *ebriosus*, 27.4 (twice); *febriculosus*, 6.4; *harundinosus*, 36.13; *imaginosus*, 41.8; *iocosus*, 8.6, 36.10, 56.1, 4; *laboriosus*, 1.7, 38.2; *morbosus*, 57.6; *otiosus*, 10.2, 50.1; *pilosus*, 16.10, 33.7; *sumptuosus*, 44.9, 47.5; *tenebricosus*, 3.11; *verbosus*, 55.20.

employed only for metrical reasons; yet one must take into consideration here the fact that *tenebrosus* is the proper formation (from the
noun stem), *tenebricosus* the improper (that is, colloquial, from the
adjective stem). Of the four adjectives in this group which do not
contain a cretic, *iocosus* is common in poetry later (though never in
epic); *morbosus* occurs only in *Priapea* 46.2; *pilosus* is not found in Vir.,
Hor., Tib., Prop., Ovid; and *verbosus* only for comic effect in Ovid.[127]
Though these four adjectives are metrically admissible in elegy or
hexameters, three definitely had no place in the later vocabulary of
these genres. A glance at the full list of the adjectives in *-osus* in the
polymetric poems, and the fact that three (*cuniculosus, harundinosus*, and
imaginosus) are *hapax legomena*, show clearly that the majority of these
adjectives are special formations, either comic in origin (*aestuosus* first
in Plautus, *Bacch.* 471, *Truc.* 350; *febriculosus* elsewhere only in *Cist.*
406), or of Catullus' own invention, or of prose origin (*morbosus*,
rustic writers; *ebriosus*, 4 times later in Cicero).

Such explanations, however, are not sufficient to explain either the
reappearance of some of these words in later poetry where meter
allows,[128] or the use which Catullus makes of them: although their
origins may be as foreign to poetry as the epic formations discussed
above were germane, they are often used with particular Catullan
effect. *Aestuosus*[129] occurs in the particularly Alexandrian and neoteric
setting of c. 7 (*oraclum Iovis inter aestuosi*, 5) and again similarly in c. 46
(*Nicaeaeque ager uber aestuosae*, 5, where, in addition, the sound of every
syllable in the line seems carefully calculated). *Harundinosus* has the
same setting (*nunc o caeruleo creata ponto | quae sanctum Idalium Vriosque
apertos | quaeque Ancona Cnidumque harundinosam | colis . . .*, 36.11-4,
where the epithet is a playfully learned attribute not unlike the *lasarpiciferis* of 7.4). *Laboriosus* (1.7) and *otiosus* (50.1) both occur in contexts
describing the setting of Catullus' poetry and literary life. These words,
at least, have a tone and purpose clearly different from that which

---

127 *Am.* 1.15.5, *verbosas leges*; *Tr.* 3.12.18 and 4.10.18, both *verbosi fori*.
128 As *aestuosus* in Hor. *Epod.* 3.18, 16.62, *Odes* 1.22.5, 1.31.5, 2.7.16; *laboriosus* in Hor.
Epod. 16.60, 17.16; *otiosus*, Hor. *Epod.* 5.43, *Odes* 3.18.11.
129 *ThLL*, s.v., records "GLOSS. καυματώδης."

their colloquial context would lead us to expect; accordingly they furnish another bridge between the vocabularies of the polymetric and longer poems. They playfully imitate, in their neoteric contexts, the poetic formations of epic from the Greek, and in their turn perhaps suggested to Catullus such a formation as the *spinosas (curas)* of 64.72, for which no real Greek parallel can be found.

The adjectives in *-osus* in the polymetrics, then, served two purposes: some (as *aestuosus*) were used by Catullus in neoteric passages to suggest the high poetic formations of the same type frequent in epic; others, being technically improper formations or words never possible in higher poetry (such as *tenebricosus, morbosus, febriculosus*), suggest both their colloquial origin and the poetic potential of the termination to create the playfully elegant combination of lightness and learning so characteristic of the polymetrics.

It has been noted that there are relatively as many *-osus* adjectives in the epigrams (3 used 5 times) as in the longer poems (7 used 8 times). In the epigrams, however, they occur in only three poems. *Formosus* (86.1, 3, 5) occurs frequently in Augustan elegy and 16 times in Virgil's *Eclogues* (but only once in the *Georgics* and never in the *Aeneid*); c. 86, its context in Catullus, may be regarded as one of the few neoteric experiments among the epigrams: since the subject is Quintia's lack of the sophisticated virtues which Catullus valued highly in both Lesbia and poetry, the polymetric vocabulary of *urbanitas* makes its rare appearance here in the epigrams (*nam nulla venustas | nulla in tam magno est corpore mica salis,* 3–4); *formosa*, repeated three times, may be regarded as a similar importation from the polymetrics. The same evaluation is true of *studiosus* in 116.1, where the context includes the only mention of Callimachus in the epigrams: *saepe tibi studioso animo venante requirens | carmina uti possem mittere Battiadae. Studiosus*, though not used by Virgil, occurs 18 times in Ovid, twice in the *Corpus Tibullianum* (3.12.15 and 3.14.5), and 3 times in Horace (*Sat.* 2.5.80, *Epist.* 1.3.6, *Odes* 3.27.29 [of Europa, *nuper in pratis studiosa florum*]). Neither *formosus* nor *studiosus* was impossible for later elegy, and both were used by Catullus in epigrams in contexts that immediately suggest the polymetrics. The only other epigram containing an *-osus* adjective is 98 (*in te, si in quemquam, dici pote, putide Victi, | id quod verbosis dicitur et fatuis,* 1–2), where there is no suggestion of anything neoteric (natively obscene invective, rather than neoteric wit, is the key-note). *Verbosus* (though occurring in Catullus also at 55.20, *verbosa gaudet Venus loquella*) is absent from the poems of Virgil, Horace, Propertius, and Tibullus but used for comic effect by Ovid three times. *Verbosus* may thus be said (though perhaps at the risk of being charged with special pleading) to be the only adjective in -*osus* found in a genuinely epigrammatic context in cc. 69–116 and to be one without any poetic function or tone. Once again, it may not be due to chance that no such adjective is found in the epigrams of Aedituus, Licinus, or Catulus.

Adjectives in -*osus* (we may summarize) were exploited in epic poetry originally to suggest certain types of Greek epic adjectives, as Catullus himself did in c. 64; yet at the same time their association with the *sermo plebeius* allowed certain of them to be used by Catullus in the lighter forms of neoteric poetry, in which they offered him a perfect means of conveying the very tone and effect such poems required— colloquial urbanity and wit derived from suggestion of the techniques and vocabulary of more serious neoteric verse. It must be for this reason that -*osus* adjectives are so common in the polymetrics (16 used 25 times). Pre-neoteric epigram, however, must have made little or no use of these formations, since it paid so little attention to epic technique (as will be discussed in greater detail later); Catullus thus has, with the exception of two neoteric experiments with the form of epigram, only one -*osus* adjective (*verbosus*) in his epigrams, and that one an adjective not used in later elegiac verse to any great extent. If relatively few such adjectives appear in elegy, the reason is that many had to be avoided as epic, while others seemed too prosaic (Tibullus is in this respect too a greater purist than either Propertius or Ovid[130]); but many remained,

---

130 Tibullus uses 7 adjectives in -*osus* 13 times (*formosus,* 4 in I, 2 in II; *fumosus,* 2.1.27; *herbosus,* 2.5.25; *iocosus,* 2.1.85; *pomosus,* 1.1.17; *umbrosus,* 1.4.1, 2.3.72; *villosus,* 2.3.76). Lygdamus has 7 used 13 times (*annosus,* 3.2.19, 3.6.58; *formosus* 5 times; *generosus,* 3.6.5; *iocosus,* 3.6.20; *rugosus,* 3.5.25; *studiosus,* 3.12.15, 3.14.5; *umbrosus,* 3.9.2). Together they have 11 such adjectives used 26 times, of which, on the one extreme of poetic diction, only 5 are found in Virgil, and, on the other, only one (*iocosus*) in Catullus' polymetric poems.

and there was in fact no small use made of these forms by the elegists, a use for which the precedent of the neoterics may have been largely responsible.

ADJECTIVES IN -*EUS*[131]

The poetic quality of adjectives in -*eus* is well established. Originally the IE adjective suffix *-eyo-, denoting material, produced such equivalents as ἀργύρεος and *argenteus*; in Latin the suffix formed, for example, adjectives from the names of trees and plants, but such formations were limited and the suffix itself was not particularly productive in the *sermo plebeius*.[132] The poets, however, exploited it and

[131] The complete list for Catullus may conveniently be given here at the start: *aequoreus*, 64.15; (*aereus*, 30.10, 64.142, 240, 291, 66.6, 68.57); *aureus*, 61.95, 63.39, 66.60; *caeruleus*, 36.11; *consanguineus*, 64.118; *ferreus*, 17.26, 42.17; *flammeus*, 61.8, 115, 64.341, 66.3; *laneus*, 25.10, 64.316; *ligneus*, 23.6; *lūteus*, 61.10, 188; *niveus*, 58ᵇ.4, 61.9, 63.8, 64.240, 303, 309, 364, 68.125; *pineus*, 61.15, 64.10; *purpureus*, 45.12, 64.163, 275, 308; *roseus*, 55.12, 63.74, 64.49, 309, 80.1; *saxeus*, 64.61; *virgineus*, 66.14, 67.28. *Aereus* requires a note of explanation. The normal form is *aerius* (ἀέριος), but *ThLL*, s.v. *aerius*, notes that -*eus* is occasionally found as a variant reading in some MSS. of the poets. No editor of Cat. had noted this alternate (except Baehrens, who has "-*eum* O" in his apparatus at 64.240), but Ellis mysteriously read -*eus* in all six occurrences (though, according to his app. crit., neither O nor G give it). Sir R. A. B. Mynors has kindly written to me (12 June 1965): "The facts are (I believe) as follows: xxx 10 -*ias* OGR; lxiv 142 -*ii* O -*ei* GR, 240 -*eum* O -*ium* GR, 291 -*ia* OGR; lxvi 6 -*io* OGR; lxviii 57 -*ii* OGR." No safe conclusion can be drawn about Cat.'s orthography from these readings, but the possibility (though not the probability) remains that Cat. may have used the -*eus* form as a more poetic variation, a possibility which, if capable of proof, would be significant. In my count of -*eus* adjectives below I have allowed *aereus* to remain, but it should be taken into account that some, if not all, of these six occurrences are doubtful. (Adjectives in -*eus* formed from Greek proper names are dealt with elsewhere: they are, of course, of a different formation, those originally from -αιος becoming -*aeus* in Latin, those from -ειος becoming -*ēus*, not -*ĕus*.)

[132] Cooper, *Word Formation*, 111: "The simple suffix -*eus* was chiefly productive of denominative adjectives denoting material, which were not rare in the classic language but were especially prevalent in the Scriptt. R. R., who formed them freely from the names of plants and trees, as *buxeus, cedreus, fageus, fraxineus, laureus, orneus*, etc. They were especially adapted to pastoral poetry, and were freely introduced by Verg. and other Augustan poets whose authority has given the class as a whole a more elevated tone. Paucker has computed that out of 190 *vett.*, 60 (more than 31%) occur first, and many of them exclusively, in poetry [Pauck., Materialien, V, p. 109]. Meanwhile the activity of the simple suffix declined; post-Hadrian literature has produced only 87 new forms, while examples in the Romance languages are rare and chiefly poetic: in Rum. they are wanting altogether." See also his list, pp. 116–18. The frequency of these adjectives in poetry is not, of course, due to pastoral, nor their introduction to Virgil and the Augustans.

extended it to denote more than simple material: it could unmistakably represent the Greek, even when the roots were unrelated (*aureus* = χρύσεος, as *auricomus* = χρυσόκομος, or *ferreus* = σιδήρεος); and it was metrically useful in the hexameter.[133]

These adjectives were used by the older poets: for example, *argenteus* appears in Livius Andronicus and Plautus, *aureus* in Livius Andronicus, Naevius, Plautus, *caeruleus* in Ennius, Plautus, and probably Naevius (Varro, *Ling.* 7.7), *ferreus* in Ennius, Plautus, and *flammeus* in Ennius, Accius, Pacuvius. Although it is impossible to determine their exact scope and purpose, it is clear at least that the older poets, considering them fitting and proper, set the precedent in their use for the later poets whose important contribution was the coinage of such forms. Norden notes: "*vipereus* neu für das metrisch unbrauchbare *viperinus*; vgl. die teils ebenfalls durch Verszwang, teils durch das Streben nach Kürzen bedingten Neubildungen Vergils *arboreus*, *frondeus*, *fumeus* (unten 593), *litoreus*, *pampineus* (unten 804, vgl. Servius zu georg. 2, 5), *pulvereus*, *rameus*, *Romuleus*, *sidereus*, *spumeus* (vgl. Servius zur Aeneis 2, 419), *squameus*, *Tartareus* (s. unten zu Vers 295), *triticeus*, *tureus* (oben 225). Dass schon die ältere Poesie hiermit voranging, zeigen Lucrezens *fulmineus* und Catulls *aequoreus*, die dann Vergil übernahm."[134]

The coinage of these adjectives was no doubt due to metrical reasons: the cretic *lītŏrālis* could be used in the form *lītŏrĕus*, *vīrgĭnālis* in the form *vīrgĭnĕus*; other adjectives, by this adjustment, could be used in all cases, as *caērŭlus* (containing a cretic in the oblique cases) and *caērŭlĕus*.[135] Catullus appears to have coined *virgineus* and *aequoreus*;[136] *saxeus* (*lăpĭdĕus* in Enn. *Trag.* and Plaut.) appears first in Catullus 64.61 and in Lucretius four times, and *roseus* four times in Catullus and in Lucretius twice; Catullus is perhaps the first poet to use *niveus*, but the

---

133 M. Leumann, "Die lateinische Dichtersprache," *Mus Helv* 4 (1947) 130: "Die Funktion des *-eus* geht bei Dichtern, teilweise in Nachahmung des Griechischen, weit über den ursprünglichen Bereich von Stoffadjektiven hinaus. . . ."

134 *Aen. VI*, p. 218.

135 E. Bednara, *ALL* 14 (1906) 592–93. Catullus, for example, has both *caeruleus* (36.11, *nunc o caeruleo creata ponto*) and *caerulus* (64.7, *caerula verrentes abiegnis aequora palmis*).

136 *ThLL*, s.v. *aequoreus*: "adi. a neotericis formatum, quo maxime delectabatur Ov., quarto demum saeclo receptum pedestribus." On *virgineus*, see Bednara (above, n. 135).

word is undoubtedly older than this usage. Metrical convenience, however, is not in itself a sufficient explanation: by Catullus' time these forms had acquired a definite poetic color.[137]

It is not necessary to discuss the context of each adjective in the list given in n. 131. Those used in c. 64 are all obviously poetic and include the coinage *aequoreus* and the forms, perhaps new to poetry, *niveus* (four times), *saxeus*, and *roseus; consanguineus* is a rare word of poetic origin.[138] It is of more interest that in the epyllion Catullus takes other adjectives in *-eus* which are not so obviously poetic constructions or which are used elsewhere without poetic color and makes them, in their new contexts, assume a poetic force: *pineus*, for instance, which is identical with the forms in *-eus* of trees and plants in the rustic writers, becomes poetic in 64.10, *pinea coniungens inflexae texta carinae; laneus* likewise appears in a formal, neoteric line to describe the Parcae at 64.316, *laneaque aridulis haerebant morsa labellis.*

In the polymetric poems such obviously poetic forms appear as *caeruleus* in the prayer of 36.11 (*nunc o caeruleo creata ponto*) and *niveus* in the mythological conceit of 58[b].4 (*non Rhesi niveae citaeque bigae*). Elsewhere in the polymetrics these adjectives have the same characteristics as certain diminutives and in this respect belong to the vocabulary of the neoteric *nugae*: they are used to connote affection as *purpureo* at 45.12, *Acme . . . | et dulcis pueri ebrios ocellos | illo purpureo ore suaviata*, in context with the diminutive *ocellos*), or to convey a tone of delicate sensuality (as *roseis* at 55.12, "*en hic in roseis latet papillis*," again with a diminutive), or in a context of homosexuality (as *laneum* at 25.10, *ne laneum latusculum manusque mollicellas . . .*, with two diminutives in the same line, in the poem beginning *Cinaede*

---

[137] Bednara implies this poetic coloring in his discussion of *niveus*, an adjective first found in poetry in Catullus: "Obwohl dies Wort zuerst bei dem Auctor ad Her. II 44 sich findet, so glaube ich doch, dass es von daktylischen Dichtern gebildet worden ist, weil dieser Prosaiker seine Redeweise mit dichterischen Wörtern zu schmücken sucht und das Adjektiv *niveus* sich sonst nur bei Daktylikern findet: Catull. Verg. Hor. Tib. Ov. Val. Fl. Calpurn. Mart. Juv. Auson.; ausserdem nur noch bei dem Prosaiker Seneca, der die Sprache der daktylischen Dichter sehr häufig nachahmt. Dazu kommt, dass der grösste Teil der Adjectiva auf *-eus* dichterisch ist; . . ." (*ALL* 15 (1908) 224.)

[138] *ThLL*, s.v. *consanguineus*: "vox primum legitur apud PLAUT, PACVV. ACC., per liberae rei publicae tempora ad modum rara, numquam in oratt. Ciceronis. . . ."

Thalle). The polymetrics also contain *-eus* adjectives used without apparent poetic color, such as *ligneus* and *ferreus* (as is also true of the *flammeus* used in an almost technical sense as a substantive of the bridal garments in 61.8 and 115, and of *luteus* in 61.10, though the latter is poetic in 61.188, *alba parthenice velut | luteumve papaver*, and the former poetic at 64.341, *flammea . . . celeris vestigia cervae*, and 66.3, *flammeus . . . rapidi solis nitor*).

In all Catullus uses 16 adjectives in *-eus* 45 times: there are 8 used 9 times in the polymetrics, 13 used 35 times in the longer poems (in c. 64 there are 10 used 18 times), but in the epigrams only one. This single instance occurs in the first line of a Gellius poem, c. 80, in a context of homosexuality and again with a diminutive, *Quid dicam, Gelli, quare rosea ista labella | hiberna fiant candidiora nive . . .*: this instance must be regarded as another experiment in the epigrams; Catullus, in dealing with Gellius' homosexual practices, allows himself vocabulary not strictly appropriate to epigram. In the avoidance of adjectives in *-eus* the epigrams once again clearly show a separate tradition: they make no use of this feature of vocabulary belonging both to older hexameter verse and to neoteric verse. This fact receives further emphasis when the role generally assigned to adjectives in *-eus* is remembered: the metrical usefulness of those adjectives to the hexameter poets would suggest that they be found in epigram far more often than in the polymetric poems. Instead, just the opposite is the case.

QUE-QUE, QUE-ET

"Polysyndetisches *que-que* ist bei Nomina ererbt . . . Die Verbindung ist altlateinisch; als Archaismus wird sie von Catull, den Augusteern und späteren Dichtern bis auf Ven. Fort. übernommen . . . Die klassische Prosa meidet sie ganz. . . ."[139] This formulation, often anticipated and repeated, has found general acceptance:[140] for later

---

[139] Schmalz-Hofmann, 656.

[140] Cf. Norden, *Aen. VI*, p. 228: "Den Hexameter mit *-que-que* zu schliessen, eine für seinen Bau sehr bequeme Praxis, hatte Ennius nach griechischem τε–τε eingeführt (bei

poets, including Catullus, the use of *que-que*, especially at the end of a verse, was either archaic after the Ennian (Homeric) type, or (later) Greek, perhaps after neoteric usage, and its total absence from prose shows that it had become entirely an artificial, in no sense colloquial, poetic mannerism.[141]

In Catullus *que-que* occurs:

    15.19: *percurrent raphanique mugilesque*

    17.9: *per caputque pedesque*

    32.11: *pertundo tunicamque palliumque*

    57.2: *Mamurrae pathicoque Caesarique*

    64.201: *tali mente, deae, funestet seque suosque*

    66.40: *adiuro teque tuumque caput*

    76.8: *haec a te dictaque factaque sunt*

On 15.19, which may serve as an example of the neoteric use of *que-que* in the polymetrics, Kroll notes that "*-que-que* entnimmt C. der von Ennius geschaffenen epischen Sprache; unbefangener Prosa ist es fremd." It may be noted, however, that its use here and elsewhere in the polymetrics is far more neoteric than Ennian: *raphani* is a Greek word, the counterpart of the Roman *mugiles*, used in the mock learned manner of the polymetrics;[142] the tone of the close of c. 15 is also emphasized by the neoteric exclamation *a!* at the beginning of the sentence (17, *a tum te miserum malique fati*). It should be observed that *que-que* is also used (with pointed epic dignity and grammatical license) with a Greek word at 57.2 (*pathicoque*), and that at 32.11 it joins the

---

Ennius 9 mal überliefert), nach dessen Muster überaus oft Vergil. . . ." For a thorough study of its use in the poets, see H. Christensen, *ALL* 15, 165–211. There is no need here to restate the details.

[141] E. Fraenkel's fine discussion of *que-que* in comedy (*Elementi Plautini in Plauto* (Firenze 1960) 199–201) demonstrates that the relatively few occurrences (11 in Plaut., 1 in Ter.) are not a colloquial feature; he concludes, "per il poeta *-que. . . .-que* era una costruzione ch'egli non impiegava mai nel comune verso parlato delle sue commedie, e solo con grande riserbo altrove, in maniera tale da rendere molto probabile l'ipotesi che egli l'abbia presa dalle clausole esametriche enniane, forse per il tramite della tragedia."

[142] For a fine example of modern learned comment, which misses the purpose and force of Catullus' line by a long way, see Ellis *ad loc.*

Roman *tunicam* and the Greek *pallium*.[143] The Greek (Alexandrian) force of *que-que* in Catullus may be seen from 66.40, where Callimachus had σήν τε κάρην ὤμοσα σόν τε βίον: there is no doubt that here it is used as a Callimachean poeticism. On the other hand, 64.201 must be taken as an Ennian archaism: the close of Ariadne's curse upon Theseus is solemn and ritualistic.[144] The only instance of *que-que* in the epigrams is 76.8, where it can be called neither neoteric nor Ennian (it does not, like the others, come at the end of its line); it would appear here to be simply a metrical convenience.[145] Otherwise Catullus restricts his use of *que-que* to the polymetrics and longer poems, where its use as a neoteric poeticism is obvious.[146]

On *que-et* Hofmann's statement may again be taken as the accepted view: "*que-et* begegnet im Altlatein (Plt. Enn. Ter. Acc. Pacuv.) meist am Versende, war also wohl damals schon ein Archaismus; . . . in der Dichtung ist *que-et* als archaische Verbindung nur dem höheren Stil angemessen, daher öfters bei Verg. Tib. al. (nicht Hor.) . . ."[147] Hofmann, in a review of Heraeus' Martial, observes the purpose for which *que-et* is used in its one occurrence in that poet, a good indication that it remained an elevated poetic mannerism: ". . . Mart. die polysyndetische Verbindung *que-et* nur an einer einzigen Stelle (7, 54, 5 *consumpsi salsasque molas et turis acervos*) bietet:

---

143 Though *pallium* is not derived from a Greek word, it always is used to designate Greek, as opposed to Roman, dress. As the commentators note, Catullus may have had Eur. *Cyc.* 328 (πέπλον κρούω) in mind; for the relationship of the poem to Hellenistic elegy, see Hezel, p. 21.

144 Kroll, *ad loc.*, notes again, "*que* . . . *que* hat Ennius nach dem Vorbilde des homerischen τε . . . τε in die lateinische Poesie eingeführt."

145 The vs. is often criticized, as Kroll, "Tonfall . . . und Ausdruck sind hölzern und prosaisch."

146 At 107.1, where Mynor's text reads *Si quicquam [quid quid O, quicquid X] cupido optantique optigit umquam / insperanti*, G. P. Goold ("A New Text of Catullus," *Phoenix* 12 (1958) 108–109), arguing solely from the corruption of the line in particular and of the poem in general, would remove the hiatus by accepting the Aldine *cupidoque* and read *Si quoi* [Ribbeck] *quid cupidoque optantique optigit umquam / insperati* [Heinsius]. See, however, M. Zicàri, "Some Metrical and Prosodical Features of Catullus' Poetry," *Phoenix* 18 (1964) 199, who argues convincingly for accepting the hiatus.

147 Schmalz-Hofmann, 663. Cf. also Kroll, *Glotta* 15 (1927) 298. See, however, Heusch, 158–60, whose argument (that *que-et* in Cat. is colloquial) is based on an unsupported hypothesis.

die Stelle klingt wohl nicht zufällig an die hohe sakrale Sprache an, zu Martials Zeit war die Verbindung, die ja schon bei den altlateinischen Szenikern fast nur im Versschluss begegnet, längst veraltet."[148]

Catullus has *que-et* twice for certain, both in the polymetrics. 28.5 (*frigoraque et famem tulistis?*) is again mock-heroic for the hardships Veranius and Fabullus have undertaken.[149] C. 44 begins as a mock prayer, reinforces the sacral tone with several archaic forms, and uses *-que et* to elevate the ancient equivalent of two aspirins at bedtime (*et me recuravi otioque et urtica*, 15).[150] *que-et* may occur again in 76.11–12 (*quin tu animo offirmas atque istinc teque reducis, | et dis invitis desinis esse miser*), but the connectives are awkward: Ellis proposed *te ipse*, which even Housman approved of,[151] though the MS authority for *teque* is good (*instincteque* O, *-toque* X); if *teque* is read (and I do not think it should be), metrical convenience must again be assumed for the *que-et*. Though the two certain instances of *que-et* in the polymetrics do not in themselves constitute certain evidence, they

---

[148] *Gnomon* 2 (1926) 253–54.

[149] Other such mock-heroic elements appear in the otherwise colloquial language of the poem, making it a good example of the effect this neoteric freedom in diction allowed: see, for instance, the last two lines (Cat. often closes, as discussed above in cc. 15 and 32, in such a way): *at vobis mala multa di deaque | dent, opprobria Romuli Remique*. Kroll hesitates about the force of *que-et* here ("*que et* ist volkstümlich, wie der Gebrauch bei Plautus zeigt (Hauler zu Phorm. 1051), für C. vielleicht schon ein Archaismus"), but there can be little doubt; he seems later to have taken a firmer stand (*Glotta* 15 [1927] 298: "Diese den Szenikern noch ganz geläufige Verbindung war wohl schon für Catull ein Archaismus.").

[150] La Penna (*Maia* [1956] 154) agrees with Heusch (*Das Archaische*, 160) in finding in the use of *-que et* in this phrase "molto probabile il valore di parodia," rightly, I think. C. P. Jones has developed the idea ("Parody in Catullus 44," *Hermes* 96 [1968] 379–83) that the poem is a mock prayer. The beginning *O funde noster* . . . continues with the ritual anaphora *seu . . . seu . . . seu . . . sive* . . . (cf. the Egnatius prayer, 39.10–14). Archaisms include *autumant* (2), *grates* (16), *recepso* (19); see Ronconi, *Studi Catulliani*, 203 (not accepted by Fordyce, who fails—in spite of several notes directly to the point—to see the purpose of the solemnity of the poem, "The piece is merely a vehicle for the pun on *rigus*").

[151] *CR* 19 (1905) 121–22. Though Heinsius is credited with *istinc teque* (he did not have O's *instincteque* before him), the construction (*atque* joining *offirmas* and the pair of verbs *reducis* and *desinis*, which are in turn connected by *-que et*) seems intolerably awkward.

nevertheless support the clear case of *que-que* in Catullus as a neoteric mannerism.

POSTPOSITION OF PARTICLES

A clear feature of neoteric style is the postposition of particles, an innovation in Latin poetry based on the conscious imitation of Alexandrian technique. Kroll (at Cat. 64.93) remarks, *"atque* steht an zweiter Satzstelle: das wagen erst die Neoteriker nach dem Vorgange der καί invertierenden Alexandriner, namentlich Kallimachos macht von der Nachstellung an den Anfang gehörender Partikeln ausgedehnten Gebrauch."[152] The fact that the postposition of particles does not occur in Lucretius and previous poetry emphasizes the remarkable interest with which the neoterics read and imitated Callimachus and their scrupulous concern with the mannerisms of Alexandrian poetic style. This innovation became a standard feature of later Latin poetry.[153]

Catullus has postponed particles 15 times, 3 in the polymetrics, 12 in the longer poems (8 of which occur in c. 64), but none in the epigrams.[154] *nam* is postponed at 23.7, 37.11, 64.301[155]; *namque* at

---

[152] Cf. Norden, *Aen. VI*, pp. 402–04: "M. Haupt hat nachgewiesen (op. I 115 ff.), dass Inversion von *et* und *atque* erst von den Neoterikern, und zwar nach dem Vorbild der hellenistischen Dichter, eingeführt worden ist; der Grund ist meist in metrischer Bequemlichkeit, häufig aber auch in dem Bestreben zu suchen, indifferente Worte von den markierten Satz- und Versstellen abzurücken."

[153] In addition to Norden's list, see Platnauer, *Latin Elegiac Verse*, 93–96. For Callimachus, see Pfeiffer's *Index Verborum s.v.* καί.

[154] We are discussing, of course, only those particles whose postposition was irregular and is thus significant (see Norden's and Platnauer's lists). It should not be disconcerting that in the epigrams *ut(i)* is postponed at 72.4, 76.21, 23, 78.4, 116.2; *si* at 75.4; *cum* at 80.3; *ne* at 74.3; and all these particles are postponed as frequently in the polymetrics and longer poems. A reading of the first five chapters of Cato's *Agr.* shows these same particles regularly postponed in early prose: *ut(i)* 3 times, *si* 3 times, *cum (quom)* twice, *ne* 7 times, *ubi* twice. It is perhaps improper to speak of postposition at all where these particles are concerned: in each of the seven cases, *ne* stands immediately before its verb.

[155] Schmalz-Hofmann, 679: "Die Nachstellung von *nam* ist . . . auf die Dichtersprache seit Catull beschränkt (nicht Enn., s. Lachmann zu Lucr. S.412 . . .); auch *namque* tritt seit Catull, häufiger seit Verg. an die 2. und gelegentlich sogar bis an die 6. Stelle zurück."

64.384, 66.65; *atque*, 64.93; *nec (neque)* 64.173, 210, 379, 68.55, 116; *at*, 64.43, 58[156]; *sed* 51.9, 61.102.[157] In most cases, Catullus' purpose, as is apparent when the instances are examined, is clearly connected with other features of neoteric style and technique—a connection which explains why postposition of particles is foreign to previous Latin poetry. Often postposition occurs in a Greek context, as in both of the poems translated from Greek (51.9, *lingua sed torpet*, where Sappho had ἀλλ' ἄκαν μὲν γλῶσσα, and *namque* at 66.65, *Virginis et saevi contingens* namque *Leonis*[158]); the simile at 61.102 also may have been taken from Alexandrian poetry.[159] Postposition also occurs after the Greek form *Pelea* (64.301, *Pelea nam tecum . . .*) and after the Greek name *Hebe* (68.116, *Hebe nec longa virginitate foret*). It is otherwise (and perhaps principally) used to allow an adjective to stand at the beginning of a line to obtain neoteric word collocation (as 64.173, *indomito nec dira ferens stipendia tauro*, and 210, 379, 68.55), an interesting result of the discovery of the possibilities of such word order; and also to allow an important word to stand first in the line for emphasis (as at 64.58, *immemor at iuvenis . . .*, or 64.93, *funditus atque imis exarsit tota medullis*). Metrical convenience may be assumed for the postposition at 23.7 (*bene nam valetis omnes*) and 37.11 (*puella nam mi*, unless special emphasis on *puella* is taken to be the reason). It is worth noting again, however,

156 *Ibid.*, 667: "nachgestelltes *at* findet sich nur bei Dichtern seit Catull (nicht Lucr. Tib. Ov.)."

157 *Ibid.*, 666: "Die Nachstellung von *sed* ist dichterisch seit den Augusteern (Niedermann, *Essais* 59–60)", a statement which should be corrected to "seit Catull". At 61.102 (*lenta sed velut adsitas / vitis implicat arbores*) *quin* may be read for *sed* (*sed* O, *-que* X); see Friedrich's argument for *quin*; *sed*, however, has the advantage of the parallel postponed *sed* at 51.9, of simplicity, and of O's ingenuousness.

158 Though this line is missing in Callimachus' text, ἀλλά is postponed to the same metrical position four lines before (φάεσ]ιν ἐν πολέεσσιν ἀρίθμιος ἀλλ[ὰ γένωμαι, 61) and no doubt justified Catullus' extreme postposition of *namque* (cf. *Ecl.* 1.14, *hic inter densas corylos modo namque gemellos*, which Norden compares with Catullus). Pfeiffer (on line 60, frg. 110) notes that no other example of ἀλλά postponed to this position seems to exist.

159 See Kroll, *ad loc.*, and at 61.34 ("Alexandrinische Dichtung fasste die Symbiose von Pflanzen als Liebesverhältnis auf"). However, Svennung, 76–77, argues that the simile must be purely Roman ("Ein Spezialausdruck der römischen Bauernsprache ist die Metapher *maritus* von Bäumen, an welche nach italischer Sitte Weinreben angebunden wurden"): in this case, Catullus may be adding a Greek touch in order to elevate the local metaphor.

that although postposition is thus allowed in the polymetrics, it was never allowed in the epigrams, not even for metrical convenience.

OPORTET, NECESSE

Axelson begins his study of unpoetic words by citing Lachmann's note on *oportet*, in which it is argued that *necessest* should be read on the grounds that *oportet* is found nowhere else in Lucretius and is avoided by other poets.[160] Axelson corrects some of Lachmann's figures and concludes, "Konstatieren lässt sich wohl nur so viel, dass *oportet* stark prosaisch geklungen haben muss und gerade deshalb in der Dichtung einen so spärlichen Gebrauch fand."[161]

It should not be inferred from this discussion that *necesse* is the poetic equivalent of *oportet: necesse* is equally unpoetic, though for Virgil (and later epic poets) it seems to have had a solemn, archaic ring. A distinction between the two words can be drawn from their use (or rejection) by the poets and can be applied with some certainty to Catullus: Terence has *oportet* 31 times, *necesse* 6 (the ratio in Plautus is similar); Lucretius *oportet* 1, *necesse* c. 96; Virgil, 1 (*Ecl.* 6.5) and 4 (all in *Aen.* in passages of an archaic solemnity); Horace, 4 (*Sat. Epist.*) and 4 (*Sat.* 3, *Ars P.* 1); Tibullus has neither (*oportet* in 3.1.14); Propertius 4 and 0; Ovid 10 and 5; Juvenal 1 and 1; Martial 1 and 7; Statius 0 and 3; Lucan 0 and 6. In general, it can be said that *oportet* is prosaic (as Axelson concludes), as can be seen from its use in comedy, its single occurrence in Lucretius and in the *Eclogues* (while not in the *Aen.*);

---

160 Lachmann at Lucr. 1.778: "accedit quod hoc ipso verbo, quod est *oportet*, ea, puto, de causa, quod ad iudicia proprie pertinet, neque Lucretius alio ullo in loco usus est, neque ceteri poetae praeter comicos eo delectantur. . . . " Lachmann's reason may be wrong (as Axelson remarks, "da es sich ja gar nicht um einen juristischen Fachausdruck, sondern um ein der Prosa überhaupt (wie auch den Komikern) geläufiges Wort handelt," p. 14), but his figures cited to show the avoidance of the word by the poets are as useful as they are impressive.

161 P. 14; also pp. 15–16: "Beispielsweise muss doch wohl hinter der Abneigung der Dichter gegen das obenerwähnte *oportet* ein besonderer stilistischer Umstand stecken: obwohl rein begrifflich für die Poesie nicht ungeeigneter als z.B. *debere*, hatte das Worte einen Nebenton, der im Vers störend klang und den nur der etwas unpräzise, aber doch genügende Ausdruck 'unpoetisch', 'prosaisch' zu charakterisieren vermag."

that *necesse*, while also prosaic, is epic, though its use restricted; and that for these two reasons both words are avoided by Virgil in the *Georgics*, by Horace in the *Odes*, and by the elegists.[162]

Catullus has *necesse* four times, all in the polymetrics or longer poems (12.16, 16.6, 61.81, 62.61), and *oportet* twice, both in the epigrams (70.4, 90.3). Though in all cases meter would seem to allow only one of the two words, and though no sure argument can be drawn from the contexts, the pattern is by this time recognizable and Catullus' use conforms with what can be observed from the occurrence of the two words in other poetry. *Oportet*, as the more prosaic of the two, is allowed only in epigram, but *necesse*, somewhat more elevated by previous poetic usage, can be used in neoteric poems: the distinction is significant, and though no conclusion can be drawn with absolute certainty,[163] it can be better understood by comparing *subito/repente*.

SUBITO, REPENTE

A stylistic distinction between *subito* and *repente* was first formulated by Löfstedt: "*subito* im allgemein von der volkstümlicheren, *repente* von der höheren Sprache bevorzugt wird."[164] This statement is too much of an oversimplification to be really useful: Löfstedt based his argument on the fact that *subito* is the Romance survival, that only it is found in the *Peregrinatio Aetheriae*, in the *Bellum Africum* (23 times), and in the conversations of Trimalchio, that *repente* alone occurs in Tacitus (50 times) and in the verse of Petronius' novel (but here as Axelson notes, only twice). In support of these facts Axelson adds that Sallust has only *repente* (18 times),[165] but he begins his disagreement by noting that the prosaic Vitruvius too has only *repente* (6 times), and then notes

---

162 Ovid is somewhat exceptional, as often, in his use of these particular words, though Prop. found *oportet* suitable on occasion: this perhaps implies some doubt as to the propriety of the two words in elegy, and it may have been for this reason that Tibullus avoided both.

163 As Axelson says of his remarks on *oportet*, "Eine subtilere Erklärung dürfte weder möglich noch nötig sein" (p. 14); he does not treat *necesse*.

164 *PA* 168.

165 Pp. 32–33.

that Caesar and Cicero use both words. "Wir werden demnach bei den einzelnen Schriftstellern auch mit einer rein individuellen Vorliebe für dieses oder jenes Synonym rechnen müssen." Clearly in prose there was not always such a well-defined distinction between the two words as Löfstedt thought.

Axelson, after making these remarks of caution, says, "Jedenfalls gehört es zur Sache, dass *subito* in der sonstigen Poesie so wenig vermieden wird, dass es vielmehr bei den allermeisten Dichtern eine weit stärkere Stellung als das Synonym hat; so besonders bei Ovid: *subito* über 50mal, *repente* nur 3mal. Ganz fehlt die letztere Partikel bei Properz, der für jene 5 Beispiele hat, wie auch bei Horaz (dessen 4 Belege für *subito* allerdings auf die Satiren entfallen). Vgl. ferner die Frequenz bei Verg. *Aen.* (14 *repente*, 26 *subito*), Tib. (1:3), Sen. (4:13), Val. (6:16), Sil. (20:23). Bei dem Archaisten Lukrez hingegen finden wir *repente* sehr viel öfter als *subito* (36:21)—eine weitere Stütze für die oben ausgesprochene Vermutung über den ein wenig altertümlichen Anstrich des erstgenannten Wortes." Here too, though, the case is somewhat overstated. The slight preference of Plautus and Terence for *subito* (Pl. 15:8, Ter. 6:4) cannot be used to show that *subito* is the more poetic of the two, and Martial (7:8) and Juvenal (2:2), for instance, made no distinction between the two words.[166] The only statement that can be made with certainty (and even this has a limited, though important, sphere of validity) is that *repente* is the older poetic word: in addition to Lucretius' preference, it should be noted that Ennius has *repente* 5 times, but nowhere does he use *subito*. Virgil, then, used *repente* in the *Aeneid*, but only once in the *Georgics* (*subito* four times), though neither occurs in the *Eclogues*. The elegists do not seem so much to use *subito* as a poeticism, but rather to avoid *repente* as too archaic and epic: of Ovid's three uses of *repente*, two occur in the *Metamorphoses* (4.402, 586) and one in the *Tristia* (3.8.8, after three couplets on Triptolemus, Medea, and Daedalus, a lofty and pathetic introduction to the poem), all three of which indicate a special concern with the tone of

---

[166] Hesitation is also expressed by Heusch, 61–62: "Doch scheint mir selbst dieses vorsichtige, vornehmlich an Sallust orientierte sprachgeschichtliche Urteil angesichts der Verwendung von *repente* bei Cicero (ca. 10mal) und Caesar (ca. 10mal) und besonders Vitruv (6mal *repente*, keinmal *subito*) für diese Zeit jedenfalls nicht zutreffend zu sein."

the word. But if this distinction held true for the elegists, it did not survive them, was not felt by many prose writers, and did not exist, for instance, in comedy.

The distinction between these two adverbs as used by Catullus is the same as that observed above between *oportet* and *necesse*. *Repente* occurs three times, only in the polymetrics and longer poems (10.3, 17.24, 63.28), *subito* only in the epigrams (76.13, 84.10). The neoteric poems once again make use of a word which had the sanction of earlier poetic usage (still felt later, though more vaguely, by Virgil and Ovid), while *subito* is confined to the epigrams.[167] Axelson is certainly correct in attributing to *repente* "ein feierlicheres, wohl auch etwas altertümlicheres Gepräge . . . (was zur Praxis des Sall. und des Tac. gut passen würde)," but it is an attribution which can only have been felt by a limited number of poets (Catullus and the Augustans), a distinction artificial and literary rather than living. The situation is identical to that of *oportet/necesse*. In both cases Catullus' usage conforms both to earlier poetic practice and to subsequent poetic convention, in the light of which the distribution of the words in the three parts of his poetry becomes meaningful.

ITA (SIC)

Axelson's thorough discussion of *ita* concludes that ". . . diese Partikel in der verfeinerten Dichtersprache überhaupt ziemlich selten ist."[168] His statistics on the use of the word present a clear picture of its gradual disappearance from poetic vocabulary. Lucretius has the

---

167 Heusch can see no distinction between the two words as used by Catullus and seems to deny that *repente* can be called archaic ("So bietet auch der Gebrauch bei Catull . . . kein irgendwie stichhaltiges Kriterium für eine geschichtliche Aufgliederung der Synonyme; und ob die nach Löfstedt "früh" eintretende stilistische Differenzierung für ihn schon gilt, bleibt auch fraglich . . ."). He sees a difference in tone between c. 17 and c. 63 on the one hand, and c. 10 ("von Kroll als ausgesprochen lässig gekennzeichnet") on the other: it is dangerous to ignore the typically neoteric and careful nature of c. 10 which puts it on the same level with c.17 or c.63, and Heusch is at fault again in not recognizing the importance of the distribution of the two words in Catullus. It should be noted that *subito* occurs in Aedituus (*per pectus manat subito <subido> mihi sudor*, 1.3) and Catulus (*cum subito a laeva Roscius exoritur*, 2.2).

168 Pp. 121–22.

particle 70 times (to which we may add that Ennius used it 3 times in the *Ann.* and 4 times in *Trag.*), but the Augustans severely limited its use. It does not appear in the *Eclogues* and is used only 4 times in the *Georgics* and 24 times in the *Aeneid*, of which half are in the formula *ita fatur* or a similar one.[169] Horace has it 25 times in the *Satires* and *Epistles*, but only twice in the *Odes*. In elegy Propertius uses it 10 times in I–II, but never in III and only twice (one of which is *atque ita*) in IV—a clear indication of its restricted use in the poet's developed diction, confirmed by the fact that Tibullus avoids the word entirely. Ovid in the *Amores* has the particle 4 times (3 of which are in the phrase *atque ita*) and in the *Metamorphoses* 30 times (half of which are *atque ita*).[170] From these figures and from Virgil's use in the *Aeneid* it might be assumed that *ita* had an epic appropriateness, but such a conscious stylist as Lucan avoided it entirely, and Silius has it only 7 times in 12,000 verses, both of whom would have followed Virgil had the word had an archaic propriety. It must be assumed that the particle was viewed by the poets (more and more severely) as prosaic.[171]

Catullus uses *ita* 9 times in the longer poems and twice in the epigrams. The three uses in 63 (44, 49, 77) are no doubt due to the demands made by the meter. Three occur in formulae (*ita me iuvent / caelites*, 61.189; *ita me divi . . . iuverint*, 66.18; *ita me di ament*, 97.1), to which may be added *ita Caecilio placeam* (67.9); and *quod cum ita sint* (68.37) is definitely colloquial[172] (prosaically used to close the letter to Manius, it should be noted—the two parts of c. 68 are very different in tone and diction). The remaining three (64.84, 315 and 75.2) are in the phrase

---

169 The distribution of these formulae of speaking (overlooked by Axelson) in the *Aen.* is indicative: one each occurs in II, V, VI, VII, but in X there are 3, in XI 4, in XII 2; and after IX there are only two occurrences of *ita* not so used. In the last books of the *Aen.* Virgil was clearly imposing new restrictions on the use of the particle.

170 Axelson omits the important (and seemingly contradictory) evidence that in *Pont.* *ita* occurs 19 times, in the *Tr.* 18 times; but this may be taken as another indication of Ovid's own increasing stylistic freedom in his last works, shared by no other (or later) poets.

171 The reason for this view is not clear. Axelson asks, "Ob man bei *ita* den Zusammenhang mit dem unbeliebten *is* empfunden und gerade deshalb das kräftigere (freilich auch metrisch bequemere) *sic* bevorzugt hat?" Perhaps there is a connection with *itaque*, which appears only 11 times in Lucr., 2 in Cat. (63.6, 35), and in subsequent poetry only in Hor. *Epist.* 1.1.10 and in Phaedr. twice (see Axelson, 92–93 and Tränkle, p. 145 n. 1).

172 See Axelson, 47.

atque ita. The majority of the occurrences of *ita* are clearly colloquial and in their contexts cause no surprise; those in c. 64 anticipate later usage.

The important fact to be observed here is that *ita* is never used in the polymetrics, even though it should have been metrically useful. *Sic,* on the other hand, occurs 7 times in the polymetrics, and is the normal poetic word.[173] Catullus here is obviously careful in avoiding the more prosaic *ita* and in using instead the poetic equivalent *sic,* care that he did not take where it was unnecessary. It is worth adding here an observation on *sicine,* a word frequent in comedy but found nowhere in poetry outside of Catullus and Propertius. Ariadne begins her tirade with this repeated, emotional colloquialism (64.132, 134), used also by Catullus himself in addressing Rufus (77.3, *sicine subrepsti mi . . .*); Propertius alone shows similar emotion.[174] These are striking examples of a colloquialism elevated for contexts of high emotion: the colloquialisms with *ita* noted above are similar (though the effect, of course, is in each case very different), but it is the phrase that constitutes the colloquialism, not the single word *ita.* As a prosaic particle it was never admitted to the polymetrics even in a colloquial phrase for a particular effect; the colloquial elements in the polymetrics are seldom simply prosaic, but are used, as *sicine* in the two instances noted here, for a particular poetic purpose.

ENIM

Poetic usage of *enim,* compared with *ita,* illustrates a distinction that must always be carefully observed and checked, for while *ita* is demonstrably prosaic (with certain exceptions explicable by the individual usage of a particular poet—e.g., Ovid's last works—or by its use with

---

[173] *Sic* is used, for instance, as the connective in similes (in Catullus, cf. 62.45 and 56, or 64.110 and 276). This particle is also used in the epigrams (5 times in 3 passages) and longer poems (3 in c. 62, 4 in c. 64).

[174] Prop. 2.15.8 ("*sicine, lente, iaces?*") and 3.6.9 (*sicine eam incomptis vidisti flere capellis*); on the latter see Tränkle, 156: "Das zeigt zugleich, dass dieser Ausdruck auch der gehobenen Dichtung nicht ganz fremd war, wo in ihr lebendiges Gespräch anklang" (the reading here is disputed, however, a fact not mentioned by Tränkle, who is also unaware that *sicine* occurs in Prop. 2.15.8). The use of *sicine* in Cat. 64 and 77 is another clear instance of how closely Catullus associated himself with Ariadne: in such a case there can be no mistaking the recall, whether conscious or subconscious.

certain other words—with *atque* or in epic formulae of speaking), *enim* is both prosaic and archaic (epic): it will thus be avoided by the elegiac poets for both reasons, but will be found in epic (though in contexts with certain other words) and satire.

Axelson again provides useful figures for the occurrence of the particle in the poets.[175] Lucretius uses *enim* about 150 times, far more than any other poet; it was frequent too in comedy. Juvenal has it over 50 times, and Horace in the *Satires* and *Epistles* 30 times. Tibullus, however, never uses it, Propertius has it only 9 times (three of which are with *neque* or *quis*), and Ovid in the *Amores*, *Ars Amatoria*, and genuine *Heroides* has only one *enim* which is not used with *neque* or *quis*.[176] Horace has *enim* 8 times in the *Odes* (not in the *Epod.*), of which two are with *neque* or *non* and two more in parentheses. Virgil has two in the *Eclogues* (one with *quis* and one in the parenthetical *fatebor enim*), 8 in the *Georgics* (two with *neque*, one in parenthesis), and 40 in the *Aeneid* (of which 26 are with *neque*, *quis*, or *sed*, 8 in parentheses, and 3 otherwise archaic, leaving only 4 not so distinguished). Ovid's *Metamorphoses* also exhibits the epic use of *enim*: 100 altogether, of which two thirds are in formulae, another 24 in parentheses, only 6 remaining (5 of which are in the last three books). This pattern is followed by later writers of epic: Lucan has *enim* only with *neque* or *quis* (20 times) except for one *at enim*; Silius likewise, but with *sed enim* often (with four exceptions, two of which are parenthetical); and similar too is the usage of Valerius Flaccus. These writers provide a control for epic usage that was lacking in the case of *ita*, which confirms the hypothesis that *enim* (in formulae at least) was a recognized feature of epic diction.

Such is the *quod enim* at Cat. 63.62, *quod enim genus figuraest, ego non*

---

175 Pp. 122–23. Axelson does not, however, make the above distinction: ". . . das von Tibull vermiedene *enim* in der Poesie wenig beliebt ist, insofern es . . . meist nur unter besonderen Bedingungen gebraucht wird. Allerdings gilt dies nicht für Lukrez, welcher *enim* häufiger als irgendein anderer Dichter verwendet, auch nicht für Horaz und Juvenal . . . ." In Horace, however, *enim* occurs mostly in the *Sat.* and *Epist.*

176 The one exception is *Am.* 3.2.73, *sed enim revocate, Quirites*: Ovid, in addressing the Romans in the circus as *Quirites*, uses the archaic *sed enim* (Quint. cites Virg. *Aen.* 1.19, *progeniem sed enim Troiano a sanguine duci / audierat*, as an example of the archaic *sed enim*; see Norden, *Aen. VI*, p. 129, who gives its force as ἀλλὰ γάρ).

quod obierim? The other two occurrences of *enim* in Catullus are not in epic formulae, but their contexts clearly indicate their nature and purpose. *Est enim leporum | differtus puer ac facetiarum* (12.8–9) and *est enim venuste | Magna Caecilio incohata Mater* (35.17–18) are both typical neoteric contexts in the polymetrics, the first characterized by the *lepores ac facetiae*, the second by its admiring reference to Caecilius' neoteric *Magna Mater*. In such contexts prosaic words invariably have no place, and the force of *enim* is to be understood from the clear pattern of its later poetic usage.[177] There is a further indication, however, of the nature of the particle in these two instances: *enim* originally had an affirmative force in Latin which can still be observed in comedy;[178] and in Virgil there are four instances of *enim* so used for archaic effect.[179] In both cases in the polymetrics *enim* is as much affirmative as it is causal, if not more so, and the emphatic position of *est* supports this observation.[180] 12.8–9 might be translated, "*There's* a boy who is . . ."; and in 35.17 it is the adverb *venuste* (a favorite Catullan pun) which receives the emphasis. The purpose of *enim* is entirely neoteric; its appearance in the polymetrics and in c. 63 might have been predicted.

IUCUNDUS/SUAVIS

Axelson characterizes *iucundus* in a brief note: "Dagegen gehört *iucundus* hauptsächlich den niederen Dichtungsarten und der Elegie

---

[177] Axelson is correct in noting that Catullus in this anticipates the later usage (and restriction) of *enim* by the poets.

[178] See W. K. Clement, "The Use of *enim* in Plautus and Terence," *AJP* 18 (1897) 402–15, who concludes that there are "14 examples of *enim* corroborative to 1 of *enim* causal in Plautus, while in Terence the proportion is 13 to 1" (p. 414); and Schmalz-Hofmann, 680–81.

[179] *G.* 3.70, *Aen.* 6.317, 8.84, 10.874. See Norden, pp. 129–30, who notes that this early force is equivalent to δή (as, for instance, at *Aen.* 8.84 *tibi enim* = σοί γε δή "in der Umgebung von lauter feierlichen Worten").

[180] On 12.8–9, *est enim leporum* . . ., cf. Schmalz-Hofmann, 614: "Voranstellung [of the verb "to be"] tritt ein bei nachdrücklicher Behauptung (*est* (*vere*) *amicus*); vielfach im Ausruf. . . ." On 35.17–18, *est* . . . *incohata, ibid.*: "Entsprechend ist der Typus *factus est* das Normale bei einfacher Feststellung der Verbalhandlung, *est factus* bei Hervorhebung oder Bekräftigung ihrer Verwirklichung."

an," and summarizes his discussion of *suavis*: "Jedenfalls muss *suavis* schon von augusteischer Zeit an als ein unfeines, für die Poesie und z.T. auch für die gehobene Prosa wenig geeignetes Wort gegolten haben."[181] The first note is far too brief to be informative, and his discussion of *suavis* ignores an aspect of the word that is clear in Catullus' use and that leads to a fuller explanation of its disappearance from later poetic vocabulary. Seen together (and with *dulcis* and *gratus*) these adjectives reveal much about Catullus' diction.

The history of these two words may be discussed together. In comedy *suavis* is used often, but *iucundus* appears only twice in Plautus (*Ps.* 238, *Poen.* 206) and never in Terence—it would seem immediately clear that *iucundus* was not an essential part of the colloquial language. It is striking, then, that *iucundus* is also absent from the fragments of Ennius, whereas the colloquial *suavis* is found twice (*suavis sonus* and *suavis homo, Ann.* 119 and 245 V.²) in addition to the epic compound *suaviloquenti ore* (*Ann.* 303). Lucretius, however, has *iucundus* 8 times (including 3 adverbs) and *suavis* 13 times (including 2 adverbs). From the early history, then, it can be assumed that the two words had entirely different backgrounds, but that Lucretius found both of them suitable for a limited use in his poem. In Cicero's poetic fragments *suavis* appears once in a line from Euripides, a positive indication that the word was still valid for someone with a taste for archaic vocabulary.[182]

The later history of the two words contrasts sharply: *suavis* disappeared entirely from satire as well as from other genres (it is not found in Tib., Prop., Ovid, Sen., Luc., Val. Fl., Sil., Mart., Juv.), though Virgil and Horace show a transition (in Horace 9 times in *Sat.* and *Epist.*, in Virgil 4 times in the *Ecl.*, once in the *G.*); *iucundus* is used effectively, though sparingly, in all genres but epic. From the fact that

---

[181] On *iucundus*, p. 35 n. 18; on *suavis*, 35–37. For *iucundus* Axelson provides only the information that it is not found in Hor. *Odes*, in Ovid's *Met.*, or in Lucan and Silius; and only once in Virg. (*Aen.* 6.363), Val. Fl., and Sen.

[182] Cicero's context (*De Fin.* 2.105) is extremely interesting (I owe this observation to W. Clausen): "Vulgo [= 'proverbially'] enim dicitur: 'iucundi acti labores'; nec male Euripides (concludam, si potero, Latine; Graecum enim hunc versum nostis omnes): 'Suavis laborum est praeteritorum memoria'." From this it is tempting to draw the neat conclusion (against other evidence) that *iucundus* is colloquial, *suavis* poetic.

suavis was also avoided by prose writers (not in Caes., Sall., Curt., Tac., Suet., though it is occasionally used throughout the works of Cicero), it can be said that the word had for some reason dropped out of formal usage (it is not infrequent, however, in either Petron. or Apul.).[183]

Catullus' use of *iucundus* indicates that the neoterics were primarily responsible for sanctioning its use in poetry.[184] Catullus has it 4 times in the polymetrics, 10 times in the longer poems, and only once in the epigrams. In the first group he uses it twice to address Calvus (*iucundissime Calve*, 14.2, and *hoc, iucunde, tibi poema feci*, 50.16), in both of which contexts the subject is neoteric poetry. 9.9 too is a typical context, 46.3 another in which the word is carefully used again (*iucundis Zephyri silescit aureis*) in a carefully constructed poem. Among the longer poems it is used 3 times in c. 64 (161, 215, 284). There is every indication, then, that the word is a neoteric innovation: it was not formerly colloquial (not in comedy) nor poetic but must have become a part of neoteric vocabulary through use in the elegant spoken language of Catullus' circle at Rome. This theory alone will explain its use by Catullus to address Calvus and Veranius (9.9), and its extension to more serious neoteric poetry, the source from which it became a part (though a small part) of later elegy and satire;[185] the same reason makes its exclusion from epic understandable.[186] It should be noted

---

[183] A. Ernout, *Rev Phil* 21 (1947) 63–64, takes issue with Axelson on the nature of *suavis*: the difference (between *suavis* and *dulcis*), he says, is not one of 'dignité' but of sense, in that *suavis* is a word of "impressions sensorielles, goût, odorat, vue," while *dulcis* is more general, abstract as well as concrete, moral as well as physical, and that while popular speech may have used *suavis* for its vividness, "cela ne suffit pas à taxer l'adjectif de vulgarité." While his definition may be right (it is hard, though, to explain in this way a use such as *seu quid suavius elegantiusve est*, Cat. 13.10), it still does not explain the disappearance of *suavis* from all poetry after Virgil and Horace, and from most formal prose.

[184] Lucretius' use of the word (8 times) does not make this assertion less true; it may have been an occasional word in poetry before the neoterics, but its later use can be explained in no other way.

[185] Hor. has it 3 times in the *Epod.*, 5 in *Sat.*, 1 in the *Epist.* and *Ars P.*; Tib. has it twice (2 more in III), Prop. has it 4 times in I and 1 in II, Ovid 2 times each in the *Am.*, *Ars Am.*, *Rem. Am.*, *Tr.*, and 4 times in *Pont.*; Juv. 6 times.

[186] *Aen.* 6.363 (its only occurrence in epic) is interesting. Palinurus begs Aeneas, *quod te per caeli iucundum lumen et auras / per genitorem oro.* . . . The word adds a personal and affective touch to an otherwise solemn line (as Norden characterizes the passage, "Affektvolle commiseratio (nach λ66 ff.) in einer kunstvollen Periode . . .").

finally that Catullus allowed the innovation only once in the epigrams, where it stands almost as a direct quotation from Lesbia (109.1, *iucundum, mea vita, mihi proponis amorem*).

Catullus' use of *suavis* can be seen as a turning point in its history. As an adjective it occurs twice (once in the polymetrics and once in c. 64), and as an adverb once again in the longer poems (61.7, *suave olentis amaraci*). It appears as another playful element of elegant neoteric vocabulary at 13.10 (*sed contra accipies meros amores / seu quid suavius elegantiusve est*). In c. 64 its context is almost unique:

> hunc simul ac cupido conspexit lumine virgo
> regia, quam suavis exspirans castus odores
> lectulus in molli complexu matris alebat,
> quales Eurotae praecingunt flumina myrtus . . .   (86–89)

To describe Ariadne here Catullus uses language particularly appropriate to the polymetrics (e.g., *molli* and the diminutive *lectulus*) and then continues with the similes to enlarge upon the *suavis odores*;[187] but such language is a normal part of more serious neoteric poetry when the effect must be one of delicacy, and to such an effect *suavis* contributes. Catullus is sparing in his use of the word, but for this reason its tone is unmistakable: as a part of neoteric vocabulary it was never admitted to the epigrams. The turning point in the use of the word occurred at this time. Its colloquial and prosaic side was felt so strongly by later writers that it was abandoned entirely in both poetry and prose, but not without leaving an indication and verification of its place in neoteric vocabulary: Virgil has it 4 times in the *Eclogues*, where such words are often met, and once in the *Georgics*; and, what is an even clearer indication, it was used twice in the *Ciris*, a belated neoteric effort (3, *suavis expirans hortulus auras*, a Catullan echo complete with diminutive, and 96, *suave rubens narcissus*, after *Eclogue* 3.63, *suave rubens hyacinthus*), and three more times in poems of the *Appendix Vergiliana*.

The following conclusions, then, can be drawn. *Iucundus* was

---

[187] Fordyce *ad loc.* notes that Helen has a θάλαμος θυώδης (*Od.* 4.121), and that "the conventional comparison . . . is enlivened, in a characteristically Alexandrian way, by the particularity of a proper name, *Eurotas* . . ."

originally urbane rather than simply colloquial (hence its very limited use by Plautus and its absence from Ennius' fragments). *Suavis* had been an archaic poeticism (hence its use by Ennius and by Cicero when he was translating the line of Euripides) but was too colloquial (often in comedy) for later verse, even as a poetic archaism in epic. Catullus, however, found both acceptable for use in his neoteric poetry (the polymetrics and longer poems only) for reasons now recognizable, and neoteric use sanctioned their later appearance (as, for instance, *suavis* in Virgil only 4 times in the *Ecl.* and once in the *G.*).

Two other synonyms must be mentioned in conclusion, *dulcis* and *gratus*, both, as Axelson says, encountered "auf Schritt und Tritt" in poetic vocabulary. *Dulcis* is used 16 times in the longer poems (7 in c. 68 alone), 4 times in the polymetrics, and as often in the epigrams; *gratus* occurs once in the polymetrics (2.11), once in c. 68 (in the prosaic phrase in the letter to Manius, *id gratum est mihi*, 9), but 4 times in the epigrams. These two words were acceptable to the established diction of Roman epigram and were for Catullus the substitutes for *iucundus* and *suavis*, words too neoteric to be used in a tradition in which innovation was not possible.

LESBIA AND THE VOCABULARY OF POLITICAL ALLIANCE

No aspect of Catullus' language has received more attention than the curious complex of words and ideas associated in the epigrams with his affair with Lesbia: *amicitia*, *fides*, *foedus*, *pietas*, and others. Certainly no other aspect has been more fully described, defined, and more clearly understood: and this more than half a century ago. On the other hand, the definite and precise associations of these words—definite, at least, for Romans of the late Republic—have been equally as long ignored by the great majority of literary critics, or, when not ignored, their implications made less precise by the few who have understood. The topic is difficult and embarrassing: first, because what has been fully described and is therefore well known to some must be discussed again in detail; and then because a certain amount of polemic seems unavoidable. However, the place of these words in Catullus' poems and the reason for their exploitation by the poet only in certain poems make it necessary to do again what has already been done thoroughly.

It is natural that, in critical studies of Catullus, the affair with Lesbia and the poems in which it is described claim the most attention; it is understandable, too, that these poems offer the widest scope for exercise of the critical imagination. Catullus is the most subjective of Latin love poets, the most personal in emotion, sincerity, and in the expression of his anguish: those who would understand him must share his emotions, and to do so must recreate from his poems the intimacy of the situations which led to their creation. The dangers for the critic in such an involvement are obvious; the work of the scholar, on the other hand (if we may use the current distinction), faces the charge of shallow coldness, and is ignored.

The concepts most frequently employed by Catullus to unify and give poetic expression to the chaos of his emotions are naturally those most discussed by critics, and suffer accordingly. Bewilderment is sometimes expressed: "To the average ancient, as to the modern reader, his *aeternum sanctae foedus amicitiae* must have remained something of a puzzle," or (on 72.3–4, *dilexi tum te non tantum ut vulgus amicam, / sed pater ut gnatos diligit et generos*), "He means only that his love had the same spiritual, nonphysical quality that a father's love possesses. In the end, the expression is fumbling. It could scarcely be expected that Catullus' contemporaries would make the correct equation of ideas. . . . It is fair to doubt that Catullus was understood—possibly because he himself did not clearly understand his own feelings."[188] Catullus is sometimes excused and rewritten, as Kroll does in his comment on *generos* (72.4): "ohne Verszwang hätte C. wohl nur die Kinder erwähnt." Most often elaborate subjectivity leads to violent misunderstanding of basic Latin words: *amicitia* comes to mean marriage.[189]

[188] F. O. Copley, "Emotional Conflict and its Significance in the Lesbia-Poems of Catullus," *AJP* 70 (1949) 26 and 29.

[189] The most recent discussion of *foedus* and *amicitia* in Catullus (P. McGushin, "Catullus' *sanctae foedus amicitiae*," *CP* 62 (1967) 85–93) may be taken here as representative of

To understand the precise meaning of *amicitia, fides, foedus, pietas,* and such words in Catullus, to appreciate the significance of their application to his alliance with Lesbia, to understand how he was able to adopt this terminology and for what reasons in what poems, it is necessary to isolate and define what was common to these words and concepts in the late Republic. Each word has a wide range of meanings, but a definite sphere of use and association is common to them all: if they are used by Catullus in the same context, or similar contexts, where each word contributes its own special significance and reference to the same general situation (the affair with Lesbia), then the sphere of reference or significance shared by them all must have been suggested purposely by the poet. For instance, if *foedus* does sometimes mean marriage in Latin, but *amicitia* never does (nor is ever normally even associated with the idea of marriage), then *sanctae foedus amicitiae* cannot refer to a metaphorical marriage, but rather must indicate a sphere of meaning common to each noun. The common area of use in late Republican Latin can easily be demonstrated, and, when the Lesbia poems are read with this area of significance in mind, all bewilderment, doubt, and misunderstanding disappear.

Such a demonstration was amply provided by R. Reitzenstein in

---

much critical discussion of the question; though this study is the most blatant in its refusal to examine the 1st century B.C. meanings of the words it deals with, it is hardly unique (since in no way original): the literature cited throughout the article should be consulted. McGushin (85) begins with a thesis: "If we can show that Catullus' relationship with Lesbia is described by an imagery consistently used in the cycle of Lesbia poems and elsewhere, then an examination of such imagery will reveal that this relationship is best explained by the view that for him it was essentially a marriage, certainly a marriage in spirit; and, further, that the love which he strove to express and found so hard to reject is that full blend of physical and spiritual feeling which finds its truest expression in conjugal love." The examination culminates a page later in the mention of ". . . that greatest example of *amicitia* between humans—marriage." This is not what Catullus says, nor any other Roman: one can search the *ThLL* article on *amicitia* without finding a single example of its use as a synonym for marriage, or even an instance where it is associated with marriage (see esp. *ThLL* I, 1898, 5–59)—Stat. *Silv.* 2.2.144–45 (*sanctusque pudicae / servat amicitiae leges amor*) is the only exception, and here the association (it is no more) arises only from the poet's self-conscious addiction to circumlocution. Had Catullus wanted to consider his relationship with Lesbia a sort of marriage, he was free to do so in precise language or allusion: Dido and Aeneas disagreed on the same question, but not because of careless or inadequate terminology.

1912 in an article far better known than read;[190] a fuller discussion of
the question could hardly be expected, yet few of those who claim to
have read it have taken notice (though to Reitzenstein himself his
demonstration seemed almost tediously obvious[191]). The work of
others (not concerned specifically with Catullus) has since enlarged his
demonstration and confirmed his general conclusions, yet scholars and
critics of Catullus have either ignored, or rephrased and restated so as
to make pallid and unspecific all these efforts. The language Catullus
uses for his affair with Lesbia is the (almost technical) terminology of
the workings of party politics and political alliances at Rome. A
demonstration of this statement is called for, but to do so is to repeat
the discussions of Reitzenstein and others: it seems best to present a
brief outline of the use and sphere of this terminology in its proper
setting, to refer to the full treatments of the subject by others, and to
hope that a discussion of the Catullan usage and an explanation of its
function and presence will be sufficient.[192]

Political historians have no doubts about the term *amicitia*: seldom
does the word mean friendship in our sense, but rather, almost always,
refers to the complex web of political alliances between leading men
that made the constitutional machinery of Rome workable and
dynamic. No one is therefore more aware of the importance of the
term than modern prosopographers: "The competition was fierce and
incessant. Family influence and wealth did not alone suffice. From
ambition or for safety, politicians formed compacts. *Amicitia* was a
weapon of politics, not a sentiment based on congeniality."[193] The

190 "Zur Sprache der lateinische Erotik," *Sitzungsber. der Heidelb. Ak. der Wiss.* [1912]
12 Abhandlung, 9–36.
191 P. 21: "So lästig es ist, Allbekanntes zu wiederholen, was vielleicht nur mir in
seinem Zusammenhang nie voll zur Empfindung gekommen war. . . ."
192 By far the most complete discussion of the language of party politics and alliances
is now that of J. Hellegouarc'h, *Le Vocabulaire latin des relations et des partis politiques sous
la République* (Paris 1963), an invaluable work; his citations of examples of the use of any
particular word should be consulted—only a few can be cited as illustrations here. In
general, see Gelzer, *Die Nobilität der Römischen Republik* (*Kl. Schr.* I 68–75); Kroll, *Die
Kultur der ciceronischen Zeit* I (Leipzig 1933) 55–62; and, though his conclusions seem weak,
Hezel, 65–69.
193 R. Syme, *The Roman Revolution* (Oxford 1956) 12. It is no coincidence that Gelzer,
among the first to investigate the intricate alliances which produced political power
during the Republic, was also the first to outline the nexus of these terms.

study of the workings of what we call party politics must trace continually the creation and dissolution of *amicitiae* between leading figures: "The old Roman substitute for party is *amicitia*, friendship. *Amicitia* in politics was a responsible relationship. A man expected from his friends not only support at the polls, but aid in the perils of public life, the unending prosecutions brought from political motives by his personal enemies, his *inimici*, his rivals in the contest for office and for the manifold rewards of public life. Friendship for the man in politics was a sacred agreement. Cicero, in writing to Crassus to clinch their reconciliation, urged Crassus to consider his letter a treaty (*foedus*). . . . Thus, as in our campaigns for nomination, friendship was the chief basis of support for candidates for office, and *amicitia* was the good old word for party relationship."[194] *Amicitia* is thus the central, controlling concept of political connections, on which all other terms and concepts of political relationships are dependent.[195]

Foedus is often used to mark the formal necessity of the obligations inherent in a political *amicitia*.[196] P. A. Brunt has conceded the technically political nature the word can have: "In professing his renewed

---

[194] L. R. Taylor, *Party Politics in the Age of Caesar* (Berkeley 1949) 7–8. Much of the book is in fact a study of such *amicitiae*, but see esp. pp. 23, 35–36.

[195] For a thorough analysis of *amicitia*, see Hellegouarc'h (above, n. 192) 48–56. It is revealing to study the occurrences of *amicitia* in Cicero's *Letters*: there is no better way of becoming aware of how common in everyday relationships, and how specific, the term was, or of how difficult it would have been to use the word, at that time and in that society, without this primary connotation. Recently, however, P. A. Brunt, writing for historians for whom the word is no mystery, has offered a corrective to the one-sided emphasis we are guilty of stressing here (" 'Amicitia' in the Late Roman Republic," *Proc. Camb. Phil. Soc.* 191, n.s. 2 (1965) 1–20): "But it is wrong to confine the sacredness of friendship to political connexions. Catullus uses the same metaphor of his relations with Lesbia, in a passage where *amicitia* stands for *amor*, just as *amor* may replace *amicitia* . . ." (p. 6). *Amicitia* can, of course, connote situations closely resembling our friendship, and, for instance, is so used often by Cicero in the *De Amicitia*, where, however, the idea of friendship under discussion is demonstrably Greek (ideal), not Roman (whatever Cicero's source may be)—see Hellegouarc'h, 42–48, and Kroll, *Die Kultur* I, 55–58. But in spite of Brunt's corrective discussion, the basic Republican sphere of the term is political: to argue against this by citing Catullus' use of the term is (as I hope will become clear) circular, and begins with an improper, though prevalent, assumption about the metaphor in Catullus.

[196] See Hellegouarc'h, *ibid.*, 38–40: "Par *foedus* l'on désigne donc, comme dans le domaine des relations internationales, les clauses qui marquent et conditionnent l'accord entre deux ou plusieurs hommes politiques" (p. 40, with the examples cited in nn. 3–6).

friendship for Crassus Cicero writes to him: *has litteras velim existimes foederis habituras esse vim, non epistulae (Fam.* V.8.5). Professor Taylor cites this to support her statement that 'friendship for the man in politics was a sacred agreement.' Although in fact many political friendships were short-lived and insincere, there is no doubt that she has hit off the meaning of the term *foedus.* Treaties were ratified by solemn oaths and to break them was perjury."[197] The use of the term in political connections (while not, as can be argued for *amicitia,* its primary use) is no doubt a metaphorical extension of its basic meaning, treaty. *Foedus* thus, when used of political alliances, always refers to a relationship of *amicitia* between equals.

Fides, on the other hand, is properly that bond which makes possible the patron–client relationship.[198] Like *foedus,* the word was often used for agreements between nations, frequently associated with *deditio,*[199] and often employed as an important element in international patron–client relationships.[200] In the late Republic, however, the concept is continually applied to political *amicitiae* between equals, and is indeed the only real basis for constancy and stability in such relationships.[201] The concept, at once concrete and moral, has been thoroughly studied.[202]

---

[197] Brunt (above, n. 195) 6. These remarks are followed, however, by the denial cited above, n. 195. But it should be noted that in the letter to Crassus cited by Brunt, Cicero mentions their *amicitia* in the very next sentence after the remark about the *foedus.*

[198] On this meaning and application of *fides* in party politics, see Taylor (above, n. 194) 41–42; Hellegouarc'h, pp. 23–35.

[199] Hellegouarc'h (above, n. 192) 34, nn. 3 and 4.

[200] See E. Badian, *Foreign Clientelae* (Oxford 1958) esp. 1–13 (also see Index, s.v. *fides*).

[201] Gelzer (above, n. 192) 71–73: " 'Treuverhältnis' entspricht dem lateinischen *'fides'.* Seine Natur ergibt sich aus Stellen, wo *fides* mit anderen Begriffen kombiniert wird, mit *patrocinium, clientela, praesidium, amicitia, hospitium.* Demgemäss finden sich auch häufig nebeneinander *amici, clientes, hospites, patroni,*" and citations in nn. 72 and 73.

[202] E. Fraenkel, "Zur Geschichte des Wortes *fides," RhM* 71 (1916) 187–99 [=*Kl. Beiträge* I, 15–26], finds it meaning "Vertrauen, Zutrauen, Glaube" only rarely (and not before Cic. *De Inv.* and *Rhet. ad Her.*) during the Republic, but rather (more "concrete", or "technisch"): "Gewähr, Bürgschaft, Versprechen; Zuverlässigkeit, Treue, Glaubwürdigkeit; bezeichnet also alles, worauf man sich verlassen kann, Garantie im weitesten Sinne, sei es dass sie in einem Akte, einer Versicherung, einem bestimmten rechtlichen Verhältnis von Personen zu einander, oder in einer Eigenschaft von Menschen oder Dingen gründet" (187). Heinze, however, argued for the basic moral character of the term, that "trust" is the basic sense from which arises the legal "guarantee" (*"Fides,"*

4

Amicitia, a political alliance analogous to an international *foedus*, based on the broad idea of *fides* or mutual trust and trustworthiness, had to bring practical advantages to each party and be reinforced continually by the conferring of mutual advantages. Hence the constant reference to *officium* (and its plural) and *beneficium* (in verse, *benefactum*): "Roman political factions were welded together, less by unity of principle than by mutual interest and by mutual services (*officia*), either between social equals as an alliance, or from superior to inferior, in a traditional and almost feudal form of clientship: on a favorable estimate the bond was called *amicitia*, otherwise *factio*."[203] "Idcirco amicitiae comparantur ut commune commodum mutuis officiis gubernetur," as Cicero himself so very clearly stated (*Sex. Rosc.* 111). Mutual services were the result or expression of unanimity: *benevolentia* (with the verb *bene velle*) has an important place in the dialogue between political *amici*, a prop to *amicitia* almost as tangible and practical as the actual *officia* or *beneficia* conferred.[204] The result of mutual favors and *benevolentia* is specifically *gratia*:[205] *gratus* commonly denotes someone who has conferred such favors, or even the situation itself (*amicitia*) in which services are rendered.[206]

All obligations involved in *amicitiae* are viewed as sanctioned by religion (as, properly, was a *foedus*); involved in this is the concept of

---

Hermes 64 (1929) 140–66). The implications of these two studies (not on all points mutually exclusive) for the use of the word by Catullus and the Augustan poets will be considered below.

203 Syme (above, n. 193) 157. Cf. Gelzer (above, n. 192) 72 ("Mit '*fides*' deckt sich vielfach die Bedeutung von '*officium*', die man mit 'gegenseitigem Nahverhältnis' wiedergeben kann. Das Wort begegnet ungemein häufig, besonders im Sinn der dem Nahverhältnis entspringenden Leistung und als gesellschaftliche und schliesslich sittliche Pflicht. Die Nuance der Gegenseitigkeit ist dabei wohl immer vorhanden."), and the citations in nn. 74 and 75. See, on *officium*, Hellegouarc'h (above, n. 192) 152–63, and on *beneficium* (*benefactum*), pp. 163–69; *beneficium* is, of course, not possible in dactylic verse.

204 See Hellegouarc'h, *ibid.*, 149–50.

205 See *ThLL* (s.v. *gratia*) VI.2, 2208, 37–84: examples of this specific usage are numerous; Cicero himself defined it (*De Inv.* 2.161), "gratia, in qua amicitiarum et officiorum alterius memoria et remunerandi voluntas continetur." On *gratia* and *gratus*, see Hellegouarc'h, *ibid.*, 202–08.

206 For the numerous examples of an *amicus* being *gratus*, see *ThLL* (s.v.) VI.2, 2260–61, 50; note esp. Plancus to Cicero, *Ad Fam.* 10.24.1, *omnis gratas amicitias atque etiam pias propinquitates . . . vincam*, and *ibid.*, 10.11.1, [*ut me praestem*] *in amicitia tua memorem atque gratum.*

pietas.[207] In the language of political alliance, he is *pius* who has fulfilled his obligations by *officia* and *benevolentia*, who is guilty of no *iniuria* against his political *amicus*. But there is another, more specific, aspect of *pietas*: it implies in respect to family connections exactly what *benevolentia* implies in respect to other connections. Thus Cicero can define *benevolentia* as an integral and essential part of *amicitia*, as distinct from *propinquitas* (*Amic.* 19, *namque hoc praestat amicitia propinquitati, quod ex propinquitate benevolentia tolli potest, ex amicitia non potest: sublata enim benevolentia, amicitiae nomen tollitur, propinquitatis manet*) and associate *pietas* with *propinquitas*, as distinct from *amicitia* (*Fam.* 10.24.1, *omnis gratas amicitias atque etiam pias propinquitates . . .*). Family connections were an important factor in Roman politics, and *pietas* an important aspect of this special sort of alliance. "The family was older than the State; and the family was the kernel of a Roman political faction. Loyalty to the ties of kinship in politics was a supreme obligation, often imposing inexpiable vendettas. Hence the role of the words 'pius' and 'pietas' in the revolutionary wars."[208]

This outline of the vocabulary of political alliances must suffice. Other words and synonyms might be added (including some that occur in Catullus), the list of examples can easily be extended, the definitions of the concepts and the connections between the words themselves can be made more detailed and precise. The purpose of this outline, however, was to define the area of use common to all the words at the time of Catullus:[209] there can be no doubt, from the frequency with which the terms occur together time and again in similar contexts, that this

[207] For instance, Cic. *Ad Fam.* 1.1.1, *ego omni officio ac potius pietate erga te ceteris satis facio omnibus*, and the examples collected by Reitzenstein (above, n. 190) p. 20 n. 34, among them Cic. *Ad Fam.* 1.9.1: *. . . te perspicere meam in te pietatem. quid enim dicam benevolentiam, cum illud ipsum gravissimum et sanctissimum nomen pietatis levius mihi meritis erga me tuis esse videatur? quod autem tibi grata mea erga te studia scribis esse, facis tu quidem abundantia quadam amoris, ut etiam grata sint ea, quae praetermitti sine nefario scelere non possunt.* On the relation of *pietas* (*pius*) to the other concepts of political alliance, see Hellegouarc'h (above, n. 192) 276–79.

[208] Syme (above, n. 193) 157.

[209] It is not difficult to illustrate the same usages and relations of the words for the century preceding Catullus: Plautus, for instance, often plays on the terminology of political alliance for comic effect. And the terminology continued even after its *raison d'être* had been lost; Syme remarks on the aristocracy under Tiberius (*ibid.*, 424), "In evil days Roman aristocratic loyalty acknowledged the ties of family, of *fides*, of *amicitia*."

area must be defined as that of political alliance, formal or informal to varying degrees. When one considers the life, the values, and the moral cast of the thought of Roman aristocratic society, the importance of this segment of Latin vocabulary and the immediate suggestiveness of these words when appearing together in any context must be obvious and compelling.[210]

It is only natural that Catullus, when betrayed by friends, should exploit the vocabulary of political alliance in his denunciations and accusations. In c. 30, Alfenus is immediately called *immemor*: it is the *memoria officiorum* or *beneficiorum* that is so frequently cited by Cicero and others as one basis for a solid *amicitia* and a source of *gratia*;[211] Alfenus' impious deeds (*nec facta impia fallacum hominum caelicolis placent*, 4) are not, in our sense, religious violations, but rather violations of the *fides* of an *amicitia*, the central idea of the poem. This sense of *fides* appears again in c. 102 (*si quicquam tacito commissum est fido ab amico / cuius sit penitus nota fides animi*, 1–2). Rufus (in c. 77) is held directly responsible for violating *amicitia*: *Rufe mihi frustra ac nequiquam credite amice . . . heu heu nostrae pestis amicitiae* (first and last lines). C. 73 is the most complete expression of these terms (a renunciation taking much the same form and expression as c. 76):

> Desine de quoquam quicquam *bene velle mereri*
> aut aliquem fieri posse putare *pium*.
> Omnia sunt *ingrata*, nihil *fecisse benigne*
> <prodest,> immo etiam taedet obestque magis;
> ut mihi, quem nemo gravius nec acerbius urget,
> quam modo qui me *unum* atque *unicum amicum* habuit.

The occurrence of such words together in such a context would make immediately clear, for a Roman reader, the only area of usage and application common to them all.

The point of the preceding pages should, by now, hardly need explication. Catullus, in what must be an early poem to Lesbia, answers her proposition of a pleasant little affair (*iucundum . . . amorem*, 109.1)

---

[210] On the significance and importance of this vocabulary in general, see Hellegouarc'h's suggestive remarks (above, n. 192) 566–70.

[211] For instance, see Cicero's definition of *gratia* quoted above, n. 205. See the uses given in *ThLL* (s.v. *memoria*) VIII, 670, or (s.v. *memor*) VIII, 656, 81—657, 17.

with an emphatic expression of something very different, *aeternum hoc sanctae foedus amicitiae* (the last line, 6). That the metaphor is definitely that of a political alliance is made clear repeatedly. Lesbia had her way, and the affair reached a conclusion which Catullus could only regard as a violation of the *amicitia* he had originally hoped for:

> Huc est mens deducta tua mea, Lesbia, culpa
>   atque ita se *officio* perdidit ipsa *suo*,
> ut iam nec *bene velle* queat tibi, si optima fias,
>   nec desistere amare, omnia si facias.   (75)

> . . . quod amantem *iniuria*[212] talis
> cogit amare magis, sed *bene velle* minus.   (72.7–8)

> nulla *fides* ullo fuit umquam *foedere* tanta . . .   (87.3)

In c. 72 a different aspect of this *amicitia* is introduced, but one which, in turn, can only be explained by the metaphor of political alliance: *dilexi tum te non tantum ut vulgus amicam / sed pater ut gnatos diligit et generos* (3–4). The embarrassment of critics and commentators with this (for us at least) strange concept disappears if it is interpreted as an extension of what has become for Catullus the controlling image of the entire affair (in the epigrams, at least): the importance of alliances by marriage between leading political families needs no documentation.[213]

The most difficult question concerning c. 76 is one that does not seem to have bothered any critic: what do the first five lines have to do with the sixth?

> Siqua recordanti *benefacta* priora voluptas
>   est homini, cum se cogitat esse *pium*,
> nec sanctam violasse *fidem*, nec *foedere* nullo
>   divum ad fallendos numine abusum homines,
> multa parata manent in longa aetate, Catulle,
>   ex hoc *ingrato* gaudia amore tibi.   (76.1–6)

---

212 On *iniuria*, see Hellegouarc'h (above, n. 192) 166: "Il [*iniuria*] convient donc mieux au vocabulaire politique. Comme le *beneficium* crée l'*amicitia*, l'*iniuria* constitue la rupture de l'*amicitia* (Cic., *Fam.*, I, 9, 18) et provoque l'*inimicitia*."

213 See, for instance, L. R. Taylor, *Party Politics* 33–34: "The relations of two houses joined by marriage frequently continued when, as often happened, there had been a divorce. Cicero maintained friendship with two former sons-in-law from whom his daughter Tullia was divorced" (p. 34).

What in fact does a man's piety, in his relations with others, have to do with Catullus' own love affair? Is it not, poetically, an ineffective and almost preposterous introduction to what is obviously an important, and sincere, personal poem?[214] The first question can be obviated by the simple (and unsatisfactory) assumption that Catullus is merely saying, "I have been true to you, Lesbia, in every fashion," but the second remains, because poetically there is little here of Catullus' usual directness in either sense or expression. If, however, it is understood that Catullus is using yet again a metaphor he has continually applied to the affair with Lesbia in his epigrams, the first five lines become not only direct and fitting, but personal as well: from the very beginning of the poem Catullus is speaking directly about Lesbia and his love, not about a general sort of piety or a vague application of it to his own situation.

Catullus, then, has portrayed his affair with Lesbia in the terminology of a political alliance: it is to be an *amicitia*, a *foedus*, based on *fides*, the concrete expressions of which are the mutual *benevolentia* and *benefacta* of the two parties, resulting in *gratia* arising from the performance of *officia*; the relationship is to be protected by divinity, as it must be religiously observed with *pietas* by both parties; and Catullus can imagine the alliance, too, as one resulting from a marriage between families, a bond of *pietas* linking the father-in-law and sons-in-law. When this relationship is broken, the metaphor is shattered by reality. Whereas at this point the two parties involved would normally become *inimici*, Catullus finds this impossible: he cannot continue in his feeling of *benevolentia*, yet cannot cease loving, a state of mind summarized in the words *odi et amo* and finding its fullest expression in c. 76.[215]

So much, I am sure, would have been the response of any Roman reader to the language of the Lesbia epigrams. To read more into the metaphor (that, for example, Catullus was actually a client of Lesbia—if

---

[214] I do not think I am manufacturing a problem. I remember very well feeling uneasy about these lines (and the whole poem) when I first read it.

[215] *Odi* may be used by Catullus in a political sense (see Hellegouarc'h [above, n. 192] 191, on *Odium-odi*), but, though it gives perfect sense if read in this way (as I think it must be read), to prove it would be difficult.

she was Clodia) would be possible but poetically unwarranted. To assume less, however (that the *amicitia*, or even the *foedus*, is merely a periphrasis for marriage[216] or an expression of some ideal of spiritual friendship) is to refuse to recognize the import of some of the most common and potent words in the Republican vocabulary and to cloud the poems in a vagueness and obscurity they are far from having.

It has been noted in passing that the terminology of political alliance is found in the epigrams, and this is so almost without exception. It is altogether true for its use in poems concerned with Lesbia (there is no trace of this metaphor in any of the polymetrics about Lesbia) and almost entirely true of the poems concerned with Catullus' *amici*: c. 30 (*Alfene immemor . . .*) is the only polymetric to address a friend in these terms. Confirmation is given by the distribution of the appropriate words: *fides* and *fidus* are never found in the polymetrics (with the exception of c. 30 and the special meaning of *fides* in 34.1, *Dianae sumus in fide*), nor are *foedus, officium, bene velle, pietas* (*pius* in the polymetrics only at 39.4, *si ad pii rogum fili | lugetur*, and 16.5, *pium poetam*, both of which are entirely without that sense of *pius* being discussed here), or *amicitia* itself. Though a few of the terms are found in the longer poems, two or more are never used together in any context to suggest the language of political alliance; and never is any such metaphor suggested by the individual use.[217]

This identification of the epigrams' political metaphor is one more indication of their special nature, but a most important one. That the

---

216 See the recent corrective remarks of H. Tränkle ("Neoterische Kleinigkeiten," *Mus Helv* 24 (1967) 87–103): "Es [*amicitia*] handelt sich um jene seltene, für die poetae novi und dann für die Elegiker so bezeichnende Übertragung des Wortes und der mit ihm verbundenen Vorstellungen von der Freundschaft unter Männern mit ihrer gesellschaftlich-politischen Bedeutung auf freie Liebesverhältnisse zwischen Männern und Frauen, so dass diese als unverbrüchliche Treuebündnisse erscheinen, ein Gebrauch, dessen Eigenart uns R. Reitzenstein im rechten Licht zu sehen gelehrt hat. Die *amicitia* gehört zu *amica* und *amator*, nicht zu *uxor* und *maritus*" (97).

217 A case might be argued for the *fidus* in 64.182 (where Ariadne asks, "*coniugis an fido consoler memet amore?*") that here too Catullus makes Ariadne reflect his own experience and language; but to argue for a metaphor (elsewhere always clearly presented by a complex of terminology) from a single word would be difficult when the simple meaning "a love of mutual trust" (as in later elegy) is available and the context is not compelling. Similarly, the *foedus* of 64.335 and 373 must be simply the bond of marriage. The *officia* of Manius/Allius in c. 68 (12, 42, 150) are hardly metaphorical.

epigrams are essentially Roman and unpoetic will be argued later; for the present we must simply add this new indication of their nature to the others so far presented. Catullus has adopted the common terminology of an important aspect of Roman political life and applied it to his affair with Lesbia, but has done so only in one group of his poems: the obvious force of this metaphor in the Lesbia epigrams makes all the more striking its total absence from such poems as 8, the end of 11, or 58, or even from c. 68 and any of the happier polymetrics concerned with Lesbia. Clearly the epigrams formed a distinct group for Catullus: a brief survey of the language of political alliance in poetry before and after Catullus can help to establish something of the nature of this group of his poems.

The first point to be raised is one that should not need discussion: the metaphor as used by Catullus has nothing to do with Greek poetry of any period, including Hellenistic epigram. The concept and its language are so thoroughly a part of a thoroughly Roman political system that its origin cannot be imagined outside of this system. Were it not that some have attempted to derive Catullus' *amicitia* from the (not uncommon) φιλία of Hellenistic epigram, this reminder would be unnecessary.[218] Again, the recurring complex of terminology in Catullus is telling.

Far more difficult is the question of what happened to the metaphor in Augustan elegy. This question demands a thorough, independent review; an answer can be suggested, but convincing proof requires a complete review of the uses of the individual terms and cannot be offered here.

The term on which all others focus is never found in elegy as a metaphor of the relationship between poet and mistress: *amicitia* never occurs in Tibullus, is used only once by Propertius (1.22.2, of a friend), and never appears in any sense in the *Amores* of Ovid. Elsewhere Ovid is sparing of its use (only once in the *Metamorphoses* and *Fasti*), and uses

---

[218] Cf. Heinze's discussion of the basic difference between the Greek πίστις (and δικαιοσύνη) and the Latin *fides* (*Hermes* 64 (1929) 163–65.), which concludes, "Während bei Plautus und, wenngleich seltener, bei Terenz, die Leute bei jeder Gelegenheit die *fides* im Munde führen, so kennt z.B. Menander nichts dergleichen."

it in a strict technical sense, for comic effect, in the *Ars Amatoria*,[219] seriously in the *Epistulae ex Ponto* (7 times) and *Tristia* (7 times). It is clear not only that Catullus' metaphorical usage was scrupulously avoided by the elegists, but that the word itself was unpoetic, to be used only when the strictly technical sense (not friendship, but a more formal alliance) was required.[220] This clearly intentional avoidance of both word and Catullan metaphor by Augustan love poets suggests that the other words we have discussed as terms of political alliance would not have been used by them to suggest that sense or metaphor at all.

Reitzenstein himself discussed "Das *foedus* in der römischen Erotik," but only to argue convincingly against Leo's interpretation of it as the *leges amatoriae* of the "Hetärenkontrakt" of Attic comedy;[221] for Reitzenstein the common use of the term in elegy for the bond between poet and mistress was to be explained and understood from its use by Catullus, but though he went on to illustrate clearly its place in the vocabulary of political alliance in Catullus, he somehow never claimed this basic sense for it in elegy (or, for that matter, even clearly for Catullus). It is perhaps this very word that has caused the uncertainty about the technical terminology in Catullus: in both Catullus and elegy good sense can be had by taking *foedus* loosely as a pact or bond between lovers,[222] but only Catullus, by associating the word with other specific terms of political alliance, made it more exact and technical.

Fides, too, occurs often in elegy, but again only in the sense of mutual trust, carefully unassociated with Catullus' metaphorical usage. Perhaps the best indication of this (without going into a detailed discussion of its individual occurrences) is Fraenkel's observation that

---

[219] Only *Ars Am.* 1. 720 (*intret amicitiae nomine tectus amor*) and 1.740 (*conquerar an moneam mixtum fas omne nefasque? / nomen amicitiae est, nomen inane fides*); cf. *Rem. Am.* 590.

[220] Virgil has it only twice, both in a technical sense (*Aen.* 7.546, *dic in amicitiam coeant et foedera iungant*, and similarly 11.321); and Horace, outside of *Sat.* and *Ars P.* (6 times), only *Odes* 2.1.4, *gravisque principum amicitias et arma.*

[221] Reitzenstein (above, n. 190) 9–15; Leo, *Plautinische Forschungen*[2] (Berlin 1912) p. 154 n. 4, and *RhM* 55 (1900) 604–05.

[222] Reitzenstein, *ibid.*, 15, "Das Empfinden hat sich seit Catulls Zeit gewandelt, das *foedus* ist zur Liaison geworden."

it occurs first in a general sense only (and even then rarely) in Augustan literature: "In Wahrheit ist diese Bedeutung ['Vertrauen, Zutrauen, Glaube'], so häufig das Wort im alten Latein ist, vor Cic. de inv. und der Rhetorik an Herennius überhaupt nicht, vor der Kaiserzeit nur ganz spärlich, als terminus technicus und in einer bestimmten Verbindung, zu belegen."[223] If, at the end of the Republic and the beginning of the Empire, *fides* was beginning to be used in a more general sense, its use in elegy as mutual trust between lovers represents a stage in this process. Heinze saw this process as one clearly illustrated by poetic usage: "Wir haben bisher Fälle einseitiger *fides* betrachtet; ich könnte nun noch von zahlreichen anderen sprechen, in denen wechselseitig die *fides* eingesetzt wird, wie etwa bei *hospites, socii, amici*, könnte dartun, wie bei den römischen Elegikern, Properz zumal, aber auch in Horaz' Oden, die *fides* der Liebenden als eine sittliche Verpflichtung erscheint, die dem Verhältnis eine ganz andere Färbung gibt, als das etwa die neimals ganz ernst genommenen Liebeschwüre in der griechischen Erotik tun."[224] Moral obligation is now the general sense of *fides*.

It must be enough merely to suggest that both the *foedus* and the *fides* between lovers in Augustan elegy are quite different from what they had been in Catullus, in spite of the superficial similarities in the way they are used; that in elegy they have been intentionally disassociated from their older technical usage, perhaps due to the more general sense in which the words were coming to be used, perhaps because the technical Roman sense of the terms was basically unpoetic; that they never occur in a metaphorical complex of terminology as they do in Catullus; and that the whole idea of *amicitia* is carefully avoided. All this would confirm the conclusion offered above about Catullus' restriction of the metaphor to his epigrams proper, and what this implies. The epigrams alone make use of what was essentially Roman and unpoetic, and in spite of Catullus' precedent, the following generation of love poets never resumed what had been for him the central metaphor of his affair. But to speak of Catullus' precedent is

[223] *RhM* 71 (1916) 187; cf. (p. 189), "Das ["blosses fides = Glaube, Vertrauen"] findet sich untechnisch zuerst in der Poesie und Prosa der augusteischen Zeit, z.B., Verg. *Aen.* 4, 12 *credo equidem, nec vana fides, genus esse deorum. . . .*"
[224] *Hermes* 64 (1929) 163.

inexact, for his poetic precedent lay, for later poets, only in certain neoteric features of his polymetric and longer poems, and in these poems Catullus too had decided that the unpoetic metaphor of political alliance had no place.

GEOGRAPHICAL AND MYTHOLOGICAL PROPER NAMES

The words geographical and mythological in the heading of this section are vague, but are intended to be so. In the widest sense, what is meant is "allusions to history or geography, used as a means of emotional communication between poet and reader," or perhaps the "romantic use . . . of history, legend or place-names."[225] Yet, as the term is understood now, Catullus is not a romantic poet, and Alexandrian is a far better term for the use of these names, if it may pass here without close definition: but though it will pass as an acceptable label for the learning of the longer poems and especially for c. 64 or c. 66, it will fail when applied to the poet of the polymetrics; and the significance of certain names will be lost entirely if the term is taken too strictly. The range of the proper names considered here extends from the most allusive, most Greek, most learned (and perhaps most romantic) to those hardly removed from Catullus' daily life and surroundings: it is only from its context that the purpose of any proper name can be seen. The significance of the geography of the opening lines of the epyllion, for example, is clear; but when does a reference to some unromantic place in Catullus' own world begin to assume this significance? Absense of a clear answer is the reason why no strict lists or counts of such names can be made and no more precise heading for this section can be found.

However, the general distribution of geographical and mythological proper names in Catullus shows clearly the relationship of the three parts of his work: long lists of such names can be compiled, naturally

225 E. A. Havelock, *Lyric Genius* 124 and 125; see his chapter "Doctus Catullus—The Romantic Scholar," 122–31, for the broadest—and most modern—interpretation of these names in Catullus' poetry.

enough, from c. 64 or c. 66, but longer still is the list from the polymetrics, in which such names might be less expected.[226] Mynors'
Index Nominum serves to give a rough estimate: there are ten full
columns in all, and a glance at any one will show that even after
allowance has been made for the names of Catullus' friends (or enemies)
or for places to which no special poetic significance should be attached
(such as Sirmio, Bithynia in 10.7, Colonia, etc.), the bulk of that
column will remain. In the epigrams, however, only fifteen such names
can be found (that is, less than half a column). The conclusions to be
drawn at this point are obvious enough: it will be sufficient here to
discuss certain general aspects of the use made of these proper names in
the polymetrics and longer poems, then to discuss certain specifics and
types, and finally to examine those few names in the epigrams. Further
conclusions will be drawn later.

One of the most convenient occasions for geographical or mythological reference offered to a classical poet was the prayer, whose
literary form demanded that the god invoked be identified first by
cult title and site of cult, or that the principle sites of worship be named,
from which he might be called. In the first two lines of c. 61, the
invocation of Hymenaeus takes this form, *Collis o Heliconii | cultor,
Uraniae genus*, and later the form is resumed,

> quare age, huc aditum ferens,
> perge linquere Thespiae
> rupis Aonios specus,
> nympha quos super irrigat
> frigerans Aganippe. (26–30)[227]

---

[226] The polymetrics are ostensibly concerned with Catullus' daily life and surroundings:
"Of the sixty lyrics and fragments which form the first part of his book, only two, a
Hymn to Diana and a little love-drama, the *Acme and Septimius*, are detached from the
immediate occasions of his daily life. Forty-six of them begin by addressing in the vocative
case some person or thing, whether friend or enemy, Lesbia's sparrow, his writing paper,
or himself." (Havelock, *Lyric Genius* 79.)

[227] Kroll on 61.1–45: "Er ist wirklichen Kultliedern nachgebildet (Wünsch RE 9,
142) und enthält den oder die Namen des Gottes (V.4f.), seine Herkunft (V.2, vgl. 34, 5),
den Wohnort (V. 1, vgl. 36, 11. 64, 96. Il. 1, 37 ὃς Χρύσην ἀμφιβέβηκας Κίλλαν τε ζαθέην
Τενέδοιό τε ἶφι ἀνάσσεις), von dem man ihn aufruft (V. 26), und die Aufforderung zum
Kommen (V. 6 ff.)," and on line 26," Hymenaios soll von seinem jetzigen Wohnsitze
herbeikommen: das ist Hymnenstil."

The prayer form, however, serves only as a setting for the literary *topos* of Helicon: it is no coincidence that Hymenaeus is the son of the muse (as introduced in the second line, *Uraniae genus*) or that the description of Helicon is entirely literary in origin and purpose.[228] In c. 36 there is a similar prayer to Venus, to whom Catullus fulfills the vow made by Lesbia:

> nunc o caeruleo creata ponto
> quae sanctum Idalium Uriosque apertos
> quaeque Ancona Cnidumque harundinosam
> colis quaeque Amathunta quaeque Golgos
> quaeque Durrachium Hadriae tabernam   (11–15)

The vow, however, was made *iocose lepide* (10) and is *non illepidum neque invenustum* (17, a proper pun); it is in this spirit that the prayer is to be taken, as is indeed indicated by the last site of Venus' worship mentioned, *Hadriae tabernam*. The first four lines of the prayer are in the high style: in c. 61 Venus inhabits Idalium (*Idalium colens*, 17), and in c. 64 two sites are repeated (*quaeque regis Golgos quaeque Idalium frondosum*, 96); anaphora is a common element in the prayer form, here used with solemn effect. Catullus uses the solemn and elevated style of prayer for the purpose at hand: the language of the poem is wittily dignified (cf. the *electissima scripta* and the *tardipedi deo*, 6–7) to fit the playfulness of the subject. Catullus' poem (and the prayer it contains) is itself the antithesis to the *annales Volusi*, which were no doubt long, turgid, and without wit, altogether *pleni ruris et inficetiarum* (19).

Geographical excursus similar to that in prayers was part of Alexandrian technique. In c. 64 the assembling of the guests for the wedding demands the highly poetic lines

> deseritur Cieros, linquunt Pthiotica Tempe
> Crannonisque domos ac moenia Larisaea,
> Pharsalum coeunt, Pharsalia tecta frequentant.   (35–37)

All is done with infinite care: the four verbs are meticulously placed,

---

228 See Kroll on 28: "*Aonius* ist seit hellenistischer Zeit allgemeine dichterische Bezeichnung für boiotisch . . .; für die hellenistischen Dichter ist die Musengrotte ein konventionelles Motiv . . . C. kennt das alles aus der hellenistischen Poesie, nicht aus Autopsie"; and on 30, "*frigerans* . . . von der kühlen Quelle: das Ganze ein hellenistisches Idyll. . . ."

one at the beginning of the passage, one at the end, one after the caesura in the first line rhyming with the one before the caesura in the last line; the nouns are likewise placed for variation of position from one line to the next, and on these proper names all emphasis (as in the spondaic ending with the proper adjective *Larisaea*) is placed. Sound is all-important: in addition to the verbs, *linquUNT* and *coeUNT*, *moenIA* and *PharsalIA* are in the same position, as are *PthioTiCA* and *TeCtA*, *CierOS* and *domOS*. The poetic quality of the proper names is to Catullus as important as the learning of the geography.[229] In the polymetrics, c. 4 contains similar lines (6–9, in which the sound patterns of 8 and 9 are again important): the subject of the *phaselus* naturally suggests a brief geographical excursus, and here too the places are distant and colored by mythological suggestion. The excursus of c. 11 begins with distant places (*sive in extremos penetrabit Indos*, 2) in a poetic context (*litus ut longe resonante Eoa / tunditur unda*, 3–4), somewhat heroic (cf. the compound adjectives *sagittiferos* and *septemgeminus*, 6–7), and stylistically elevated (again the anaphora, *sive . . . seu . . . sive . . . sive . . .* at the beginning of lines 5, 6, 7, and 9); but at line 9 the scenes become suddenly more real, more Roman, and with the mention of the *Caesaris monimenta magni* (10) the reality of the present is imposed: within itself the excursus suggests the movement and changes of tone of the whole poem, the final generalizing simile (22–24) even finding its antecedent in the general conclusion of the excursus (*quaecumque feret voluntas / caelitum*, 13–14). It is among such poems that c. 39 must be seen. Catullus could not find an excuse for the smiling Egnatius even if:

> si urbanus esses aut Sabinus aut Tiburs
> aut pinguis Umber aut obesus Etruscus
> aut Lanuuinus ater atque dentatus
> aut Transpadanus, . . . (10–13)

Again there is anaphora, again the epithets (*pinguis, obesus, ater atque dentatus*), but the whole effect is comic, made so by the parody of

---

[229] See Kroll on 55: "Die Häufung geographischer Namen (vgl. Cir. 463, die Propemptika, Musai. 46) dient nicht bloss der Entfaltung von Gelehrsamkeit, sondern auch einem poetischen Zweck. . . ."

elevated style. Geographical allusion serves the same purpose in c. 37, when at the end Egnatius is introduced with the mock-heroic address *cuniculosae Celtiberiae fili* (18), in which the epithet *cuniculosae* adds much to the effect.[230] Finally, in c. 55 Catullus records his search for Camerius:

> te Campo quaesivimus minore,
> te in Circo, te in omnibus libellis,
> te in templo summi Iovis sacrato. (3–5)

The anaphora of *te* conveys the tone so clearly that the familiar Roman scenes become, comically, as remote, and the search as heroic, as in any epic setting. The mythological excursus of the other Camerius fragment (58[b].1–4), with its anaphora *non . . . non . . . non . . . non . . .*, serves the same comic purpose.

Alexandrian fascination with geographical learning and the "romantic use . . . of history, legend or place-names," taken together with the obvious delight of the poet in the sound as well as the associations of such names, can all be seen behind their use in the longer poems. In the polymetrics these same explanations can often be assumed (as in c. 4), but in other cases pathos results (as in c. 11), or what amounts to parody of a higher style produces a comic effect (as in c. 39 and c. 55). Only passages of extended geographical excursus have been dealt with above, but single geographical or mythological allusions are as frequent in the polymetrics as in the longer poems—too frequent for detailed examination here.[231] By insertion of such allusions into the

---

230 With the phrase *cuniculosae Celtiberiae*, compare *Nicaeae . . . aestuosae* (46.5): *cuniculosus* is both an *-osus* formation (suggesting epic) and a diminutive; it is a Spanish word (so Pliny, *NH* 8.217, and see Ernout-Meillet s.v.), perhaps in this passage felt to be a burlesque equivalent to a heroic Greek form, fitting the mock-heroic address to the Spaniard Egnatius; and it is a pun on a comparable form of *cunnus*.

231 Their purpose is much the same. *Magnanimi Remi nepotes* in the conclusion of c. 58 is as pathetic and bitter as the first three lines are affecting or *glubit* is shocking. *Romuli nepotum* in the first line of the poem to Cicero (49) can be nothing but comic and provides the best reason for not taking the poem as a sincere offering of thanks. *Adoneus*, used of Mamurra in 29.8, is a sharper reproach than any other in the same poem (the other geographical and mythological allusions in this poem, poetic and heroic for comic effect, make it worth study: *ultima Britannia, cinaede Romule, amnis aurifer Tagus*). Two other references are worth discussing here as illustrations of this principle. *Apheliotae* (*Furi, villula vestra non ad Austri | flatus opposita est neque ad Favoni | nec saevi Boreae aut Apheliotae*, 26.1–3) concludes a comic list of the winds with an obscure Greek name which in later

The Poetic Vocabulary

context of his daily life and personal concerns, Catullus manages shifts and changes of tone and dimension which serve any purpose he may have. In this the polymetric *nugae* can be seen as an extension of serious neoteric poetry, but it is again obvious that only the *nugae* allowed him this extension, whereas the epigrams did not.

Catullus' use of certain types of Greek names and Greek inflection must now be considered. His use of adjectives formed from Greek names in *-αιος* and *-ειος* shows clearly the close relationship of the polymetrics and longer poems.[232] 13 of these forms are used 14 times by Catullus, and with the exception of two in the polymetrics, all in the longer poems. Their poetic quality needs no explanation: it is sufficient to observe only the contexts of the three in c. 64, or of *Oetaeus* in the simile of 68.54, or of *Cyllenaeus* in 68.109 (*quale ferunt Grai Pheneum prope Cyllenaeum*, where the Alexandrian *ferunt* is coupled with the poetic form *Grai*, and the adjective itself makes a spondaic line). The two used in the polymetrics are worth notice. *Pegaseus* occurs in the comic mythological excursus of 58b.2 (*non si Pegaseo ferar volatu*). C. 38, addressed to the neoteric poet Cornificius

---

Latin is found only as a technical term needing explanation (see *ThLL*, s.v.: the Latin equivalent is *subsolanus*): Cicero's point, that such an obscurely named wind is representative of neoteric preciosity, is well taken here (*ad Att.* 7.2.1: '*flavit ab Epiro lenissimus Onchesmites*': hunc σπονδειάζοντα si cui voles τῶν νεωτέρων, pro tuo vendito); but it is obvious that Catullus is enjoying himself equally as much as is Cicero. *Si placet Dionae* (56.6) is a learned variation on the colloquial *si dis placet* (see Kroll *ad loc.*); Catullus, using a literary cult title (Theoc. 15.106, Κύπρι Διωναία), underlines the point of the final line by referring to the appropriate deity in the high style, but thereby emphasizes the tone of the poem itself (*res est ridicula et nimis iocosa*, 4): it is tempting to speculate on a possible connection with Caesar here (cf. Virg. *Ecl.* 9.47, *ecce Dionaei processit Caesaris astrum*).

[232] For the spelling of these place names in Greek and Latin, see Housman, "*ΑΙΟΣ* and *ΕΙΟΣ* in Latin Poetry," *JP* 33 (1914) 54–75. His rule is given on p. 56: "Adjectives in *-αιος* are formed from feminine substantives of the 1st declension. Adjectives in *-ειος* are formed from substantives of the 2nd and 3rd declensions and from masculine substantives of the 1st." In Latin, those in *-αιος* become *-aeus*, those in *-ειος* become *-ēus*. Catullus has the following forms: *Androgeoneus*, 64.77 (a hapax); *Ariadnaeus*, 66.60 (a Catullan coinage afterwards used only of the star itself); *Beroniceus*, 66.8 (on the ending, cf. *Penelopeus* below); *Cycneus*, 67.32 (which, if the emendation is correct, may be a particularly playful, learned allusion to local geography: see Kroll *ad loc.*); *Cyllenaeus*, 68.109; *Idaeus*, 64.178; *Larisaeus*, 64.36; *Lethaeus*, 65.5; *Oetaeus*, 62.7, 68.54; *Pegaseus*, 58b.2; *Penelopeus*, 61.223 (on the ending see Housman, 73: perhaps the Grk. adj. in *-ειος* derived from the alternate Πηνελόπεια); *Rhoeteus*, 65.7; *Simonideus*, 38.8. To these proper adjectives should perhaps be added the neoteric coinage *labyrinthēus* (64.114), though the *-ειος* formation does not appear in Greek, acc. to L.S.J.

and requesting, with typical terseness and wit, some scrap of poetic sympathy in a time of dire need, ends *paulum quidlubet allocutionis,* / *maestius lacrimis Simonideis,* 7–8. The use of the Greek form of the proper adjective here is probably more than a metrical convenience: it implies all the Greek learning that the neoteric Cornificius could muster for the occasion, an effort, undoubtedly, not unlike Catullus' poetic letter to Allius, but naturally of a more playful sort.[233]

Greek proper names are often given Greek inflections by Catullus, but apparently, always for a particular reason.[234] In the longer poems such inflections are found only in cc. 63, 64, and 66, where they refer directly or indirectly to a Greek original. In c. 66 Catullus has *Athon* (46) at the end of the line where Callimachus had Ἄθω (a genitive); *ut Calybon omne genus pereat* (48) is a direct translation of Χαλύβων ὡς ἀπόλοιτο γένος; *Arsinoes Locridos* (54) is Callimachus' Λοκρίδος Ἀρσινόης; *Callisto* (66), the only such dative in Latin, must represent Καλλιστοῖ;[235] and the other two Greek inflections in the poem, *Booten* (67) and *Tethyi* (70), must likewise represent the original forms.[236] In c. 64 Catullus emphasizes the remoteness of subject and the novelty of neoteric style by these inflections. He is the first Roman poet to use the metonymy *Amphitrite* for the sea (64.11), but the possibility of its having been so used first by a Hellenistic poet is given support by the fact that Catullus gives it the Greek inflection *-en*.[237] The Greek genitive singular, *Phasidos*, balances the adjective of Greek formation *Aeeteos* in a spondaic line and emphasizes the poetic remoteness of scene (*Phasidos ad fluctus et fines Aeeteos,* 3). *Cierŏs* (35), with the Greek

---

[233] The allusion is, of course, playful, and the answer expected from Cornificius would be equally playful. Horace's reference to the dirges of Simonides (*Odes* 2.1.37–38, *sed ne relictis, Musa procax, iocis* / *Ceae retractes munera neniae*) should not be taken to imply that Catullus here asked in earnest for such somber songs, *iocis relictis*.

[234] See the list given by Fordyce on 64.2, to which should be added from Riese's list (p. XXVIII) *Amastri* (4.13), *Amathunta* (36.14), *Ancona* (36.13).

[235] On this form, see Fraenkel, *Gnomon* 34 (1962) 259.

[236] On the doubtful dative *Hydrochoi* (66.94), see Pfeiffer *ad loc.*, who decides that Catullus must have written *Hydrochoo*. Callimachus has the nominative Ὑδροχόος. Mynors' genitive *Hydrochoi* must depend on *proximus*, unparalleled (Fordyce *ad loc.*) in Latin, but formed after a Greek construction with γείτων and therefore probably right.

[237] Kroll, *ad loc.*: "*Amphitrite* 'Meer' hier zuerst, doch lässt der Gebrauch bei Oppian und Dionys. Perieg. (und Ovid?) einen Rückschluss auf hellenistische Dichter zu, bei denen diese Metonymien (zuerst Il. 2, 426) häufig sind."

nominative singular ending, is perhaps used, as suggested above, for the partial rhyme with *domōs* in the following line, both words immediately preceding the caesura (though such a rare literary name would naturally keep its Greek form). In c. 63 the only Greek terminations are *Cybeles* and *Cybebes* (12, 20, 35, 68) and *Attin* (88), used to emphasize the foreignness of the cult. Catullus, rather than using such terminations freely,[238] introduces them only in these three of the longer poems, and in these poems only for a particular poetic purpose.

In the polymetrics these terminations are all found in passages discussed above. C. 4 has two, *Cycladas* (7) and *Amastri* (13); c. 11 has *Arabas* (5); c. 36 has *Ancona* (13) and *Amathunta* (14);[239] the accusative *Acmen* appears in c. 45.1, 21, a fitting contrast to the Roman Septimius. In this respect too these passages appear as extensions of the neoteric style of the longer poems (it hardly needs noting here that no Greek inflections of proper names appear in the epigrams[240]), and the restraint and purpose with which Catullus employed these forms is again obvious, a feature of neoteric art at its best.[241]

What of the epigrams? When the names of Catullus' friends have been excluded, only some fifteen proper names remain, most of which, like *Syriam* (7) and *Ionios* (11) in the Arrius poem (84), are without any

---

[238] Cf. Fordyce at 64.2: "in earlier Latin verse Greek names are normally given Latin inflections; such exceptions as *Hectora* in Ennius are few. Catullus uses Greek terminations freely."

[239] The proper Latin *Ancona*, *-ae* is always used by prose writers, but *Ancon* (Ἀγκών) always by poets (Luc., Sil., Juv.); Cicero *Ad Att.* 7.11.1 has the accusative *Anconem* (see *ThLL*, s.v.). *Amathus* is not mentioned by any prose authors: Ovid has the Greek acc. *-nta* (*Met.* 10.220), Virgil only the nom. (*Aen.* 10.51).

[240] *Tethys* (88.5) is of course a Greek termination, but no Latinized form of the name occurs; on the context, see below.

[241] That Greek terminations had been a part of poetic diction earlier is clear from Varro (*Ling.* 10.70): *Accius haec in tragoediis largius a prisca consuetudine movere coepit et ad formas Graecas verborum magis revocare, a quo Valerius ait: Accius Hectorem nollet facere, Hectora mallet* (Morel, *FPL* 41); but it can be doubted that they were used with such a clear purpose as by Catullus. The disputed passage in Horace, *Sat.* 1.10.17–21 (*quos neque pulcher | Hermogenes umquam legit, neque simius iste | nil praeter Calvum et doctus cantare Catullum. | 'at magnum fecit quod verbis Graeca Latinis | miscuit.'*), is in point here: it seems doubtful that Horace here is finding fault with Catullus and Calvus themselves, but rather only with the bedraggled rear-guard of the neoterics, such as Hermogenes himself, who must have carried neoteric technique to tedious extremes (the later *Culex* or *Ciris* can represent such productions). Catullus is as sparing in his use of Greek words as he is purposeful in restricting Greek terminations of proper names.

special significance. A Gellius poem (88), however, contains the lines
*ecquid scis quantum suscipiat sceleris? | suscipit, o Gelli, quantum non
ultima Tethys | nec genitor Nympharum abluit Oceanus* (4–6), lines which
must be regarded, as in the case of other elements in other Gellius
poems, as an experiment in the epigrams. The force of *o* has been
commented on before, and *genitor* is in keeping with the high poetic
style.[242] *Tethys* appears in 64.29, and is used for the sea (with a Greek
inflection) again in 66.70; the sea nymphs appear again in 64.17, and
Oceanus in 61.85, 64.30, 66.68. The total effect of the lines is epic and
elevated: it is remarkable to find such a neoteric passage, properly at
home in the polymetrics, in the epigrams. A similar line occurs in c. 115,
where Oceanus again appears (. . . *prata arva ingentes silvas altasque
paludes | usque ad Hyperboreos et mare ad Oceanum*, 5–6): Catullus
suddenly ascends to stylistic heights to emphasize the immensity of
Mamurra's holdings, an epic immensity brought to its conclusion with
the Ennian echo of the final line *non homo sed vero mentula magna
minax.*[243]

The only other proper names of this sort in the epigrams are more
in the nature of proverbs than of poeticisms.[244] *Harpocrates* (74.4,
102.4) is a clear example: in the poets he is never named again, though
Ovid does refer to him.[245] *Croesus* enters 115.3, where Kroll correctly
observes, "Croesus' Reichtum war sprichwörtlich (Otto, Sprichw.
98)," and compares the line with the *divitias Midae* (24.4).[246] One final
curiosity occurs in the epigrams: *Mentula conatur Pipleium scandere*

---

[242] See *ThLL*, s.v.: "*genitor* primitus est vocabulum poetarum vel sublimioris dictionis . . . invenitur inde ab ENN. et ACC. (non ap. comicos), in prosa oratione his locis . . ." (these places are very few).

[243] Enn. *Ann.* 621 V.[2]: *machina multa minax minitatur maxima muris*; Catullus' triple alliteration of *m* makes the reference perfectly clear. The epic tone demands *altasque* for the *saltusque* of the MSS in 5 (and removes the hypermetric *-que* from *paludes*).

[244] On the significance of *Satrachi* and *Paduam* in c. 95, see W. Clausen, "Callimachus and Latin Poetry," *Greek, Roman, and Byzantine Studies* 5 (1964) 188–91.

[245] *Met.* 9.692, *quique premit vocem digitoque silentia suadet*. Also in *Anth. Lat.* 346.6 (Baehrens); see Otto, *Sprichwörter* 160.

[246] Croesus is rarely mentioned by the poets (once in Hor. *Epist.* 1.11.2, twice in later Ovid, also in Juv., Stat., Mart.: see *ThLL*, s.v.), though Propertius showed a certain affection for him (3 mentions, one of which is in a particularly neoteric line, *Lydus Dulichio non distat Croesus ab Iro*, 3.5.17): it would seem that his name was too proverbial to have been used often by the poets, even for the common theme of wealth.

montem (105.1). Again the subject is Mamurra, and again (as in 115.8) there is an Ennian echo (*Ann.* 215V.[2], *cum neque Musarum scopulos. . .*), perhaps justifying the obscure allusion to the *Pipleius mons*. The name, however, never became an accepted reference in the Roman poets; accordingly it can perhaps be concluded that here it is not to be considered a genuine neoteric poeticism.[247]

URBANITAS AND THE VOCABULARY OF THE POLYMETRICS

It is a well known and much commented upon fact that Catullus introduced the word *basium* in Latin literature, a fact sometimes misinterpreted to mean that *basium* had previously been foreign to the Latin language.[248] *Basium* was not used again in Latin until Martial, Juvenal, and Petronius—a certain indication of its colloquial, if not somewhat obscene, nature. *Suavium*, the principal word for kiss in comedy, also occurs in Catullus, but then disappears from poetry (only in Prop. 2.29.39, Hor. *Epod.* 3.21, never in Petronius, Martial, or Juvenal).[249] These two words are often cited to illustrate the colloquial nature of Catullus' shorter poems; but their distribution in the polymetrics and epigrams is overlooked, and the difference between them, as far as can be observed, is ignored.

[247] However, cf. Callimachus, *Hymn* 4.7–8: ὡς Μοῦσαι τὸν ἀοιδὸν ὃ μὴ Πίμπλειαν ἀείσῃ / ἔχθουσιν, τὼς Φοῖβος ὅτις Δήλοιο λάθηται; and Ap. Rhod. (1.25) states that Calliope bore Orpheus σκοπιῆς Πιμπληίδος ἄγχι. It is strange that the Roman poets did not make more use of a place name used by the Alexandrians in such contexts. See Kiessling-Heinze at Hor. *Odes* 1.26.9 (*Piplei dulcis*): the name occurs elsewhere in poetry only in Mart. 11.3.1, 12.11.3, Stat. *Silv.* 1.4.26, 2.2.37.

[248] See G. Highet, *Poets in a Landscape* (New York 1957) 3, ". . . a word which this poet picked up and made into Latin to amuse his sweetheart." The accepted view is given by Ernout-Meillet, *Dictionnaire Etymologique*[4] (Paris 1959) s.v., "L'apparition tardive du mot laisse supposer un emprunt, celtique? Catulle, qui semble l'avoir introduit dans la langue écrite, était originaire de Vérone"; Ernout (*Él. dial. lat.* (Paris 1928) 119–20) had previously thought it a word from "un dialecte de l'Italie du nord, ombrien ou voisin de l'ombrien." J. Whatmough (*Poetic, Scientific, and other Forms of Discourse* (Berkeley 1956) 50–51) assures us that "this word was thoroughly acclimatized in Latin, as the derivatives and intervocalic -*s*- show," but the reasoning behind this is to me unclear. But that the word, so little used in literary Latin, became the common Romance word is enough in itself to show that Catullus did not introduce it into the language.

[249] See Axelson, 35; *osculum* is the accepted literary and poetic equivalent.

Basium and its derivatives occur 9 times in the polymetrics, but once only in the epigrams.[250] This single occurrence is in a Juventius poem (99), which also contains the two uses of the diminutive *suaviolum* (99.2, 14), an indication of the general delicacy and preciosity with which Catullus wrote his poems to *mellitus Iuventius*.[251] As a literary innovation *basium* was restricted to the polymetrics. In addition to the diminutive *suaviolum*, *suavium*, the colloquial commonplace, is restricted to the epigrams (79.4, *si tria notorum suavia reppererit*; 78ᵇ.2, *suavia comminxit spurca saliva tua*, both contexts of commonplace bitterness), though the verb *suavior* is found twice in the polymetrics (9.9, 45.12). *Osculum* is used once, significantly at 68.127 (*oscula mordenti semper decerpere rostro*), where either of the other two would have been inappropriate; but the playful construction *osculatio* is found among the polymetrics in another Juventius poem (48.6, *nostrae seges osculationis*, which may be compared with the invention *basiatio*, 7.1, *quaeris quot mihi basiationes*). It is not sufficient to term *basium* and *suavium* colloquial and to consider their occurrence in the shorter poems another indication of the low diction of these poems: Catullus obviously made a definite distinction between the two, reserving his own contribution to the literary language entirely for the polymetrics (and to one pointed use in the epigrams). Where Catullus had found the word is a question that cannot be answered with absolute certainty, but to picture him scouting it out in the northern Alps and then using it in poems which reflect his personal addiction to *urbanitas* is to misunderstand the poet completely. In Catullus' poems, the proper domain for the vocabulary of Rome's smart set has not been sufficiently recognized.

Certain words obviously belong in a discussion of the vocabulary of urbane Rome: *delicatus*, *dicax*, *elegans*, *facetiae*, *ineptiae*, *lepos*, *sal*,

---

250 *basium*, 5.7, 13, 7.9, 16.12, 99.16; *basiare*, 7.9, 8.18, 48.2, 3; *basiatio*, 7.1.

251 Cf. the other diminutives in the poem. It may be noted again here that this poem is unique among the epigrams in that 6 of its 8 pentameter lines have an adjective before the caesura modifying the noun at the end of the line—preciosity of technique as well as of vocabulary and tone. *Mellitus* is a word which can be associated primarily with the language of the polymetrics: it occurs of the sparrow at 3.6, of Juventius' eyes at 48.1, and again here—a further indication of the tone of the poem. Hezel (p. 51) even suspects that the poem is a translation of a Greek original.

urbanus, and *venustus,* with their other forms and opposites, all have their well-documented place,[252] and other words used by Catullus may be inferred from their associations and contexts to be similar. It should be noted that such words (unlike, for instance, the use of diminutives) did not form part of a neoteric *Programm;* but their avoidance by later poets only emphasizes the singular use Catullus made of them, a use which again cannot be set down to a poetically unsophisticated tendency to colloquial cliché.

In comedy these words had sometimes been used to give vent to an accusation of rusticity or overrefined urbanity, and occasionally are used together in comic profusion, but they are not common enough to be considered a part of the *sermo plebeius:* they clearly belong to a restricted group.[253] An indication of the place these words had in Catullus' society can be gathered from one section of Cicero's *Pro Caelio,* when finally, to emphasize the uselessness of Clodia's set, he uses their own language with pointed condescension.[254] It is not necessary here to discuss the range of meaning and application of these words in Catullus:[255] as has been often recognized, in every case they

---

[252] For a recent discussion of *urbanitas* (with bibliography), which also touches on Catullus, see R. G. Austin, *Cicero: Pro Caelio*³ (Oxford 1960) 53–54; and on *facetus,* W. J. N. Rudd, "Libertas and Facetus," *Mnemos.* 10 (1957) 328–32.

[253] Cf. Plaut. *Mostell.* 15, *tu urbanus vero scurra, deliciae popli, rus mihi obiectas?* For the words used together, cf. *Poen.* 234 (*callida et docta et faceta*), *Mil.* 907 (*lepide et sapienter commode et facete*) and 1161 (*lepide et facete, laute*). Terence never uses *deliciae, delicatus, dicax, inelegans, facetiae* or *infacetiae,* or *lepos* (but *lepidus* often), and the other words only a few times each; Plautus is somewhat freer (e.g., *lepos* 6 times, *lepidus* very frequent), but hardly enough for them to be considered common.

[254] 28.67: *Quam volent in conviviis faceti, dicaces, non numquam etiam ad vinum diserti sint . . . Quam ob rem excutiemus omnis istorum delicias, omnis ineptias . . . Vigeant apud istam mulierem venustate. . . . Cf. Austin ad loc.,* "Cicero uses the adjectives deliberately: they can be smart and fashionable men-about-town . . . at dinner parties, but in the witness-box they will look like silly country bumpkins."

[255] See Austin, 53: "The poetaster Suffenus (22), *bellus ille et urbanus,* becomes *infaceto infacetior rure* the moment he starts to scribble—he is no longer then *venustus* or *dicax,* the significant terms that imply *urbanitas.* The napkin-stealer (12) plays a trick that is *res invenusta;* the minx who wittily catches Catullus out (10) in *non sane illepidum neque invenustum;* the death of Lesbia's sparrow affects all men who are *venustiores;* above all, Quintia, whom so many think *formosa* (86), has no real claims to beauty, 'nam nulla venustas, nulla in tam magno est corpore mica salis'—there is the indefinable ingredient of *urbanitas*— what lacks wit and sparkle is clumsy and rustic." Fordyce, at 43.8, says that these words "are the clichés which, though their nuances must elude us, reflect the attitudes and values

are used of Catullus' friends and society in a way that makes their association with this society certain. Often, however, they are applied to Catullus' poetry or to the poetry of his circle; a collection of these instances indicates further that it is the *nugae*, or polymetric poems, which are meant.

> Hesterno, Licini, die otiosi
> multum lusimus in meis tabellis,
> ut convenerat esse delicatos:
> scribens versiculos uterque nostrum
> ludebat numero modo hoc modo illoc,
> reddens mutua per iocum atque vinum.
> atque illinc abii tuo lepore
> incensus, Licini, facetiisque . . . (50.1–8)

It is clear that the after-dinner poetry of Catullus and Calvus was what can be called the *ludus poeticus* (*lusimus in meis tabellis*), in which a variety of meters was used (*ludebat numero modo hoc modo illoc*) in writing the little verses (*versiculos*), all of which implies poetry exactly like Catullus' polymetrics, the *nugae*.[256] The tone of such poetry is established by *delicatos*, which can cover a wide range of meanings from willful to naughty,[257] and especially by the *lepos* and *facetiae* which so aroused Catullus:[258] the nature of this poetry is evident not only from Catullus' description of it, but from the words he uses to describe it and its effect. The same can be seen from the defense of his verse in c. 16: while the poet himself is *pius* and *castus*, his *versiculi*

---

of Catullus' society, a society which puts a premium on attractiveness (*venustas*), discrimination (*elegantia*), piquancy (*sal*), metropolitanism (*urbanitas*), and has only scorn for the dull, the insensitive, the clumsy and the provincial."

256 See H. Wagenwoort's fine synthesis and discussion of the *ludus poeticus* (*Studies in Roman Literature, Culture and Religion* [Leiden 1956] 30–42) in which he establishes that "the *ludus poeticus* requires *otium*" and "is especially a youthful game"; a contrast can be made between *ludus* (*carmen argutum et breve*) and *seria* (*continuum et longum*), cf. Pliny *Ep.* 7.9.9, but the term is always relative. On the correlation between *nugae* and *ludus* he says, "*Nugae* is practically synonymous with *ludus*" (cf. Hor. *Sat.* 1.9.2, *Epist.* 1.19.42, 2.2.141): "The scholiasts, at any rate, make no difference between *ludus* and *nugae* (cf. Schol. Veron. on Virg. *Ecl.* 6.1)."

257 See Fordyce *ad loc.* Cicero suggests that the word was particularly appropriate in Clodia's circle (*Pro Caelio* 19.44, *amores autem et deliciae quae vocantur* . . .).

258 The commentators compare, with good reason, Sall. *Cat.* 25.5, *prorsus multae acetiae multusque lepos inerat* ("von der gesellschaftlich gewandten Sempronia," Kroll).

(again implying the polymetric *nugae*—the word occurs only here and in c. 50) are *molliculi ac parum pudici*, and for a reason: *qui tum denique habent salem ac leporem* (16.7), again words whose backgrounds are obvious. Similarly, his verse is *lepidus* (6.17, *ad caelum lepido vocare versu*), as is his *libellus* (1.1); and his poems are playfully called *ineptiae* (14ᵇ.1); again he uses fashionable terms. The same terms are used to disparage poetry which does not conform to neoteric standards of wit and elegance: the *annales Volusi* are *pleni ruris et inficetiarum* (36.19), just as Suffenus, when he begins to write, becomes *infaceto infacetior rure* (22.14), a man otherwise *venustus et dicax et urbanus* (22.2), *bellus et urbanus* (22.9); in c. 36 Lesbia had made a vow which was not *illepidum neque invenustum* (36.17) and had made it *iocose lepide* (36.10), words to which she must have been much addicted and which Catullus applies both to individuals whose conduct is acceptable and to acceptable poetry. Finally, when Catullus mentions Caecilius' *Magna Mater*, he does so with a word summarizing all the wit, charm, and seductive elegance of neoteric verse, *venuste* (35.17). These words, then, not only appear in profusion in his poems, but almost every description of his poetry employs them as the sole means of conveying its purpose and nature. Such details need no further emphasis, but it is important to note what became of such words in poetry after Catullus, and to what extent he himself actually employed them in the whole corpus of his work.

Some of these words could not be used in dactylic verse: *delicatus*, *elegans* and *inelegans*, *facetiae* (though not *facetus*), *infacetus* and *infacetiae*, *ineptiae* (though not *ineptus*), and *invenustus* (though not *venustus, -tas*) were all excluded from the vocabulary of epic or elegy. Virgil, however, uses none of their available forms in any of his poetry. Axelson comments on *lepidus* and *venustus*: "Ein paar Lieblingswörter des Catull sind bekanntlich *lepidus* und *venustus*, wie er auch die zugehörigen Adv. und Subst. gebraucht. Von diesen Ausdrücken, die freilich vor allem in der Umgangssprache der republikanischen Zeit florierten, aber auch z.B aus der Prosa Ciceros bekannt sind, nimmt die übrige Dichtung so gut wie gänzlich Abstand."²⁵⁹ Lucretius has *lepidus* once

---

²⁵⁹ P. 61: "in der Umgangssprache der republikanischen Zeit" is perhaps too broad a formulation, as has been argued above.

and *lepos* 11 times, but with the exception of Horace's *Ars Poetica* 273 (where the context shows its purpose, *si modo ego et vos / scimus inurbanum lepido seponere dicto* . . .) it does not appear again until Martial; *venustus* likewise is not found again until Martial. *Dicax* never appears in the elegists or Horace; *facetus* only in Horace's *Satires* 3 times and once in the *Epistles*; and *urbanus* (apart from its literal meaning, someone who lives in the city) only 3 times in the *Satires* and twice in the *Epistles*. *Sal* in the sense of wit appears only in Propertius (3.21.28, of Menander) and in the *Satires* and *Epistles*, but *salsus* and *insulsus* never (except for Hor. *Sat.* 1.9.65). *Ineptus* in Horace also occurs only in the *Satires* and *Epistles* (4 times), but is used 2 times by Propertius, once by Tibullus (*ineptus amor*, 1.4.24; also 3.16.2), and 6 times by Ovid. Without exception all these words were considered fitting only for the diction of satire, too colloquial for more than occasional use in elegy, and were never admitted to lyric or epic. Horace uses none of the cretic words in his *Odes* or *Epodes*, where they would have been metrically admissible: it is safe to assume that they too would have been beneath the dignity of epic or elegy.

The distribution of these words in Catullus shows that their proper domain is the polymetrics, where the 20 forms (9 basic words) are used a total of 50 times; none occur in the longer poems, and only 3 forms are used 6 times in the epigrams.[260] The reason for this distribution can only be that the diction of the longer poems did not allow such words, that they were not part of the neoteric *Programm* in serious poetry (just as they had no place in later epic or elegy); and that previous Roman epigram had made no use of them, an understandable circumstance. In the longer poems Catullus is as careful in avoiding these words as any of the poets after him. It is a mistake, however, to consider these words in the polymetrics merely as unpoetical colloquialisms, because there is every indication that Catullus used them purposefully, and the fact that they are virtually excluded (except for special effect) from the epigrams supports this. Like *basium*, they are employed with wit and daring as a special feature of the polymetric *nugae* and are in themselves the essence of the new occasional verse

---

[260] *lepidus*, 78.1, 2; *venustas* and *sal* in 86.3, 4; *venustus* again in 89.2, 97.9.

which Catullus and the neoterics invented: it is for this reason that they so often are used to express the very nature of this new poetry.

Another word which can be associated with this vocabulary is *bellus*, whose place and associations in Catullus' poetry have not been properly understood.[261] In comedy it is found only once in Terence (*Ad.* 590, cf. Donatus), and in Plautus, though more common, always with a touch of urbane delicacy (as *bellus, lepidus, Capt.* 956; *bella aut faceta, Truc.* 930; *bellam et tenellam, Cas.* 108). Axelson notes that Lucretius has the adjective and adverb once each, that it is missing from all later epic and appears only very occasionally in later elegy:[262] its use in poetry thus parallels the other words belonging to the vocabulary of *urbanitas*. It is clearly associated with this language in c. 12 (where it is used of Asinius the napkin thief, *manu sinistra / non belle uteris*, 1–2, who is contrasted with his brother, *est enim leporum / differtus puer ac facetiarum*), in c. 22 (*bellus ille et urbanus*, 9, of Suffenus), and in c. 43 (of the shortcomings of Ameana, *nec bello pede*, 2, and *ten provincia narrat esse bellam?*, 6, which calls forth the exclamation of disgust, *o saeclum insapiens et infacetum!* 8). Such contexts leave no doubt about the associations of the word for Catullus. It occurs 9 times in the polymetrics and never in the longer poems (again exactly as is the case with the other words discussed above); in the epigrams it is used 6 times in 4 different poems, a fact which has led to a misunderstanding, because each of the four poems is one in which Catullus obviously experimented (for different reasons) with vocabulary belonging properly to the polymetrics and having no precedent in epigram. At 69.8 (*nec quicum bella puella cubet*) *bella puella* is the "feste Formel", but the poem itself is experimental: three of the first four lines (and also line 9) have the adjective before the caesura modifying a noun at the end of the

---

[261] Riese's oversimplification is typical: "*bellus* steht in der Umgangssprache, während *pulcher* dem höheren Stil angehört (p. XXVI). Cf. Fordyce at 3.14: "in the shorter poems Catullus uses *pulcher* only twice, and both times for a particular reason—once in speaking of Lesbia (86.5) and once probably to make a pun on her brother's name (79.1). Otherwise his word is the popular *bellus*, an old word (a diminutive made from *bonus* before it assumed its classical form) which in the Romance languages has outlived its literary rival." The term "shorter poems" again obscures the interpretation of the distribution of the word.

[262] Twice in Tib. (1.9.71, 3.19.5), once in Ovid (*Am.* 1.9.6, *bella puella*, "feste Formel"), never in Prop.: Axelson, 35.

line, a feature of neoteric collocation rarely found in the epigrams (as is discussed below); a diminutive adjective occurs in a form with the emphatic (and colloquial, to use the term with caution here) prefix per- (*aut perluciduli deliciis lapidis*, 3); *deliciae* too is a word with connotations of urbanity.[263] A variation of this "feste Formel" is found in c. 106 (*cum puero bello praeconem qui videt esse*, 1), where pederasty is the issue, and it is not surprising to find *bellus homo* in a Juventius poem (81.2), where it is a pointed repetition of Juventius' words at 24.7–8 ("*qui? non est homo bellus?" inquies. est: | sed bello huic neque servus est neque arca*). C. 78, in which *lepidus* occurs twice in the first two lines, has *bellus* three times in the next two (*Gallus homo est bellus: nam dulces iungit amores, | cum puero ut bello bella puella cubet*), a repetition of formulae already observed. It is important to observe, then, that in the epigrams *bellus* occurs only in certain well-defined formulae, and that far from being used freely, it only occurs in contexts where effeminancy or sensuality are to be emphasized—that is, in contexts where the language of the polymetrics serves a definite purpose. *Bellus* is not a colloquialism used by a poet either careless or ignorant of poetic diction: it is a word, properly a part of the urbane and suggestive language of the polymetrics, carefully used for a calculated effect.[264]

There is another group of words which may be briefly considered here. Abstract nouns in *-tio* were, under certain conditions, a particularly productive class in the *sermo plebeius*: they are common in the rustic writers to designate agricultural pursuits; they are often used by Plautus and Terence, where they frequently appear to be coinages for comic effect; they are common also in Cicero as a means of translating Greek technical terms.[265] They are, however, generally avoided in

---

263 *deliciae* is not found in Ter., though common in Plaut., and is rare in later poetry (in Virg. only *Ecl.* 2.2, 9.22; in Hor. twice, *Epist.* 1.6.31, *Odes* 4.8.10; in Prop. 3 times, in Ovid 19 times—only once in *Met.*, 2 in *Fast.*—and never in Tib.); on *delectare* see Axelson, 106. Catullus has *deliciae* 5 times in the polymetrics, never in the longer poems, and elsewhere in the epigrams only 74.2, a Gellius poem.

264 Cicero's hexameter *flavit ab Epiro lenissimus Onchesmites* is often cited without the introductory phrase: *ita belle nobis . . . (Ad Att.* 7.2.1). *belle* is perhaps as pointed as anything in the joke.

265 For a detailed discussion, with references and a list, see Cooper, *Word Formation* 1–17, who again overstates the case for their importance in the *sermo plebeius*; cf. Schmalz-Hofmann, 790–91, who finds the majority more technical than vulgar.

literary prose and seldom found in poetry.[266] In Catullus 14 nouns in
-*tio* are used 17 times, all, with one exception (*iocatio*, 61.120), in the
polymetrics.[267] *Basiatio* and *osculatio* have been mentioned above:
others are similar in tone and purpose. *Vocatio* is never found elsewhere
in the sense Catullus gives it, an invitation to dinner; *aestimatio* too is
given a concrete meaning by Catullus.[268] More indicative of his purpose, however, is the way in which the words are used. All occur at
the end of their lines, where the emphasis is obvious (the only exception
being 6.11, a line containing two such nouns, *tremulique quassa lecti |
argutatio inambulatioque*). Coinages such as *fututio* and *irrumatio* are as
witty in their formations as their meanings are blatant. Again Catullus
is not to be accused of colloquial or unpoetic vocabulary: all these
nouns are used with precision and wit and are an essential part of the
inventive urbanity of the polymetric vocabulary.

[266] Schmalz-Hofmann, 791: "Während die Augusteer nur wenig Verbalia auf -*tio*
bieten (z.B. Vergil nur 6, darunter *ratio seditio superstitio*), überwuchern dieselben im
Spätlatein sowohl in der Dichtung (Prud. z.B. hat nicht weniger als 50) als in der Prosa..."
Most nouns in -*tio*, however, contain a cretic.

[267] *oratio* (44.11) and *natio* (9.7) are not included in this count. The complete list is:
aestimatio, 12.12; *allocutio*, 38.5, 7; *ambulatio*, 55.6; *approbatio*, 45.9, 18; *argutatio*, 6.11;
basiatio, 7.1; *cogitatio*, 35.5; *esuritio*, 21.1, 23.14; *fututio*, 32.8; *inambulatio*, 6.11; *irrumatio*,
21.8; *osculatio*, 48.6; *vocatio*, 47.7; *iocatio*, 61.120.

[268] See Ellis and Fordyce *ad loc.*

II· THE ROMAN POETIC TRADITIONS

THE ROMAN POETIC TRADITIONS

THE NEOTERIC ELEGIACS AND THE EPIGRAMS PROPER

Meter

There are several questions fundamental for an understanding of Catullus' work which are seldom raised, or if raised, are a source of embarrassment and disagreement among scholars. One such question concerns his metrics. No one doubts the refinement of meter evident in his polymetrics,[1] an ease and naturalness difficult to understand when one considers that Catullus was among the first to experiment with these meters in Latin. On the other hand, his pentameter couplets have been almost universally criticized for their metrical roughness and lack of elegance. Wheeler summed up this condemnation and suggested a reason for it: "The position of the Catullian distich in the development of that metre at Rome is the only feature of his elegiac work about which there is substantial agreement. It is recognized that he was less successful in this metre than in any other. He was consciously endeavoring to transplant the Greek distich, but the result did not commend itself, in all respects, to the ears of those who succeeded him in the next generation. The distich was a form which required time and the touch of many poets before the best results could be achieved. Catullus stood too near its beginnings . . ."[2] If Catullus' apparent failure with the distich is to be explained by the difficulty of transplanting a Greek meter into Latin, why, it may be asked, was he more successful in the polymetric forms, in which Latin poetry was far less experienced?

[1] Cf. Sedgwick, *Mnemos.* 3 (1950) 64: "Here the keynote is metrical polish and refinement." P. 65: "No poet gives a stronger impression of complete ease, and mastery of verse-technique, from the simplest hendecasyllables to the galliambics of 63 and the sustained artistry of 61—to many the very summit of Latin lyric."

[2] A. L. Wheeler, "Catullus as an Elegist," *AJP* 36 (1915) 160; for other recent comments of this nature, see Sedgwick (above, n. 1) 65 n. 2, and D. A. West, "The Metre of Catullus' Elegiacs," *CQ* 7 (1957) 102 and nn. 7 and 8.

And did Catullus really stand "too near its beginnings," or is the simple fact of the matter not rather that the distich, being an Ennian introduction, is equally as old as the hexameter? How then is it possible that Catullus appears so accomplished and so fluent in his hexameters, a meter long established at Rome, when his pentameter couplets are so rough? Norden raised this embarrassing question, but apparently found no difficulty worth discussing: "die Hexameter in Catulls c. 62 sind die melodiösesten in lateinischer Sprache, während seine Pentameter noch viele Härten zeigen, die erst die folgende Generation beseitigte (z.B. 91, 2 in misero hoc nostro hoc perdito amore fore mit den vielen schweren Synaloephen, 110, 4 quod nec das nec fers, saepe facis facinus mit den fünf Monosyllaba in den ersten, dem mehrsilbigen Wortschluss in der zweiten Hälfte)."[3] Attempts have been made to explain away or excuse the metrical rudeness of the pentameter couplets, but never has the fundamental question been fairly faced. If no less of a critic than Norden, sensitive to style and meter as he was, could see the hexameters of c. 62 as the most melodic in the Latin language, and yet balk at the quality of the distichs, surely we must try to find an explanation which does not excuse the distichs on the grounds of their (supposed) early place in the history of that meter in Latin or of the difficulty Catullus presumably felt in trying to transplant the Greek distich.

W. B. Sedgwick is perhaps the only scholar to have posed the question as one demanding an answer from the literary tradition rather than as one to be explained away; he finds that Catullus, in his lyrics, was an innovator, but that in his distichs he stands "not at the beginning but at the end of a period. . . . The lyric tradition exemplified in Catullus seems to have been started by Laevius, *ca.* 90 B.C., who, without great poetical merit, seems to have had considerable metrical facility; no doubt Catullus' work differed little in kind from that of his contemporaries. In the bulk of their work Catullus and his school must have been regarded as innovators (Cicero's νεώτεροι): but in the *shorter* elegy at least this was far from the case. Here Catullus followed a tradition, but a different one, which went back a century, with an

---

[3] Gercke-Norden, *Einleitung*, I 4, p. 28.

established technique based on the metrical practice of the second century, starting from Ennius' *saturae* (including his epitaphs in elegiacs)."[4] This suggestion represents a considerable advance in our understanding of the problem: it first takes account of the obvious fact that the distich was not a recent immigrant to Rome (a fact so often ignored by those who strangely want to excuse Catullus on these grounds and who even more strangely ignore his success with the novel lyric meters); secondly it discards an assumption often made but lacking visible means of support, that Catullus was trying to transplant the Greek couplet. We will be justified, then, in our attempt to carry this line of reasoning further, first examining certain of the rough features of the meter of the distichs, then contrasting the distichs with the hexameter poems, trying to understand such differences as are obvious and to explain them in the dim light of the tradition.

Before we can begin with the metrical details of the distichs, another question must be posed to clarify and test Sedgwick's hypothesis. If, as he says, Catullus represents an earlier tradition in his distichs (one in which he was a follower), but in his lyric poems he stands as an innovator (one of the νεώτεροι), then we are faced with a paradox: Catullus' neoteric poetry, by common agreement, includes four poems in distichs,[5] three of which at least (65, 66, 68) are neoteric productions *par excellence*. The only solution to this paradox is that there must be an obvious difference between the meter of these neoteric distichs and that of the epigrams themselves (cc. 69–116), because it would not seem possible that Catullus was an innovator in his neoteric distichs in all respects but meter. If it can be shown clearly that in important and indicative features Catullus' epigrams differ in meter from his neoteric distichs, then Sedgwick's hypothesis may stand as proved. Statistics for each group may be compared without conversion: the neoteric elegiacs have 325 lines, the epigrams proper 319 lines.

It seems strange that such differences as appear so obvious between

---

[4] Sedgwick (above, n. 1) 66.

[5] In the following pages, c. 67 will be considered as a proper member of this group of neoteric elegies, for the present without further discussion.

the epigrams themselves and the longer neoteric distichs have not been previously observed: but no studies of Catullus' metrics or of the development of the distich in Latin poetry take account of the possibility that these two groups of poems might belong to two different traditions and therefore show different characteristics. All such metrical studies present figures and statistics for the distichs as a whole, and often the hexameter poems (cc. 62 and 64) are also included. It has therefore been necessary to restudy the whole matter and to compile new sets of statistics.

The excessive number and harsh quality of the elisions in the distichs are most often pointed out to show Catullus' deficiency in this meter. D. A. West, who has most recently acted the apologist for the elegiacs, concludes that ". . . this feature is felt by Catullus to be particularly appropriate in passages where he is discussing some intense emotion of his own,"[6] and there is much to be said for this view. West cites the well-known line *quam modo qui me unum atque unicum amicum habuit* (73.6) as an example of an emotionally intense final pentameter; he mentions too the large number of elisions found in another highly charged personal poem, c. 76, and that "When, in poem 68, five strange elisions occur in one couplet [*Troia (nefas!) commune sepulcrum Asiae Europaeque, | Troia virum et virtutum omnium acerba cinis*, 89–90] after thirty lines which have offered only nine elisions, either this is the work of chance, which is unlikely, or else this couplet with its four Greek proper names and its five elisions is in rhythm as in sense a link between the declamatory poetry of mythology, that precedes, and the plain poetry of personal sorrow that follows." Examples of such emotional elision may easily be multiplied from the distichs, but, as one further case worthy of note, three lines from the hexameter epyllion c. 64 may be quoted, from Ariadne's emotional speech:

> certe ego te in medio versantem turbine leti
> eripui, et potius germanum amittere crevi,
> quam tibi fallaci supremo in tempore dessem. (149–51)

[6] P. 102.

In a poem which contains an average of only one elision every 3.1 lines, the five elisions, including the irregular *cert(ē) ĕgo*,[7] must be due to the sudden release of Ariadne's emotions in a situation which perhaps is closely paralleled in Catullus' own personal life.[8]

West rightly refers to a remark by Sedgwick to support his argument, a remark which may be amplified: "In his frequent elisions, which are not at all characteristic of his other poetry, he represents the actual pronunciation of the day; the avoidance of it is a deliberate poetical artifice. The most extreme cases can be paralleled from lines in Plautus and Terence, written for stage presentation, which would have been intolerable if they had not reflected actual pronunciation . . . It is really the Ovidian practice which is divorced from nature."[9] If, as seems most likely, elision does represent actual pronunciation, then Catullus may be seen to have followed a tradition in his distichs which was to some degree removed from what at any rate came to be the poetic practice (hence the more realistic personal emotion which can be conveyed by excessive elision). What this poetic practice was at the time when Catullus himself was writing can be seen only by comparing certain figures for elision in his own work and in the work of other poets, but in any such comparisons we cannot speak of Catullus' elegiacs to include all the poems 65–116 (as even West does): the epigrams proper must be compared with the neoteric elegiacs (65–68) and also with the neoteric hexameters of c. 64; each in turn must be separately studied in the different traditions of Roman poetry to which they may belong.

Figures for the total number of elisions per 100 lines are given for

---

[7] The elision -(ē) ĕ- is rare. According to Platnauer (*Latin Elegiac Verse*, 74), *quare ego* occurs in *Corp. Tib.* 3.4.49, *te ego* in Prop. 2.20.11, Ovid *Am.* 2.10.3; *certe ego*, however, in Ovid some dozen times.

[8] It is interesting to speculate on the possible significance of Ariadne's reference to her *germanum* here together with her wish not to desert her lover; while it is impossible, of course, to reconstruct the facts of Catullus' life at the time of his brother's death and his later (?) break with Lesbia, or to be sure when c. 64 was written, the many seemingly personal elements in the story of Ariadne can be developed into a convincing parallel. In any case, it seems clear that the elisions in these lines serve to emphasize sudden emotional release.

[9] Pp. 67–68.

representative poets by E. H. Sturtevant and R. G. Kent,[10] from which a selection will serve to sketch a background for Catullus' practice. Plautus and Terence represent what may have been close to the normal colloquial practice with 150 elisions per 100 lines; Lucilius likewise has 133. Ennius,[11] however, is remarkable for limiting his elisions to only 22: "From this it seems that elision was a phenomenon of the popular speech which did not find immediate acceptance to its fullest extent in the dignified style of the epic."[12] How remarkable Ennius' restriction was can be seen from Lucretius' (48 per 100 lines in Bk. I) and Virgil's practice (28 in *Ecl.* 1–6, but 46 in *G.* I, 48 in *Aen.* I, and 56 in *Aen.* XII). Horace's *Satires* show a far higher proportion of elisions (43 per 100 lines in I, 46 in II) than do his *Epistles* (19 in I, 20 in II) and must be regarded in this respect too as the more colloquial (Virgil's similar proportion in the *Georgics* and *Aeneid* cannot of course be attributed to the same reason). The Augustan elegists have from 14 elisions per 100 lines (Tib. I) to 24 (Prop. I–II, 9).[13]

In this setting Catullus must be seen. Sturtevant and Kent give 47 elisions per 100 lines, but this figure represents all the hexameter verses of the elegiac distichs and for our purposes is misleading. The epigrams proper (69–116) have 75.7 elisions per 100 lines, far higher than even Lucretius or Horace in his *Satires*. The neoteric elegiacs (65–68), however, contrast strikingly: 44.8 elisions per 100 lines. This still represents something of a compromise, because the hexameter epyllion c. 64, the neoteric masterwork, shows only 33.3.[14] The picture given by these totals finds further support in the analysis of the

----

[10] "Elision and Hiatus in Latin Prose and Verse," *TAPA* 46 (1915) 148. The figures include prodelision of *est* and *es*, which has also been included for purposes of comparison in my figures for Catullus.

[11] In reference to both Lucilius and Ennius, "The figures cover all fragments amounting to two complete dactylic hexameter verses . . ." Sturtevant and Kent, 148.

[12] Sturtevant and Kent, 149.

[13] I have not seen it observed that, in the hexameters of the *Apocolocyntosis* (a total of 49 lines), not a single elision occurs: these verses are a brilliant parody of mannered epic style, a *tour de force* not sufficiently appreciated as such.

[14] It should be noted that c. 62 (the hexameters which Norden called "die melodiösesten in lateinischer Sprache") has a very high proportion, 68.4 elisions per 100 lines, an indication of the natural and native quality of the song sung by the two choruses at the wedding banquet. The refrain has been ignored in this count.

individual neoteric elegiacs. Excluding now prodelision with *est* or *es*[15] and calculating on the basis of the number of lines per elision, we find that in the epigrams proper there is one elision every 1.5 lines; c. 76, noted often for its numerous elisions, has 27 in its 26 lines, slightly less than one line per elision. At the other end of the scale, the epyllion has only one elision every 3.1 lines.[16] Of the neoteric distichs, c. 66, the translation of Callimachus' *Coma*, exactly reproduces this proportion (3.1), and the poem which accompanied it, c. 65, has one elision every 4 lines. C. 67 has one elision every 2.5 lines, and c. 68 is similar (2.4). Within c. 68, however, a clear stylistic difference must be noted in the matter of elision (a difference which, taken with others, supports the assumption that originally at least c. 68 represents two separate poems): in lines 1–40 there are 22 elisions, or one every 1.8 lines; in lines 41–160, however, there are only 44 elisions, or one every 2.7 lines. 68.1–40 thus agrees with the epigrams proper (nothing surprising in view of its colloquial epistolary style), while the second part of the poem (or the second of the two original poems) agrees closely with the average for the neoteric distichs (65–68), 2.7 lines per elision.

This same relative frequency can be observed in certain types of elision. The epigrams proper show 78 elisions of final long vowels, a proportion of one every 4 lines (c. 76 has 9 final long vowels elided, or one every three lines); in cc. 65–68 there are only 30 instances (one every 11 lines) and in the epyllion only 25 (one every 16 lines). Similarly, the elision of a final long vowel before an initial short vowel is far more freely allowed in the epigrams (10 instances) than in the neoteric distichs (only one example: 66.25, *tē ˘go*, where, incidentally, *te* has been supplied in the text) or in the epyllion (3 instances).[17] Elision of a short vowel at the end of a dactylic word before an initial short

---

[15] Prodelision in the distichs remains fairly constant: there are 33 in 69–116 (319 lines) and 25 in 65–68 (325 lines); on the other hand, c. 64 (408 lines) has only 6 instances of prodelision, while c. 62 (57 lines without the refrain) has 9.

[16] C. 62 has one elision every 1.9 lines.

[17] The three instances in the epyllion are all in passages of an emotional nature: 70, where Catullus addresses Theseus directly by name, *illa vicem curans toto ex te pectore, Theseu, | tot(ō) ănimo, tota pendebat perdita mente*; 149, *cert(ē) ˘ego*, in a passage discussed above, one of five elisions in a space of three lines; 372, *quar(ē) ăgite*, a colloquial phrase used by the Parcae to continue again suddenly with the *optatos amores* immediately following the dire prediction of the end of Troy.

vowel is rare, though legitimate, in Augustan elegy:[18] there are only 5 cases in Catullus' neoteric elegiacs (and 7 in c. 64), but 13 in the epigrams.

From these figures certain general conclusions may be drawn before a more difficult point is considered. West apologizes for Catullus on two grounds: ". . . in many details his metre resembles that of the Augustan Elegists," and ". . . some of the points in which Catullus differs from the Augustans are signs not of incompetence or indifference but of a deliberate adjustment of metre to content."[19] While the first point is true for certain aspects of Catullus' meter, it would be rash and almost impossible to extend such an apology very far: the figures given above for different types of elisions are enough to show that, while in his neoteric productions Catullus approaches Augustan usage, it is only an approach—albeit a particularly relevant one when compared to the difference of the epigrams proper from Augustan usage. In every aspect there is still a gap between the neoteric elegiacs and the Augustan rigidity in the matter of elision. West's second point is also true; but, besides being a matter of subjective interpretation, it fails to take any account of the tradition Catullus may have been following. We may agree with Sedgwick (as West does) when he writes: "But how can we suppose that Catullus, a master of every other sort of verse, was in elegiacs a complete failure? The fault must surely lie in the critics: the verses must be excellent of their kind."[20] It only remains to ask what was their kind? The answer, suggested by Sedgwick himself, sees Catullus at the end of a tradition of Roman epigram, which may be called pre-neoteric epigram. The study of Catullus' elisions, however, indicates that this is true only for the epigrams proper: the neoteric elegiacs agree closely on all important points, both in total number of elisions and in specific types, with the hexameters of the neoteric epyllion. The outlines of so much are clear: there are, of course, notable exceptions, both in Catullus' use in the neoteric elegiacs of elements more fitting to the epigrams, and in neoteric restrictions appearing in the epigrams. It may be assumed that Catullus found it

[18] See Platnauer, *Latin Elegiac Verse*, 73.
[19] West, 98.   [20] Sedgwick, 65.

somewhat difficult to break away from the tradition of pre-neoteric epigram even in his neoteric distichs, but it is obvious from the study of elisions that he did so, just as it is obvious that he was occasionally able to introduce neoteric refinements into the epigrams. A full discussion of the tradition must be postponed until other stylistic features have been examined; it is sufficient here only to suggest the lines along which our study is tending.

One final aspect of elision in Catullus must be examined, that of elision at the halfway point in the pentameter. Of this only two examples are to be found in the Augustan elegists, both in Propertius;[21] in Catullus, however, there are 4 certain instances in c. 68 and 11 in the epigrams,[22] to which may be added 67.44 and two more in the epigrams (97.2, 99.8) where the readings are in dispute. Not only are these disputed readings important (removal of the elision only adds to the number of even more disputable cases of hiatus at the halfway point in the line), but the question of Catullus' precedents in this practice is debatable. The most thorough discussion of these elisions is by M. Zicàri,[23] who finds them "so characteristic of Catullus' technique" and says: "At least for the epigrams . . . it is hazardous to speak of imperfect technique and not rather of conscious adherence to a *particular* technique."[24] This technique Zicàri argues to be that of pre-Hellenistic elegy:[25] he had noted that "in point of fact, elision at the diaeresis of the pentameter is far from rare in Alexandrian epigram," but since Callimachus, "who himself also employs elision at the diaeresis of the pentameter in his epigrams (30.6 and 42.6 Pf.), does not do this elsewhere," and since "the regrettably scanty fragments of Alexandrian elegy confirm this difference in the handling of the

---

[21] Platnauer, 88, finds only Prop. 1.5.32 and 3.22.10, both discussed below.

[22] 68.10, 56, 82, 90; 71.6, 73.6, 75.4, 77.4, 88.6, 90.4, 91.10, 95.2, 99.12, 101.4, 104.4.

[23] "Some Metrical and Prosodical Features of Catullus's Poetry," *Phoenix* 18 (1964) 193–205 (esp. 194–97).

[24] P. 194. Zicàri would remove the elisions from 67.44, 97.2, and 99.8, and, though I do not agree (the resulting hiatus is more difficult than the elision), I cannot defend the elisions: but the following discussion may help the case for their propriety.

[25] Zicàri notes that in Theognis elision at the diaeresis occurs in twenty-five per cent of the first 500 pentameters (p. 195).

pentameter in the two genres," he concludes rightly that Alexandrian verse cannot be the source of Catullus' practice. The theory that pre-Hellenistic elegy was Catullus' precedent has the obvious disadvantage of all such explanations, that of seizing upon a distant tradition whose influence on the poet's work can hardly be called pervasive. Then, too, as Zicàri seems to realize, there are only a few cases of this elision where a Greek influence can be inferred in Catullus:[26] the rest of the pentameters with elision at the halfway point are far removed from Greek sense or style. A precedent which is more pertinent and far more extensive can be suggested after an examination of the cases.

Zicàri's argument that "Catullus keeps before his mind's eye the elegiac couplet as it was composed by the early Greek elegists" seems based primarily on the cases of elision of *-que* (68.56, 95.2, 99.12) and *atque* (68.82, 73.6), which he finds identical to junctures of the same sort found after the *penthemimeres* in the hexameter poets:[27] "Such hexameters, though common enough in Lucretius, Virgil, and the post-Augustan epic writers, are however excessively rare, or rather could be said to disappear completely, in the elegy." His choice of a precedent for Catullus seems based on a tenuous connection: "It is not surprising that this type can be matched in hexameters belonging to the epic tradition, inasmuch as the epigrammatists and the early Greek elegists, who are followed here by Catullus, in treating the pentameter (from this point of view) as the hemiepes, are themselves connected with this same tradition, which means that such verses are ultimately affiliated to the Homeric hexameter." That Catullus has five instances of elision of *-que* and *atque* at the halfway point of the pentameter is a fact; Zicàri's observation that this elision was common at the end of the first *hemiepes* in Latin epic hexameters is a good one. But it is far simpler and less far-fetched to dismiss Greek hexameter and elegy, and to see Catullus' elision at the halfway point in the pentameter (when compared to elision at the *hemiepes* of the Latin epic hexameter) as

---

[26] Zicàri's eagerness to press "Grecizing" in the matter of these elisions may be due to his similar explanation of hiatus in Catullus, where he may be on firmer ground.

[27] He cites as examples Ovid *Met.* 2.400, *saevit enim natumque obiectat et imputat illis*, and Virg. *Aen.* 6.394, *dis quamquam geniti atque invicti viribus essent*.

representing a stage of stylistic development before the pentameter had developed strict rules of its own. The situation with the Homeric hexameter and the early Greek elegists is a parallel phenomenon, but there is no need or reason to see Catullus as a follower of the early Greek elegists. It is important to recognize the clear fact that Augustan elegy shunned this elision, and to view this as a peculiar refinement paralleled by Callimachus' avoidance of it in his non-epigrammatic distichs: Catullus too avoided it in cc. 65 and 66, which must have been conscious and intended. Therefore it may be argued that Catullus allows elision at the halfway point of the pentameter when he follows a Roman tradition, one which had good precedent by analogy with hexameter practice and which could easily have been common in pre-neoteric epigram as well, whereas his avoidance of this elision elsewhere is an intentional refinement, due perhaps to Callimachean influence, and one observed almost without exception by the Augustan elegists. There is no need to force the early Greek elegists onto the stage at this point. If further examination supports this argument, and if such a hypothesis succeeds in explaining more of the cases of this elision than does the one which keeps the early Greek elegists before Catullus' mind's eye, then it may stand as the simpler explanation and find its place among other pieces of evidence which together explain and illustrate the various traditions in which Catullus wrote.

Since it is proposed to explain elision at the halfway point in the pentameter as entirely Roman, representing a pre-neoteric stage in the development of the distich, it is necessary first to discuss the four instances of this elision in c. 68: it is with these instances that Zicàri begins his analysis of this elision, and these lead him to the supposition that Catullus followed early Greek elegiac technique. He argues that Callimachus has this elision only in his epigrams; that no instance occurs in Alexandrian elegy; but, though c. 68 comes close to epigram in other respects, it is still basically an Alexandrian elegy; thus this device must be due to the pre-Hellenistic elegists. The basic points of this argument are sound and can be retained; the conclusion may easily be altered.

The four instances in c. 68 are:

> *muneraque et Musarum hinc petis et Veneris* (10)
> *cessarent tristique imbre madere genae* (56)
> *quam veniens una atque altera rursus hiems* (82)
> *Troia virum et virtutum omnia acerba cinis* (90)

Two of the lines make the elision with *-que* and *atque*, a category assumed by Zicàri without explanation (so also, in the epigrams, 73.6, 95.2, 99.12). W. Meyer has shown that *-que*, when occurring as the syllable following what must be regarded as a necessary caesura, could be regarded by late poets as an independent particle (not as an attached enclitic).[28] This license, which must have its ultimate explanation in the nature of the spoken language, is to be assumed here: the halfway point in these two pentameters occurs before the *-que* (*tristi | qu(e) imbre* and *una at | qu(e) altera*)—there is, in fact, no "elision" at this point. Propertius, in one of the only two instances of this elision in all Augustan elegy, makes the elision with *-que: Herculis Antaeique Hesperidumque choros* (3.22.10). The explanation of the license is the same.

68.10 occurs in the epistolary part of the poem (1–40), in which the higher frequency of other pre-neoteric elisions has been noted above. The elision of the final syllable of a first declension genitive plural (*Musarum*) occurs also at this point of the pentameter in 88.6 (*Nympharum*) and 90.4 (*Persarum*), both Gellius epigrams: all three are proper names.[29] The first three occurrences of this elision in c. 68 may hardly

[28] "Zur Geschichte des griech. und latein. Hexameters," *Sitzungsber. der bay. Ak. der Wiss.* (1884) 1045–46: see also Norden, pp. 176 and 428 n.1. Meyer cites the rule that in the developed Latin hexameter a third-foot feminine caesura must be accompanied by masculine caesurae in the second and fourth feet, and shows that where one or both of the accompanying caesurae are neglected (in 8,060 verses of Lucan, in Manilius IV, Stat. *Silv.* V, Columella, Val. Fl. IV–V, and Claudian), the third foot trochee is formed with *-que* as the short syllable in every case but one (Man. 4.470, *ad decumam nec quarta nec octava utilis umquam*, involving intractable numbers)—"also ist que als selbständiges Wort zu behandeln und in diesen . . . Versen männliche Caesur anzunehmen."

[29] The actual pronunciation of *-arum* (*-orum*) might have been closer to contraction than to elision (this, along with the whole question of elision "blurring" a caesura in Latin verse, still needs thorough study): it may well be incorrect to speak of elision at all in these three instances. The blurring of the main caesura by the elision of *-orum* at 64.252 can be compared: *cum thiaso Satyrorum et Nysigenis Silenis*, certainly a properly elegant neoteric line.

be called irregular or regarded as impossible if they were found in Augustan elegy; nothing points to early Greek elegy, but rather to the character of the Latin language and to a verse technique natively Latin.

The elision at the halfway point in the pentameter at 68.90 may be considered the only unusual example of this phenomenon in the neoteric elegiacs 65–68: yet its poetic purpose is obvious. The line was cited above in connection with its three elisions (with two others in the preceding hexameter) as an example of the emotional quality conveyed by prosaic elisions; the unusual elision of a dactylic word before a short vowel (*omni(a) acerba*) is called by Platnauer "though quite legitimate, rare."[30] It is significant that both these irregular elisions occur again in a line notorious for its elisions, *quam modo qui me unum atque unic(um) amicum habuit* (73.6),[31] a line, furthermore, often taken to show the emotional quality of Catullus' excessive elisions and therefore natural and natively Roman.

In the epigrams proper the great majority of lines with this elision are found in poems clearly a part of Roman epigrammatic tradition. C. 104, for instance, ends with the line *sed tu cum Tappone omnia monstra facis*, which would be a fine example for those wishing to illustrate the rudeness (both literal and stylistic) of Catullus' distichs: in addition to the elision, the first half begins with three monosyllabic words and is entirely spondaic; the previous line had ended *perdit(e) amarem* (one of the ten instances of a final long vowel elided before an initial short syllable in the epigrams—only one such elision occurs in the neoteric elegiacs).[32] The elision occurs again in the final line of the

30 *Latin Elegiac Verse*, 73. As noted above, there are only 5 examples of this elision in the neoteric elegiacs (none in 65, one in 66, 3 in 68), 7 in c. 64 (the same proportion as the neoteric elegiacs), but 13 in the epigrams proper.

31 Platnauer, 73: "Cretics in -*m* are not elided before an initial short vowel except for 'huic ego, vae, demens narrabam flumin (um) amores' (Ov. *Am*. III 6.101)—a unique instance."

32 *Perdite* itself is not found in Virg., Tib., Prop., Ovid, no doubt because of the necessity of eliding it before a short vowel. But it is notable that such a common and useful word as *perditus* in the erotic vocabulary of Plautus and Terence is found only once in Prop. (1.13.17), Tib. (2.6.51), and Ovid (*Am*. 3.6.80); in Virgil only *Ecl*. 2.59, 8.88, and once, significantly, used by Dido of herself in direct address (*Aen*. 4.541); Catullus uses it twice of Ariadne in c. 64 (70, 177). The word *perditus* may have been too colloquial for the poets.

invective epigram 71, *illam affligit odore, ipse perit podagra*, where the perfectly balanced word order demanded it. Again, the elision occurs in 101.4 (*et mutam nequiquam alloquerer cinerem*), the one line for which Zicàri finds no explanation. No further discussion, however, is necessary when one realizes that this poem is a literary development of Roman funeral epigram, and thus, to have been successful, should have contained stylistic elements in no way foreign to such epigram. One need only recall that it is written *prisco . . . more parentum* (7).[33]

It is not necessary to cite additional lines which contain elision at the halfway point of the pentameter: it should be clear that if a source or precedent is to be found for this elision in Catullus' distichs, it is likely that we need look no further than to the Roman epigram existing and fully developed by the time Catullus wrote. Of the nature of this epigram, as far as it can be known, more will be said later; it must be sufficient for the present simply to suggest the different character of the two groups of Catullus' distichs. Catullus' use of elision points to two separate traditions; and certain types of elision, such as the elisions at the halfway point of the pentameter, suggest an explanation of the double tradition, but one which must be illustrated and tested further.

Thus far the emphasis has been on the epigrams proper and on types of elision which can most easily be assumed to have been a part of the pre-neoteric tradition of epigram. We may now consider two metrical features which Catullus undoubtedly acquired from Callimachus and

---

[33] The only other elision at the halfway point in the pentameter in Augustan elegy (Prop. 1.5.32) may be explained in the tradition of pre-neoteric epigram: *quare, quid possit mea Cynthia, desine, Galle, | quaerere: non impune illa rogata venit.* Quare is an unpoetic word in elegy (though possible but rare in epic and didactic verse) as is shown by its avoidance by Tibullus (though Lygd. 3.4.49, where it is elided with a following short syllable, *quar(ē) ĕgo*); in Ovid once each in *Am., Ars Am., Pont.,* though 5 in *Met.,* 10 *Fast.,* 4 *Tr.* (in the *Her.* once in III, once in XVI, twice in XX!); in Hor. only *Sat.* (6 times) and *Epist.* (once); Virgil has it only once in *G.,* 4 times in *Aen.* (never in *Ecl.*). It is a model unpoetic word. Prop. has it 7 times, 6 of which occur at the beginning of the hexameter, 4 of which are the final couplets of poems. It may be said to be a favorite Catullan word (it is, of course, equally common in Lucr. and satire), occurring in all groups of his poems, 26 times altogether. In addition, the hexameter of Propertius' couplet begins *spondee spondee dactyl dactyl,* the least frequent sequence (only 1.3% of his hexameters—in Tibullus only 2 examples, 0.5%: see Platnauer, 36–37). Augustan readers may have been reminded of Catullus' epigrams (or of older Latin epigram in general), and were certainly aware of the lack of Augustan polish and stylistic formality of this final couplet.

which therefore emphasize the neoteric tradition of cc. 65–68. The first of these is now well known and needs little comment here. Hermann's Bridge—the avoidance of caesura after the fourth trochee—has an important history in both Greek and Latin hexameter verse. Homer violated this bridge once in every 1000 lines, but Callimachus invariably respects it.[34] The Latin poets, however, with some notable exceptions, are indifferent to it, though a strong stop or sense break was avoided at this point in the line. As Norden points out, Cicero in the *Aratea* has the weak caesura in the fourth foot only twice, Catullus in the epyllion never, and Tibullus in his first book only once; Virgil, on the other hand, has it once every 28 lines in the *Eclogues*, every 32 lines in the *Georgics*, and every 31 lines in the *Aeneid*.[35] Tibullus' attitude toward this caesura is clearly implied in his only use of it in Book I, "*hanc tibi fallaci resolutus: amore Tibullus | dedicat et grata sis, dea, mente rogat*" (1.9.83–84), on which Norden comments (p. 428), "wo der weichliche Rhythmus des Verses ἀνειμένος, *resolutus* ist, wie es der Dichter selbst zu sein vorgibt." It is equally important, however, to note that the single instance of this caesura occurs in a dedicatory couplet, which, if it was to be stylistically convincing, must reproduce the style of actual dedicatory epigrams, a style which differed from the refined and artificial distichs of the literary elegists. It is no coincidence, then, that a parallel for this caesura is to be found in a similar dedicatory couplet of Propertius, "*has pono ante tuas tibi, diva,: Propertius aedis | exuvias, tota nocte receptus amans*" (2.14.27–28). It is beyond question that Catullus, in observing Hermann's Bridge completely in c. 64, was following Callimachus:[36] it must then follow that

---

34 P. Maas, *Greek Metre* (Oxford 1962) 60, 62.

35 Norden, *Aen. VI*, p. 427: "Dagegen hat Vergil, gemäss seiner schönen Vermittlung zwischen archaischer Freiheit und moderner Strenge, diese Nebencaesur zwar nicht mehr so oft wie Ennius und Lucrez, aber doch auch nicht so selten wie Catull und Tibull. . . ." For complete percentages of this caesura in the Augustan elegists, see Platnauer, *Latin Elegiac Verse*, 10.

36 How Catullus was made aware of Callimachus' regard of Hermann's Bridge is not clear, but there are two possibilities: either he made the observation himself (consciously or even unconsciously, by ear), or Parthenius pointed it out to him. Cicero's surprising regard of the bridge in his *Aratea* (only two violations) can have nothing to do with Parthenius, but may well have been an (unconscious) aural imitation of Aratus, who has only 5 violations (4 with a postpositive monosyllable, 1 with an elision—see Maas, *Greek Metre*, 62). Aural imitation of Callimachus is therefore entirely possible for Catullus, but

the neoteric elegiacs will show the same observance, whereas the epigrams proper will conform to the pre-neoteric tradition of epigram in disregarding the bridge (as in the dedicatory epigrams of Tibullus and Propertius just mentioned). This is indeed the case: Hermann's Bridge is neglected but once in the neotericeleg iacs (68.49), but four times in the epigrams proper (73.5, 76.1, 84.5, 101.1).[37] The neglect in c. 68 causes no trouble: we have observed other elements of meter in c. 68 which belong to the epigrams proper. The other four occurrences are indicative. 73.5 (*ut mihi, quem nemo gravius nec: acerbius urget*) precedes the notorious final line *quam modo qui me unum atque unicum amicum habuit* (with its excessive elisions including the two irregular ones discussed above). C. 76, with its 30 instances of elision, begins with a violation of Hermann's Bridge, as does c. 101, a literary version of Roman epitaph. The latter, because of this violation, even leads Norden to comment: "Dass Catull die Phrase *multa per aequora vectus* nicht geprägt hat, ergibt sich mit Wahrscheinlichkeit aus der für seine Praxis höchst seltenen trochaïscher Caesur im 4. Fuss."[38] However this may be, there can be no doubt that the strict observance of Hermann's Bridge in the epyllion and the neoteric elegiacs, and its neglect in the epigrams proper show the marked difference between these two groups of poems in the same meter, and furthermore that the contexts of the instances in the epigrams, together with the implications suggested by the dedicatory couplets of Tibullus and Propertius cited above, point clearly to the pre-neoteric tradition of the epigrams proper.

The spondaic line is another metrical feature exploited by the neoterics from the example of Callimachus and the Alexandrians, and one which also requires little comment here. Cicero's verdict (*Ad Att.* 7.2.1) connecting spondaic endings with the neoterics is often cited, and the frequency of such lines in the epyllion c. 64 is a sign of the neoteric masterwork. The Augustan elegists either avoid such endings

---

it would seem more likely that Parthenius instructed him on this point: as is clear from Virgil's practice, there was no inherent metrical reason to observe this bridge in Latin.

[37] See Zicàri, 194–95.

[38] Norden, p. 228, on *Aen.* 6.335, *ventosa per aequora vectus* (see also similar phrases at G. 1.206, *Aen.* 1.376, 6.692, 7.228).

entirely (Tibullus) or used them sparingly and only under certain conditions (either with Greek proper names or with Greek hiatus) to emphasize their Greek origin:[39] doubtless they felt such lines to have no place in distichs, but Catullus, under the spell of neoteric novelty, felt no such qualms. 12 Spondaic lines occur in his distichs, and for this too he had the precedent of Callimachus.[40] D. A. West has pointed out that all but 3 of the 12 spondaic lines in the distichs of Catullus occur in the neoteric elegiacs: 1 at 65.23, 4 in 66 (3, 41, 57, 61), 4 in 68 (65, 87, 89, 109).[41] It should be noted that Catullus offers no apology for the five in the translation of Callimachus (66) and in the poem accompanying it (65): none of these occur in contexts with Greek proper names. In c. 68, however, he seems to have felt it necessary to do what the Augustan elegists came to do: the first spondaic line occurs in a line with the names of Castor and Pollux, the others all consist of a proper name (*Argivorum, Europaeque, Cyllenaeum*). Of the three occurring in the epigrams proper, one (116.3) may be regarded as a marked neoteric intrusion (occurring in the line following a mention of Callimachus, *carmina uti possem mittere Battiadae*), and another may be taken in a similar way (*Caelius Aufillenum et Quintius Aufillenam*, 100.1, where the proper names either necessitated, or perhaps gave Catullus the excuse to play with, a neoteric device); the last (76.15), it seems to me, cannot be understood in this way at all, but must rather have been allowed solely for its sonorous and unrelenting effect (*una salus haec est, hoc est tibi pervincendum*). It is perfectly clear once again how great a difference in traditions exists between 65–68 and 69–116. It is true that Catullus could, on occasion, experiment with neoteric metrical devices in the epigrams proper, just as on occasion he introduced into them neoteric vocabulary in an experimental way, but it was seldom that such experiments were tried, and the epigrams remained firmly in the older Roman tradition.[42]

[39] For the occurrences in Prop. and Ovid, see Platnauer, *Latin Elegiac Verse*, 38–39.

[40] See Pfeiffer on fr. 303: 9 spondaic lines occur in the *Aetia*, and they are, of course, far more frequent in the *Hecale*.

[41] P. 101.

[42] It is worth adding one more metrical point, which occurred to me as an independent proof of the validity of the preceding discussion (*CP* 62 (1967) 219). In Augustan elegy a monosyllable before the halfway point in a pentameter line must be preceded by either

Word Order

One last technical feature must be discussed. Recent studies of poetic word order have left no doubt about the innovations in traditional patterns which were due to the neoterics: it is now possible, with absolute certainty, to identify certain arrangements of attribute and substantive within a line as neoteric; and these can be used as a final test of the hypothesis developed above. If the neoteric elegiacs belong to a different tradition from that of the epigrams proper, then neoteric word order will predominate in the first group, while the second will show only those patterns that had been employed to some extent before the neoterics.

Three studies may be singled out as the most important for the Latin poets, those of Norden,[43] Patzer,[44] and Conrad,[45] the last two being the most comprehensive. From all the types of attribute and substantive collocation examined in these studies, only a few—those most indicative of neoteric innovation—need be discussed here. Two clarifications must be made at the outset, necessitated by the fact that the rules of the game have not been clearly established. First, we will adopt here Patzer's system of classifying the different types of word order, but will use our own symbols: thus, for example, . . . A/ . . . S will

a long monosyllable or a pyrrhic word (see Platnauer, *Lat. El. Verse*, 23). Catullus observes this rule in 65–68, but in the epigrams proper violates it 5 times (76.26, 91.6, 92.2, 93.2, 109.2). There is no clearer indication of the different stylistic natures of these two groups of poems.

F. Cupaiuolo (*Studi sull'esametro di Catullo* (Napoli 1965) 51–52, a book which unfortunately was available to me too late to be of any use in this study) notes that Catullus was the first to have restricted the use of a monosyllable before the third-foot caesura in the hexameter; he is wrong in attributing this restriction to the example of Homer (it is inevitable in the development of accent/ictus in the Latin hexameter), and his explanations of the five occurrences of this hexameter in c. 64 are unnecessary—in each case the monosyllable is preceded by a long monosyllable or a pyrrhic word.

[43] Norden, *Aen. VI*, Abhang III, 391–98. Norden discusses only two of the types of word order dealt with here: a verse enclosed by attribute and substantive, and the disposition of two attributes and two substantives in one verse.

[44] H. Patzer, "Zum Sprachstil des neoterischen Hexameters," *Mus Helv* 12 (1955) 77–95.

[45] C. Conrad, "Traditional Patterns of Word Order in Latin Epic from Ennius to Vergil," *HSCP* 69 (1965) 195–258. This, being the most recent, contains useful bibliography. It is also by far the most systematic, thorough, and imaginative examination of the subject.

represent a line in which the attribute precedes the caesura (for simplicity's sake always taken to be the penthemimeral) and the substantive stands at the end, and . . . A/ . . . S . . . represents a line in which the attribute precedes the caesura (penthemimeral) and the substantive stands in the second main position after that (always, for the present purpose at least, immediately after the bucolic diaeresis).[46] The second difficulty arises from the obvious fact that certain lines may be counted under several headings. Thus, *flavus quam molli praecurrit flumine Mella* (67.33) may be counted either as an example of A . . . / . . . S, or of . . . A/ . . . S . . ., or of the concentric type *abBA*. As a result of this difficulty, Patzer, who is not concerned with the type *abAB* and who therefore counts such lines only as examples of the . . . A/ . . . S type, finds 94 such lines in Catullus 64, whereas Conrad, who counts the *abAB* type separately, states that there are only 76 examples of the . . . A/ . . . S type in the same poem. It is important here only that our figures be internally consistent: we will, however, count first the total number of lines in which significant word order appears (thus, a line which may illustrate three separate types will only count as one) and then discuss certain types, in which one line may appear and be counted three different times. Other minor difficulties pass without mention: the results will remain substantially the same nevertheless.[47]

Six types of word order have been selected as those most frequent in Catullus' neoteric epyllion. In Table I the frequency of these types in Catullus' epyllion is compared with Ennius, Cicero's *Aratea*, Lucretius, and Virgil. The difficulty of exact count may be seen in the varying figures given for Catullus by Norden, Patzer, and Conrad; unless otherwise noted, the figures for the other poets are taken directly from Conrad's work. The significance of the figures for each type will be

---

[46] Conrad's system is not only more complete than Patzer's, but also offers the clearer historical explanation for the different patterns of word order. It has not been adopted here, however, because Patzer's notation is simpler, and for the few types of word order considered here this simplicity does not imply distortion of the essential facts.

[47] For instance, should the line *uvidulam a fluctu cedentem ad templa deum me* (66.63) be taken primarily as type A . . . / . . . S or type . . . /A . . . S? Often, particularly with the help of Conrad's perspective, the poet's intention can be distinguished from accident or metrical necessity; sometimes, however, it cannot, but the few doubtful cases have been either counted or omitted so as not to affect the proportions.

TABLE I

Type	Catullus 64			Ennius	Cicero's Aratea	Lucr. III	Aen. VIII
	(Norden)	(Patzer)	(Conrad)				
...A/...S	—	94	76	9	47	30	92
.../A...S	—	70	71	27	55	82	110
...A/...S...	—	50	36	1	36	25	17
A.../...S	21	25	24	4	24	12	13

Norden gives:

abAB *and* abBA	58 (1 every 7 lines)	Ennius: 0 Lucr. I: 8 Lucr. VI: 9 } (1 every 140 lines) Virg. *Ecl.*: 39 (1 „ 21 „) „ *Geo.* I & IV: 66 (1 „ 16 „) „ *Aen.* I & VI: 38 (1 „ 43 „)	

TABLE II

	...A/...S	.../A...S	...A/...S...	A.../...S	abAB	abBA
cc. 65–68	32	15	13	7	11	8
cc. 69–116	10	10	4	1	1	0

discussed below, but it is immediately obvious that Catullus made far greater use of each type than had Ennius or Lucretius. Cicero's *Aratea* comes closest to Catullus' epyllion: whatever the orator may have thought of the νεώτεροι in his later life, he somehow anticipated, to a certain extent, the neoterics' discoveries of the expressive possibilities of word collocation.[48]

[48] Cicero's position in the history of Latin poetry needs a thorough re-examination. The *Phaenomena* cannot be later than 85 B.C. (written by Cicero *admodum adulescentulo*, *Nat. D* 2.104), and it is now thought by some that the *Prognostica* must have been written at the same time, not in 60 B.C. (see K. Büchner, *RE* (2) 7, 1237, supported by D. R. Shackleton Bailey, *Cicero's Letters to Atticus*, at 2.1.11; however, see also A. Traglia, *La lingua di Cicerone poeta* (Bari 1950) 10–14). How he came to anticipate certain stylistic developments of the neoterics is not clear; but how far he was from understanding the poetic possibilities of, for instance, expressive word order, Conrad (*passim*) demonstrates time and again.

A general impression of the marked difference between the neoteric distichs and the epigrams proper can be had by comparing the total number of lines with indicative patterns of word order in each group. Of the 161 hexameters of cc. 65–68, 69 show one (or more) of the six patterns (42.8%). On the other hand, the epigrams 69–116 (165 hexameters) contain only 25 lines with any of these types (15.1%). Three of the four neoteric epigrams show a common high percentage (in c. 65, 54%; in c. 66, 45%; in c. 68, 44%); whereas c. 67 is decidedly lower (only 29%), but still closer to the other three poems in its group than to the epigrams. The difference between the two groups of poems in distichs, however, is even greater than these percentages show, as an analysis of each type of word order will make clear.

In Table II I give the frequency of each type of word order in the neoteric distichs and in the epigrams; in these figures one line may have been counted several times. It will be clear immediately that the patterns *abAB* (interlocking) and *abBA* (concentric), which were particularly exploited, if not invented, by the neoterics (see Table I), are together used 19 times in the neoteric elegiacs, but only once (100.7, *cum vesana meas torreret flamma medullas*) in the epigrams.[49] The only genuine golden line in these poems occurs at 68.29 (*frigida deserto tepefactet membra cubili*). The type A . . . / . . . S is likewise a neoteric innovation (or exploitation),[50] of which the only example found in the hexameters of the epigrams proper is *iucundum, mea vita, mihi proponis amorem* (109.1). The type . . . A/ . . . S . . . is found only once in Ennius, though it is more common in Lucretius; there are three times as many in the neoteric elegiacs as in the epigrams. If

---

[49] The rarity of the types *abAB* and *abBA* in Hellenistic poetry led Norden to suppose the influence of rhetoric on the neoterics here (pp. 395–96). This supposition was not accepted by Patzer (pp. 87–89), who examines in further detail some Hellenistic distichs (esp. Euphorion, fr. 9.10–15 (Powell) and Hermesianax fr. 7.21–26 P.). See, however, Conrad, p. 239: "The two patterns of interlocked word order which have been discussed are constructed on patterns of distribution of substantive and attribute that we have already seen in our earlier discussion."

[50] Norden, p. 391: "Diese Wortsymmetrie gehörte zu den wohlerwogenen Kunstmitteln, durch welche die Neoteriker die Eleganz ihrer Verse erhöhten." Norden finds only 3 examples in the first 900 lines of Lucr. I; the figure 12, given by Conrad for Lucr. III, may be reduced to 10 for the present comparison, as he includes 2 examples of *noun . . . / . . . gen.*

these four types, all of which are neoteric, are taken together, 39 examples are to be found in cc. 65–68, but only 6 in cc. 69–116.

The remaining two patterns of word order are those which are most common in the epyllion, but nevertheless they cannot be called neoteric: they had been a feature of the oldest Latin hexameter. Thus, 27 examples of the type . . . /A . . . S are found by Conrad in Ennius, and 82 in Lucretius III:[51] "This feature of Homeric style which had become a distinguishing feature of epic style by the Alexandrian age, was carried over by Ennius into Roman epic, along with the hexameter itself. The pattern remained a standard feature of Latin epic style."[52] It may be argued that it remained rather a feature of the Latin hexameter: the attribute, coming immediately after what was most often the main "sense" caesura of the line, neatly framed the last half of the line with its substantive at the end, a feature whose usefulness was not confined to epic. It is therefore no surprise to find this pattern 10 times in the epigrams, and only a little more often (15 times) in the neoteric distichs. Almost exactly comparable are the figures for the type . . . A/ . . . S: this appears less frequently in Ennius (9 times) and Lucretius III (30 times) than the previous pattern, which the ratio in Catullus' distichs (10 times in 69–116, 32 times in 65–68) reflects.[53]

A brief note may be added here on one type of word order in the pentameter. In the neoteric elegiacs, the attribute stands as the last word in the first half of the line and the substantive at the end of the

---

[51] Conrad, 203–07, compares Ennius, fr. 1, *Musae quae pedibus magnum pulsatis Olympum*, with Homer, *Il.* 1.530, . . . μέγαν δ' ἐλέλιξεν Ὄλυμπον and 8.443, ἕζετο, τῷ δ' ὑπὸ ποσσὶ μέγας πελεμίζετ' Ὄλυμπος; in Homer, "this pattern of separation is by far the most frequent of all, . . . appears even more frequently in the *Argonautica* of Apollonius of Rhodes, . . . [and] had in fact become such a standard feature of epic hexameter style that Theocritus employed it with a notably greater frequency in those Idylls and parts of Idylls where dialect and other factors indicate that he was writing in the epic tradition" (p. 204).

[52] Conrad, 206.

[53] Shackleton Bailey (*Propertiana*, p. 57 n. 1) notes that 44% of the hexameters in Prop. I take the form . . . A/ . . . S, and 30% in IV; Tibullus I had 13% of its hexameters of this type, Ovid *Ars Am.* I 12%. Catullus' neoteric elegiacs thus stand mid-way between these two extremes with almost 20%, while his epigrams have a percentage of this type decidedly less than even Ovid with 6.25%. The figures for the individual neoteric elegiacs may be noted, however, for comparison with Propertius: 65, 45.5%; 66, 23.4%; 68, almost 20%; 67, only 5%.

line (. . . A/ . . . S, as above) 57 times (35%), but in the epigrams only 29 times (18%).[54] This observation, besides supporting the figures presented for the hexameters of the distichs, is important for what it shows about certain of the epigrams: in only five of these does this type of word order occur in more than one line, and these five poems are all ones in which neoteric vocabulary has been found. Two of these poems are Gellius epigrams (in c. 80, 3 of the 4 pentameter lines have this pattern, and in c. 88, 2 of the 4), one is the Iuventius epigram c. 99 (6 of the 8 pentameters), another is the epigram on Cinna's *Zmyrna* (c. 95, 2 of the 4 pentameters), and the last is the Rufus epigram c. 69 (2 of the 5).

It has been established, then, that in representative points of technique there is a marked difference between the two groups of distichs, and that in every case cc. 65–68 agree with Catullus' technique in his epyllion and with what can be said with certainty to have been neoteric practice; the epigrams proper, on the other hand, with the exception of certain poems which must be regarded as experimental, agree with an older tradition, one which sometimes seems similar to Ennius' practice (as in the case of the two types of word order . . . A/ . . . S and . . . /A . . . S), but which often is strikingly different (as in the case of elisions). It seems likely, therefore, that Sedgwick's hypothesis, when qualified, is correct, and that the epigrams proper represent a tradition of Roman, pre-neoteric epigram, in following which Catullus was its last representative among serious poets. We must now see what is known of such a tradition, and how much of it can be restored.

THE TRADITIONS

The history of the elegiac couplet in Latin begins, appropriately, with Ennius. It is likely that the earliest couplets we possess (*Varia* 15–24V.[2]) were also the first in Latin, just as Ennius introduced to Rome the

---

54 For the neoteric elegiacs the figures are: 65, 6 (50%); 66, 14 (29.8%); 67, 8 (33.3%); 68, 29 (36%). It should be noted that type . . . A/ . . . S occurs in only one of the 20 hexameters of the first part of c. 68 (lines 1–40) and in only one of the pentameters of this part.

dactylic hexameter. It was in Saturnians, for instance, that Naevius wrote his own epitaph (if he did); he was attacked by the Metelli also in the same meter; and meters other than the pentameter couplet must have been popular and prevalent.[55] It is understandable, then, that our fragments of the distich before Catullus are so scanty: the meter was not a popular one, nor, on the other hand, was it soon put to serious literary uses. Ennius' four examples are all epitaphs, but epitaphs never intended to mark a burial; they are literary productions which, because of their very nature and subject, were not to inspire other poets to extensive production. Proper epitaphs (like that of Pacuvius, recorded with admiration by Gellius, 1.24.4) continued to be composed in other meters or in prose, and, despite Ennius' name as a precedent, even literary epitaphs in distichs must have been a rarity. Any other use Ennius may have made of the distich is not known; it is possible, though questionable, that he wrote short erotic poems, but there is no evidence that he used the elegiac couplet for such pieces.[56] What became of the distich in the generation or so after Ennius is not known, but it seems likely that, being a literary innovation and having a precedent for its use perhaps only in epitaph, it lay dormant.

Ennius' epigrams themselves show little difference in style from his epic hexameters. Alliteration, native to Saturnian verse, is used, and archaism is frequent. The tone is elevated and formal, as in the last couplet of the epigram given to Scipio, *si fas endo plagas caelestum ascendere cuiquam est, | mi soli caeli maxima porta patet.* The terseness

[55] See, for instance, the Saturnians, iambic senarii, and trochaic septenarii collected by Buecheler, *Carmina Latina Epigraphica*; the survival of the latter for popular lampoons (cf. the *Versus Populares* 1–5, Morel, *FPL* 92) makes it likely that it was so used much earlier (see E. Fraenkel, "Die Vorgeschichte des Versus Quadratus," *Hermes* 62 (1927) 357–70).

[56] See Wheeler, *Catullus and the Traditions*, 66 ("There are hints that Ennius, Accius, the tragic poet, Quinctius Atta, the author of *togatae*, and perhaps Lucilius, the great satirist, attempted the small erotic poem") and p. 256 n. 9: Pliny (*Ep.* 5.3.6) includes Ennius and Accius among those who wrote *lusus* (. . . *quorum non seria modo, verum etiam lusus exprimere laudabile est,* 5.3.4), but it may be argued that Pliny does not have only short erotic poems in mind: he is justifying his addiction to all forms of lighter literature (*facio non numquam versiculos severos parum, facio; nam et comoedias audio et specto mimos et lyricos lego et Sotadicos intellego,* 5.3.2). On the general question of the extent to which Ennius used the couplet, one can say no more than Vahlen (*Ennianae Poesis Reliquiae*[2], ccxvii): "Haec unica fuisse epigrammata aut haec cum aliis continentem librum epigrammatum Ennii exstitisse quis hoc aut negabit aut affirmabit."

and expressiveness of Catullus' epigrams may be seen in Ennius' own epitaph (*nemo me lacrimis decoret nec funera fletu / faxit. cur? volito vivos per ora virum*), which in its form resembles Catullus 85 (*odi et amo. quare id faciam fortasse requiris? / nescio, sed fieri sentio et excrucior*): initial statement, rhetorical question, final answer. In Catullus the suggestion of alliteration of *f-* may be no accident: though there is no question of conscious imitation, it seems certain that Catullus in this most epigrammatic of all his epigrams found himself echoing an ancient form.

The obvious Roman character of Ennius' epigrams—so basically Roman in style in spite of the fact that the meter itself was new to Rome, and so like the style of the epic hexameter, which, too, remains Roman for all that Ennius did to transplant Homeric verse—might make a further observation unnecessary were it not that a misunderstanding of an essential point might arise shortly. This point is that Ennius, in these verses, owed nothing to Hellenistic epigram. Though, as Clausen points out, Ennius knew "the poetry of Callimachus, or at least some part of it,"[57] there is nothing in these epigrams that has the least releationship to Callimachean epigram, or, in fact, to any Hellenistic epigram. Though we have assumed that the novelty of the meter and the restricted use to which the pentameter couplet was put by Ennius caused it to lie dormant for a generation or so, the beginnings of epigram at Rome are entirely Roman, and this Roman character, it will be argued here, remained basic and unchanged even for Catullus, even after the arrival in Rome first of Hellenistic epigram and then of Callimachus.

Among the first poems we have in the pentameter couplet after Ennius are the five epigrams by Valerius Aedituus, Porcius Licinus, and Q. Lutatius Catulus, four of which are preserved by Aulus Gellius (19.9) and one by Cicero (the Roscius epigram of Catulus, *Nat. D.* 1.79). It is perfectly clear that the immediate source and inspiration for these poems is to be found in Hellenistic epigram: in fact, it may be assumed that here is the explanation for the revival of the couplet, that

---

57 W. Clausen, "Callimachus and Latin Poetry," *GRBS* 5 (1964) 187. In the preceding discussion Clausen suggests that Ennius' purpose in alluding at the beginning of his *Annals* to the opening of the *Aetia* was "polemical and anti-Callimachean: he designed to confute Callimachus, *alter Hesiodus*, in something like Callimachus' own oblique style" (p. 186).

this new interest in Hellenistic epigram gave the couplet a purpose and place in Latin poetry which it had not had when introduced by Ennius. Such an explanation, however, begins with the supposition that the hiatus between Ennius and these three poets was an historical fact and not a mere chance of survival; and it must be balanced and corrected by what can be gathered from the poems themselves and from the few other epigrams in distichs from the same period (all of these poems are, of course, the best witnesses for the unpredictable and unreliable chances of preservation). As a broad working assumption, subject to later qualification, we may say that in the epigrams of Aedituus, Licinus, and Catulus is to be found the reason for what appears to be a sudden revival and extension of the use of the pentameter couplet: Hellenistic epigram had been discovered by Roman *literati*.

The nature of this Hellenistic intrusion is subject to serious misconceptions. If, around the last half or quarter of the second century B.C., Hellenistic epigram was the primary reason for new interest in the previously dormant couplet, how (it may be asked) is it possible to argue that in the epigrams of Catullus there is so little, in vocabulary and in points of style, of Hellenistic innovation and so much of what can only be called a native Roman character? If these three writers of epigram (and there must, as will be shown, have been many others) were translating Hellenistic originals a generation or so before Catullus, is it not far simpler to see Catullus (as in fact he has so often been seen) also transplanting the Greek couplet into Latin? Yet the fact remains that all the evidence we have assembled thus far shows just the opposite, that Catullus had little or no interest in Hellenistic epigram when he was writing his own.[58] If this evidence is to be accepted and properly understood, it is necessary to examine again the nature of this sudden intrusion of Hellenistic epigram, to clarify if possible from the scant remains just what the generation of poets before Catullus made of their new interest, and just what their epigrams really were.

The dating of the five examples of Hellenistic-inspired epigrams is a question which cannot be settled with any exactness. It may be argued,

---

[58] This is not to say, of course, that he wasn't interested at all in Hellenistic epigram: the polymetric poems do show this interest.

however, that the dates usually given and accepted are altogether too late, that there is every likelihood that these poems, and therefore the beginnings of the genre at Rome, were quite a bit earlier than is usually supposed. All too often Catulus' *floruit* (his consulship in 102 B.C.) is carelessly taken as the approximate date of all five epigrams, implying that the genre, and its development, preceded Catullus by only a generation.[59] If Catulus' poem to Roscius "betrays a youthful admiration," then it "must have been composed some years before he became consul—not later, let us say, than 102 B.C. and probably nearer 130 B.C."[60] Such a subjective argument for the date of the poem is the best that can be had, but something better can perhaps be done for the other two poets. One piece of evidence is that both Gellius and Apuleius (*Apol.* 9) give the three poets in the same order—Aedituus, Licinus, Catulus—which may (or may not) imply a chronological anthology available in later times, or may at least suggest an order of precedence based on age. Though 130–120 B.C. may be taken as a *floruit* for Licinus (as Wheeler takes it, though there is little concrete evidence on which to base such a *floruit*), it is important to remember that if Licinus' lines (Morel, *FPL* 44–5) on Terence (who died in 159 B.C.) were to have relevance, they could not have been written long after his death, say (conservatively) by 150 B.C. Licinus, then, must have been active by 150. One further indication is that Aedituus, and only he, is given the epithet *veteris poetae* when all three poets are introduced by Gellius (19.9.10), implying that he is older than either of the other two and supporting the argument that Gellius and Apuleius give the three names in a chronological order. It seems safe to say, then, that by 150 B.C. Hellenistic epigram was being imitated

<hr/>

[59] K. Quinn (*The Catullan Revolution*, 12), for instance, says only, "For several decades prior to 70 B.C., we find traces of interest in a third kind of poetry . . .," and gives no further indication of date except the mention that Catulus was consul in 102 B.C. Scholars are almost without exception content to date the poems to the end of the second and beginning of the first centuries B.C.: e.g., J. Wight Duff (*A Literary History of Rome*[3] [1953] 180), "About 100 B.C. Lutatius Catulus and Valerius Aedituus, as well as Porcius Licinus, composed epigrams. . . ." The acceptance of a late date is perhaps due to the questionable assumption that these poets were part of a circle centering around Catulus.

[60] Wheeler, *Catullus and the Traditions*, 69 and 257 n. 17. But Roscius was born *ca.* 134 B.C. (Bardon 117): only the years 120–115 B.C. are acceptable.

by Roman poets, and that the period of activity spanned by our three poets must have been a long one.

Whether or not these poets formed a circle (and I do not believe they did),[61] it is generally recognized that their interests and the general milieu of their times made this intrusion of Hellenistic epigram entirely natural.[62] The details of this process, however, are entirely unknown, and the fragmentary nature of the evidence can easily lead to dangerous oversimplification. Little is known about the three poets whose five epigrams survive, and it is an easy matter to fit them neatly into a group or circle and to think of them as forming a movement dedicated to this new literary influence. It must be remembered, however, that all three were amateur poets, dilettantes whose interest in things Hellenistic extended to philosophy and rhetoric,[63] and that undoubtedly there were many others active in the same ways. The few facts available can illustrate only the general trend. Antipater of Sidon, whose epigrams were well represented in Meleager's *Garland*, had been a friend of Catulus,[64] and, if the date of his death may be placed around 125 B.C.,[65] he may well have been influential in initiating

---

[61] An important question, though subsidiary to the present discussion. Büttner (*Porcius Licinus und der Litterarische Kreis des Q. Lutatius Catulus*, Leipzig 1893) had supposed that there was such a circle, but H. Bardon (*La Littérature Latine Inconnue* I, Paris 1952) argues convincingly against it on the grounds that there is no real evidence for such a circle (pp. 123–24); that the Licinus mentioned as a client of Catulus by Cicero (*De Or.* 3.225) was not the poet, since Licinus, who attacked Terence and the Scipionic circle so violently, was anti-aristocratic and "se présente comme un Marianiste" (p. 128); that there is no evidence to connect Aedituus with such a circle (p. 131). Finally, Bardon concludes that Büttner's theory is ". . . la construction très subtile, très érudite, et très fragile, d'un philologue intelligent. Les poètes, que nous venons d'étudier, admettons, pour le mieux, qu'ils ont connu Catulus et qu'ils lui ont communiqué leurs oeuvres. Assurément, il n'y a pas de communauté profonde de réflexion qui unisse ces hommes, comme auparavant Laelius, Scipion, Térence et Panétius" (p. 132). The question, however, is far from settled.

[62] For a good summary of the political and social background of these poets and of the conditions suitable for the arrival of Hellenism at this time, see A. Rostagni, *Storia della Letteratura Latina* I (Torino 1949) 306–11. It may be noted that Rostagni is among those who accept Büttner's theory of a literary circle around Catulus.

[63] For Catulus, at least, this is amply documented: see Bardon, 115–17, for a summary of the evidence.

[64] Cic. *De Or.* 3.194, . . . *Antipater ille Sidonius, quem tu probe, Catule, meministi.* . . .

[65] Little is known of Antipater's life, nor when he actually came to Rome. For the date of his death (or the collection of his epigrams), see A. S. F. Gow and D. L. Page, *The Greek Anthology: Hellenistic Epigrams* I (Cambridge 1965) xvi; one of his epigrams can be

Catulus' (and no doubt others') imitation of Hellenistic epigram. Catulus kept this interest throughout his life: the poet Archias, who did not come to Rome until 102,[66] lived for some time with Catulus and later with his son.[67] It is not necessary to argue that Meleager's *Garland* was important for the beginnings of Hellenistic epigram at Rome: Antipater had preceded it by at least a quarter of a century, and other anthologies had no doubt been circulating.[68] The *Garland* itself was only another aspect (one we happen to know about) of a growing influence. If, as is suggested above, Aedituus may be supposed to have written as early as 150, this influence had been already felt at Rome when Catulus was born (c. 150 B.C.) and must have been widely spread among amateur *literati* by the time he began to write. Care must be taken, therefore, lest the simplicity of the evidence as we have it suggest a corresponding simplicity of the historical situation: the intrusion of Hellenistic epigram preceded any circle which may have formed around Catulus and, in all probability, extended beyond any one circle of poets which lack of evidence may allow us to reconstruct.

What this interest in Hellenistic epigram meant for the technical development of Latin poetry can be inferred from the five epigrams themselves. In discussing these poems, however, it must be remembered that there is hardly enough to allow more than general conclusions about stylistic features, and that any statement made below must be regarded as tentative at best, however likely it may seem. The following

---

dated "with high probability to about 150 B.C.," and another "refers to the sack of Corinth (146 B.C.)" (xv).

[66] Cic. *Arch*. 3, *Roman venit Mario consule et Catulo*.

[67] Cic. *Arch*. 3, *vivebat cum Q. Catulo et patre et filio*.

[68] On the date of the *Garland*, see the latest word by Gow and Page (*Hellenistic Epigrams* I, xiv–xvii), who conclude, ". . . it seems, in default of further information, reasonable to guess that Meleager's *Garland* was compiled in the early years of the first century B.C." (xvi). On the probability of previous anthologies: "It is not necessary to consider here the sources from which Meleager compiled his *Garland* beyond noting that the belief once held that he was the first anthologist is no longer tenable. Papyrus scraps of anthologies of sufficiently early date make it plain that he had predecessors . . ." (xvi). Reitzenstein recognized that these epigrams were not influenced by Meleager, ". . . dem Meleager im Geiste, nicht in der Kunst ähnlich sind die sicher nicht vom ihm beeinflussten Epigramme des Catulus und seiner Klienten . . ." (*RE* 6, 96).

text of the poems is, with one change,[69] that of Morel (*FPL*, pp. 42–43, 46):

Valerius Aedituus:

1) Dicere cum conor curam tibi, Pamphila, cordis,
    quid mi abs te quaeram, verba labris abeunt,
per pectus manat subito <subido> mihi sudor:
    sic tacitus, subidus, dum pudeo, pereo.

2) Quid faculam praefers, Phileros, quae nil opus nobis?
    ibimus sic, lucet pectore flamma satis.
Istam nam potis est vis saeva extinguere venti
    aut imber caelo candidus praecipitans;
at contra hunc ignem Veneris nisi si Venus ipsa
    nulla est quae possit vis alia opprimere.

Porcius Licinus:

Custodes ovium teneraeque propaginis, agnum,
    quaeritis ignem? Ite huc; quaeritis? ignis homost.
Si digito attigero, incendam silvam simul omnem,
    omne pecus flammast, omnia quae video.

Q. Lutatius Catulus:

1) Aufugit mi animus; credo, ut solet, ad Theotimum
    devenit. Sic est, perfugium illud habet.
Quid, si non interdixem, ne illunc fugitivum
    mitteret ad se intro, sed magis eiceret?
Ibimus quaesitum. Verum, ne ipsi teneamur
    formido. Quid ago? Da, Venus, consilium.

2) Constiteram exorientem Auroram forte salutans,
    cum subito a laeva Roscius exoritur.
Pace mihi liceat, caelestes, dicere vestra:
    mortalis visus pulchrior esse deo.

---

[69] Baehrens (*FPR*) adopted *teneraeque* in Licinus, line 1, and noted, "teneraeque *P Victorius*: vendere *codd.* vernaeque *R Ungerus* . . ."; Morel accepted Hosius' *tenerae*. Without the *-que*, sense and style are lacking: if the meaning is "guardians of *lambs* . . ." (Loeb Gellius), one may ask what shepherd has ever been responsible only for lambs (as opposed to sheep *and* lambs), and why the poet should make such a distinction; if the meaning is "guardians of sheep *and* lambs . . .," the expression, involving two nouns and an appositive phrase all without a connective, is extremely awkward and unnatural. *Teneraeque* (or *vernaeque*) must be read, and is notable for the violation of Hermann's Bridge; but even so, a caesura may have been heard before the *-que*.

    For the present purposes, only one other reading need be noted (Aedituus 2.2): *pectore codd.*, *pectoris* Baehrens.

The archaic quality of the verse is clear: there is in certain points a great difference between these distichs and those of Catullus, a generation or two later (if not more). Two obvious points will suffice to show how much closer these epigrams are to Ennius than to Catullus. First, alliteration is frequent in both the poems of Aedituus, which is understandable if it is correct that he may have written as early as 150, or even earlier; in the other two poets, however, archaic alliteration is not to be found. Second, a final -s, in both Aedituus (3 times) and in Catulus (twice) can be dropped before a following initial consonant to allow a short syllable. In Catullus, the only example of this occurs in 116.8 (*tu dabis supplicium*), where Catullus may have been quoting a phrase from an epigram of his opponent Gellius in order to emphasize the very roughness of his verse. Cicero (*Orator* 161) says that suppression of a final -s "iam subrusticum videtur, olim autem politius," and specifies exactly to whom this refinement was due: "ita non erat ea offensio in versibus quam nunc fugiunt poetae novi." Both Lucretius and Cicero took advantage of this liberty:[70] it was presumably Catullus and the neoterics, as Cicero implies in 44, who had thought it rustic.

In two other important aspects already discussed for Catullus, however, the tradition represented by these epigrams obviously constituted a precedent for his epigrams proper (though not for his neoteric elegiacs). Elision is frequent in the five epigrams, and often is strikingly like some of the more notorious lines of Catullus (cf. lines 2–3 of Licinus, *quaeritis ignem? ite huc: quaeritis? ignis homost. | si digito attigero incendam silvam simul omnem*). Though the quantity of the five epigrams is not sufficient to allow much trust to be placed in the figures, the total number of elisions nevertheless may be taken as a fair indication of the general picture: there are 19 elisions in the 24 lines (79 elisions per 100 lines), which compares with the average of 75.7 elisions per 100 lines in Catullus' epigrams proper, but contrasts with the average of only 37.1 per 100 lines in his neoteric elegiacs. When it is remembered that Ennius has only 22 elisions per 100 lines in his hexameters, it may be assumed that these epigrams owed nothing to the

---

[70] C. Bailey (*Lucretius, De Rerum Natura* [Oxford 1947], vol. I, p. 124) finds final -s suppressed 8 times in Cicero's *Aratea* and 49 times in Lucretius (77 times in Lachmann's text).

developed hexameter literary tradition. It may also be noted (though this again is subject to chance) that in Catulus 1.1 a long final vowel is elided before a short initial vowel (*mī ănimus*): only one instance of this occurs in Catullus cc. 65–68, but in cc. 69–116 there are 10 instances.

In the matter of word order, too, the five epigrams resemble Catullus' epigrams. Of all the significant types of word order discussed above, there is not a single example in these 24 lines. It was observed, however, that the most common type of word order in Ennius was . . . /A . . . S, which has the effect of marking off the last half of a line as a unit. Though the type . . . /A . . . S does not occur in these epigrams, there is a tendency to keep the unity of the last half of the hexameter line by putting the noun after the caesura and an attribute (a genitive) at the end of the line (thus Aedituus, 1.1, *Dicere cum conor | curam tibi, Pamphila, cordis;* or 2.3, *istam nam potis est | vis saeva extinguere venti*); and Catulus once has a noun at the beginning of the line and its adjective at the end (2.3). In not making use of the two common types of poetic word order in Ennius, the epigrams again show their independence from the developed hexameter tradition. There is, however, a definite concern for word order, though not for the Ennian types or those exploited later by the neoterics. In the Licinus epigram, *quaeritis* is emphatically placed at the beginning of each half of the pentameter, and a form of *omnis* ends the third line and stands again at the beginning of each half of the following pentameter. Bardon has commented on the effectiveness of the word order in Catulus' Roscius epigram: "Le style, simple et pur, n'ignore pas quelque recherche, avec la spirituelle reprise de *exorientem* par *exoritur*, le parallélisme de *exorientem Auroram* et de *a laeva Roscius*, la correspondance de *mortalis* et de *deo*, en place antithétiques, mais dominés tous deux par *caelestes*, au vers précédent."[71] It cannot be denied that these poets were conscious of word order or that what they achieved had a natural spontaneity often lacking in later mannered verse; yet their obvious concern for effective word placement makes all the more striking the fact that not a single type of word order exploited later by the neoterics appears in any of their lines. Clearly these epigrams are far removed from Catullus' neoteric

[71] Bardon, 117.

elegiacs. The distance, however, between these five poems and his epigrams proper is not at all great: in word order, as in the matter of elisions, Catullus obviously followed precedent in his epigrams 69–116 and willfully ignored what technical and stylistic features he and the other *poetae novi* had developed as a trademark of their smooth and polished neoteric verse.

Before further discussion of these five epigrams, it is necessary to consider some important evidence for the widespread popularity of Hellenistic epigram in Italy during the generation or so before Catullus, evidence which is more often than not overlooked or ignored. In 1883 fragments of nine epigrams (three of them almost complete), found on a wall of the small theatre at Pompeii (datable to 75 B.C.), were published and immediately recognized by Buecheler ("Pompejanisch-Römisch-Alexandrinishes," *RhM* 38 [1883] 474–76) as significant examples of the same sort of epigram represented previously only by the five poems we have been discussing. Buecheler's enthusiasm was hardly contagious, and the importance of these epigrams has been almost universally ignored by scholars writing on the beginnings of Hellenistic epigram at Rome. The text of the three more complete epigrams is:[72]

CIL 4.4966 (= *CLE* 934):

...t [?] ui me oculei pos<t>quam deducxstis in ignem
...vim vestreis largificatis geneis
...non possunt lacrumae restinguere flam<m>am
...cos .?. incendunt tabifican<t>que animum.

CIL 4.4967 (= *CLE* 935, 1–2):

...veicinei [vesci nei?] incendia participantur
...flammam tradere utei liceat.

CIL 4.4971 (= *CLE* 935, 14–6):

sei quid amor valeat nostei, sei te hominem scis,
commiseresce mei, da veniam ut veniam.

---

[72] The text of these three epigrams offered here includes only what can be established with certainty. For the other fragments, a complete catalogue of restorations and interpretations, a full discussion of the discovery of the *graffiti*, the work that has been done on them, and the state of the text as we now have it, see my article to be published in *Yale Classical Studies*, vol. 21.

Whoever was the Tiburtinus who composed the first epigram, and whoever was the anonymous inscriber and author of the others,[73] they obviously reflect Hellenistic subject matter in Roman dress. Buecheler observed the essential points: ". . . diese Epigramm gehört nach der Abwerfung des schliessenden *s* (*largificati*'), nach den lautlichen Formen, nach den neuen, das heisst für alte Zeit sonst nicht nachweisbaren Lexeis *largificare, tabificare* (Accius *leto tabificabili*) in die sullanisch-ciceronische Periode, ist nicht nach 700/54 verfasst—wohl verstanden das Epigramm."[74] Even if the first epigram is as late as Buecheler thinks possible, it nevertheless clearly reflects the same poetic practice as the five epigrams discussed above. To Buecheler's observations, we may add that a long vowel is elided before a short vowel in the first line (*mē ŏculi*) and again in the fragment *CIL* 4.4969 (line 3, . . . *sumptī ŏpus est a* . . .), that another final *-s* is suppressed in another fragment (*CIL* 4.4973, line 2, *multa opu(s) sunt* . . .), that elision is generally frequent, and that the hiatus *te hominem* (*CIL* 4.4971, line 1) reflects colloquial usage (as in Plautus) and indicates that the poet had little concern for the metrical practices which had even then become established for hexameter poetry. On the other hand, it is equally obvious that the source of inspiration of these poems was Hellenistic epigram: for the first poem Buecheler notes as parallels *Anthologia Palatina* 12.91, by Polystratus, and 12.92, by Meleager, both of which contain the theme of the poet's eyes and the fire of love, and were included in Meleager's *Garland*;[75] yet the epigram is a free

---

73 All the epigrams appear to have been inscribed by the same hand, but it is probable (as I have argued—see n. 72) that the signature, which appears only with the first, indicates that the remaining poems may have been composed by the anonymous inscriber. Buecheler considered the second epigram an answer to the first, which, if true, also implies a second poet. 74 Buecheler, *RhM* 38 (1883) 475.

75 12.91 begins Δισσὸς Ἔρως αἴθει ψυχὴν μίαν and concludes:

Καίεσθε, τρύχεσθε, καταφλέχθητέ ποτ' ἤδη·
οἱ δύο γὰρ ψυχὴν οὐκ ἂν ἔλοιτε μίαν. (lines 7–8)

12.92 concludes:

τί μοι νενοτισμένα χεῖτε
δάκρυα, †πρὸς δ' Ἱκέτην αὐτομολεῖτε τάχος†;
ὀπτᾶσθ' ἐν κάλλει, τύφεσθ' ὑποκαόμενοι νῦν,
ἄκρος ἐπεὶ ψυχῆς ἐστὶ μάγειρος Ἔρως. (lines 5–8)

Gow and Page (*Hellenistic Epigrams*) print 12.91 as Polystratus I, and note that he seems to

adaptation of the two possible originals, not a translation in any sense of the word.[76] Its source is Hellenistic, but the treatment and the technique are entirely Roman.

The great importance of these epigrams lies in the fact that they show the extent to which Hellenistic epigram must have been read and imitated in Italy at the end of the second century B.C. and the beginning of the first. The technique bears little similarity to serious poetic developments. The poems are clearly second-rate, amateur productions which come from a provincial town. It is likely, therefore, that the influence of Hellenistic epigram was widespread, that the majority of those who were attracted by it were amateur poets, and that for this reason little of it has survived. The paucity of the evidence has in turn led to an oversimplification of the picture. From the time of Aedituus, as early as 150, if not earlier, down to the Pompeian *graffiti*, there must have existed a great interest in epigram based loosely on Hellenistic models but written in a verse natively Roman. The best of this production was good, and Gellius may be believed when he says that Aedituus, Licinus, and Catulus represent the best; at the same time, their verses must not be read or studied in a vacuum, but rather must be seen only as a part of the tradition to which they so obviously belong, that of amateur epigram.

To reach a final conclusion about the nature of the five epigrams and about the tradition to which they belong it is necessary only to consider their relation to the originals which inspired them. The first poem of Aedituus, as was pointed out originally by K. P. Schulze,[77] derives from the same ode of Sappho that Catullus translated (c. 51). Two points should be observed. The first is that Aedituus used Sappho's poem only as a beginning for what cannot be called even a loose translation, whereas Catullus translated as precisely as meter and

---

have been contemporary with Antipater of Sidon (both refer to the sack of Corinth in 146 B.C.). They print 12.92 as Meleager CXVI and find it an obvious variation on Poly-stratus' epigram.

[76] Buecheler, 475: "Dass jene Epigramme bei Gellius freie Uebersetzungen griechischer Originale sind, daran zweifelt wohl niemand . . . Dasselbe gilt von unserem Gedicht."

[77] *Fleckeis. Jahrb.* 131 (1885) 631.

language allowed. The second point is that Catullus kept the original meter, but Aedituus recast his original in two pentameter couplets. The second epigram by Aedituus is closely paralleled by an anonymous Hellenistic fragment,[78] and the theme is a commonplace in Hellenistic epigram. Certain parallels for the theme of fire and the poet's eyes have been noted above for the first epigram from Pompeii, and other parallels can be found for Licinus' epigram, the theme of which is similar to Aedituus' second.[79] No single Hellenistic epigram, however, can be said to be the original from which any of these Latin epigrams were translated: they are merely conflations of many originals from which they take the commonplace theme of fire, but little of precise content. Catulus' two epigrams illustrate the same situation. The second, which certainly is personal and Roman in content, has a theme borrowed from Theocritus,[80] but the borrowing, no more than a suggestion of theme, is without verbal parallel. Catulus' second epigram is obviously inspired by an epigram of Callimachus (41 Pf.), but here again, although the similarities of theme are striking, there are few verbal parallels. The first two lines of Callimachus' epigram are far more subtle than Catulus': only half of his spirit has vanished, but whether Love or Death now possesses it the poet does not know (Ἥμισύ μευ ψυχῆς ἔτι τὸ πνέον, ἥμισυ δ' οὐκ οἶδ'/εἴτ' Ἔρος εἴτ' Ἀΐδης ἥρπασε, πλὴν ἀφανές). Catullus, however, has simplified the conceit: he has no doubt as to where his spirit has gone, he knows that all of it, not a half, has left him; and he substitutes for Callimachus' metaphysical Love and Death the name of the object of his affection. Callimachus' poetic playfulness has become a concrete reality. The

---

[78] συνοδηγὸν ἔχω τὸ πολὺ πῦρ/τὸ ἐν τῇ ψυχῇ μου καιόμενον (in O. Crusius, *Herondae mimiambi*[5] [1914] 125); A. Turyn (*Hermes* 62 [1927] 494) sought to justify Baehrens' *pectoris* (for *pectore*) from this fragment.

[79] Cf. *Anth. Pal.* 9.15 (attributed to Callimachus) and 5.57, 96, 139, 176; 12.82, 83 (all attributed to Meleager). Bardon notes (p. 127 n. 5) that "Le thème de l'amour qui consume les amants est cher à Méléagre"; and Day (*Latin Love Elegy*, 103), similarly, that the epigram of Licinus "is simply a synthesis of Meleager's variations upon the theme of Love's consuming fire."

[80] This was recognized by Reitzenstein, *RE* 6, 96:

Ἀὼς ἀντέλλοισα καλὸν διέφανε πρόσωπον,
πότνια Νύξ, τό τε λευκὸν ἔαρ χειμῶνος ἀνέντος·
ὧδε καὶ ἁ χρυσέα Ἑλένα διεφαίνετ' ἐν ἀμῖν. (Theocritus, 18.26-8)

fact that these three poets, like the poets of the Pompeian *graffiti*, did not translate but only borrowed the themes they found in Hellenistic epigram, has often been recognized; it is the significance of this fact which has not received sufficient emphasis.[81]

Furthermore, confusion has resulted from ignoring certain essential points. We have observed in some detail that there is a real difference in technique, vocabulary, and style between Catullus' epigrams proper and his neoteric elegiacs and that the latter resemble his neoteric productions in these features; that the epigrams of Aedituus, Licinus, and Catulus and those from Pompeii are Roman in style and technique, and that in this they are similar to Catullus' epigrams proper; and that though the earlier poets' epigrams are based loosely on Hellenistic epigrams, they are in no sense translations of their Greek originals and do not show close verbal parallels with these originals, but simply adapt from them prevalent themes which are often introduced into settings otherwise Roman. It is important to state these facts as clearly as possible in order to deal with certain confusions. It has often been assumed that the three writers of Hellenistic epigram before Catullus are "Alexandrian". Bardon, for example, writes: "Avec Catulus, l'Alexandrinisme s'impose à Rome. Les Alexandrins n'avaient agi, jusqu'alors, que par intermittence, et à l'ombre des classiques. Maintenant, en s'inspirant d'eux, Catulus affirme son goût pour un art dégagé di tout utilitarisme; il vise au raffinement maniéré du style; bref, il proclame la gratuité de l'oeuvre littéraire."[82] A confusion of terminology is partly at fault. "Alexandrian" should properly be applied only to Callimachus and those poets, whether contemporary or later, who felt and acknowledged the force of his literary doctrine; "neoteric" should be limited to the first group of Roman poets of whom the same can be said, that is, Cicero's *poetae novi*. "Hellenistic", on the other hand, is a looser term having reference only to a fairly long historical period and involving no particular literary creed.[83]

---

[81] See the statement by Buecheler above, n. 76; and, for instance, Bardon, 119, "Catulus n'a donc pas traduit Callimaque; il l'a adapté,—et transformé: il a substitué une âme à une autre."

[82] P. 119.

[83] See W. Clausen, "Callimachus and Latin Poetry," *GRBS* 5 (1964) 187: "It is a

The confusion, however, often extends beyond the terminology and represents a misunderstanding of the literary history and traditions. The fact that Catulus translated an epigram of Callimachus is no indication of a special interest in that poet. W. Clausen has argued: "But Callimachus had little or no influence on Latin poetry until the generation of the New Poets. . . . Sometime before he committed suicide in 87 B.C., Lutatius Catulus rendered one of Callimachus' epigrams (41) into Latin; but this, the diversion of an idle hour, should not be taken as evidence of any serious interest in Callimachus' major poetry or in his esthetic views. Catulus was a Roman aristocrat with a taste for Greek poetry, an elegant amateur. He would have read many Greek epigrams; one, by Callimachus, pleased him especially, and he made a version of it."[84]

At this point we may shift our attention back to Catullus. Whereas the Roman writers of Hellenistic epigram had adapted only the theme of their originals and had ignored verbal and stylistic translation, Catullus can be seen doing just the opposite. C. 70 has often been compared with Callimachus 25 Pf.:

> Ὤμοσε Καλλίγνωτος Ἰωνίδι μήποτ' ἐκείνης
> ἕξειν μήτε φίλον κρέσσονα μήτε φίλην.
> ὤμοσεν· ἀλλὰ λέγουσιν ἀληθέα τοὺς ἐν ἔρωτι
> ὅρκους μὴ δύνειν οὔατ' ἐς ἀθανάτων . . .

> Nulli se dicit mulier mea nubere malle
>   quam mihi, non si se Iuppiter ipse petat.
> dicit: sed mulier cupido quod dicit amanti,
>   in vento et rapida scribere oportet aqua.

Catullus has ignored Callimachus' final image entirely, and even the theme of the first couplet has been so obscured that, were it not for one technical feature, the model for Catullus' poem would hardly have been recognized: this feature is one which does not appear in the earlier

mistake, not uncommon in our literary histories, to employ the terms "Hellenistic," "Alexandrian," "Callimachean" interchangeably. The poetry of Catulus, Valerius Aedituus, Porcius Licinus, and Laevius might be called Hellenistic; but it had little to do with the New Poetry, which is Callimachean in its inspiration."

[84] P. 187.

epigrammatists, direct translation of an obvious point of style. Catullus refers to his original not by the repetition of theme (as did the earlier pre-neoteric epigrammatists) but by rendering Callimachus' anaphora "Ὤμοσε . . . ὤμοσεν· ἀλλά by *dicit . . . dicit: sed.* Such interest in verbal imitation is entirely neoteric: the only surprise is to find it here in the epigrams proper which, as we are arguing, are in the tradition of pre-neoteric epigram. It is usual for Catullus, when imitating, translating, or in any way making use of Greek epigram, to do so in his polymetrics. A complete demonstration of this point is unnecessary here. Reitzenstein, after noting how few parallels there are between Catullus' epigrams and Greek epigrams, says: "Dagegen zeigen die πολύμετρα 1–60 häufiger Berührungen mit dem griechischen E., so z.B. 3 die Klage um den toten Lieblingsvogel, 4 die angebliche Unterschrift unter das Votivbild seines Schiffes, 56 gedacht wie eine Unterschrift unter ein Bild Caesars und Mamurras, die dichtend auf einem Pfühle liegen (vgl. etwa A.P. XVI 306.307). Die Reihe wächst, wenn wir an die Verwendung des E.s als Briefchen, als kurze erotische Erzählung oder als Entrüstungs- und Spottgedicht denken. Die metrische Form macht für Catull keinen Unterschied, πολύμετρα und ἐλεγεῖα stehen sich gleich, das E. ist zum kurzen Gedicht geworden."[85] It was Catullus' practice, as a neoteric, to turn Greek originals into polymetrics: in so doing he could adapt neoteric features of style to reproduce verbally corresponding features in the originals (as has been observed above with a unique example from the epigrams proper). It is for this reason that Catullus kept the Sapphic stanza in his translation of Sappho (c. 51), whereas Aedituus, not in the least concerned with reproducing the original, was free to adapt it loosely in his pentameter couplets.

More will be said shortly of Catullus as a neoteric. It has been suggested that Hellenistic epigram had arrived in Rome as early as 150

---

[85] *RE* 6, 102. Owing to neglect of its context, the final sentence is one of the most misquoted ever written (see, for instance, Svennung, p. 24). It is commonly cited to mean that there is no difference between Catullus' polymetrics and epigrams, which is what it does say when isolated. What it means in context (and it will be admitted even by German-speakers that the context is no model of clarity) is that metrical form made no difference to Catullus when he turned (Greek) elegiacs into (his own) polymetrics.

and that it was popular and widely practised by amateur poets for at least the next seventy-five years, poets whose technique shows no interest in the developing technique of serious poetry and who themselves were unconcerned with the stylistic niceties of the verse they were freely adapting. It has also been suggested that this intrusion of Hellenistic epigram gave the dormant Latin couplet, previously used only by Ennius for literary epitaphs, a *raison d'être* and a new life, and it has been argued that this new life was so thoroughly successful (far more so than our fragments at first suggest) that Catullus was faced with an impossible situation: to write epigram he had to write for the most part according to the terms of an established tradition, and these terms were anything but reconcilable with neoteric innovations. Catullus did, however, accept these terms, though he used the same meter for four longer poems which, not being epigrams in the proper sense, represent a union of neoteric style with the pre-neoteric verse form. Before we can outline the arrival of Alexandrian verse in Rome, however, another use which had developed for the pentameter couplet must be briefly discussed; and, after that, the first seeds of polymetric verse.

There is little which can be said with certainty about the epigram ascribed variously to a Papinius, Pompilius, or even Pomponius (Morel, *FPL* 42):[86]

> Ridiculum est cum te cascam tua dicit amica,
> fili Potoni, sesquisenex puerum.
> dic rusum pusam: sic fiet 'mutua muli',
> nam vere pusus tu, tua amica senex.

For the present purposes it is only necessary to point out that this epigram shows certain characteristics common also in Catullus' epigrams. The vocabulary shows no relation to poetic usage: *cascus* (the strange word which caused the poem to be cited by Varro, *Ling.* 7.28), though also employed by Ennius (*Ann.* 24 V.[2]), did not become part of the poetic vocabulary; *sesquisenex* (compare Catullus' *sesquipedalis*) and *pusus* are similarly prosaic. The proverbial expression

---

[86] For a complete and cautious discussion, with all the evidence and arguments for date and author, including a new text of the epigram, see Bardon, 52–53.

mutua muli (sc. *scabunt*) is similar to Catullus' *hoc est quod dicunt: ipsa olera olla legit* (94.2).[87] An attempt to date the epigram is a hopeless undertaking. It can be said only that it represents another use to which the distich had been put by the end of the second century: it is more than likely that invective came to be practised more and more in this meter, but, as is the fate of all such amateur and occasional poetry, little has survived to indicate the extent to which it had been popular. Catullus' invective epigrams, differing as they obviously do in poetic quality and allusion from his polymetric invectives, may be seen to represent this tradition, a tradition which he could not change. It is unfortunate that this tradition of invective epigram in distichs is even more obscure than that of Hellenistic epigram, but it is impossible to doubt that Catullus' invective epigrams represent it fairly.[88]

The sudden intrusion of Hellenistic literature inspired other forms of verse as well. Laevius, about whom we are poorly informed,[89] was no doubt the first to use Greek lyric meters for Latin verse: he did this, however, in the early part of the first century, long after Hellenistic literature had first come to Rome. Two characteristics of the thirty fragments which have survived are notable: the great variety of the meters employed in the poems, and the riotous inventiveness and playfulness of the vocabulary. These two characteristics have led to the common supposition that Laevius is a direct forerunner of Catullus, both in the use of polymetric forms and in vocabulary. Wheeler, for instance, writes: "[Laevius'] use of diminutives, of compounds, and of Greek loan-words are all striking characteristics of Catullus. In other respects also Laevius was breaking ground for Catullus and other

---

[87] See Otto, *Sprichwörter*, 232–33. For the other proverbial expressions in Catullus, see Kroll's *Register* s.v. *Sprichwort*: most of the instances there noted, however, would hardly fall under the heading of New England "sayin's" (many of them are rather poeticisms, as 70.4, *in vento et rapida scribere oportet aqua*): of the examples in the polymetrics, only 22.21 (*sed non videmus manticae quod in tergo est*) would so qualify; the others, though to a certain extent proverbial, all include Greek names, a significant distinction between the use of such expressions in the polymetrics and epigrams.

[88] Two more fragments of pre-neoteric epigram survive (the single hexameter of Atta and the epigram of Pompilius, giving his literary genealogy, both Morel, *FPL* 42), but of these nothing particular can be said.

[89] For the best summary of Laevius' date and work, see F. Leo, "Die Römische Poesie in der Sullanischen Zeit," *Hermes* 49 (1914) 180–88.

poets of the following generation. Like them he turned away from Ennius and the older Roman poets to the Hellenistic and Alexandrian Greeks. . . . There are glimpses of technique common to the Alexandrians and Catullus . . ."[90] Laevius himself has frequently been viewed as a neoteric.[91] While it cannot be denied that his experiments with meter may have interested Catullus or that his vocabulary does resemble that characteristic of Catullus' polymetric poems, it must be argued here that too much emphasis has been placed on circumstantial similarities. A list of the parallels in the vocabulary of two poets, however long and however close the similarities, will not suffice to prove a dependent relation if their intentions and sources can be demonstrated to be entirely different. Before the importance of the place of the neoterics and their contribution can be understood, we must re-examine, as briefly as possible, the sources for Laevius' interest in metrical variety and the intention behind his vocabulary, both of which will be seen to be substantially different from those which inspired Catullus and the other neoterics.

Laevius' meters may be divided into two groups, those native to Roman dramatic verse and those whose origins are to be found in Hellenistic verse.[92] The first group, the smaller, needs no explanation: it is clear that Laevius owed a great deal to Roman drama, both tragedy and comedy;[93] it is also clear how little, if anything, Catullus

---

[90] *Catullus and the Traditions*, 75.

[91] See H. de la Ville de Mirmont, *Étude Biographique et Littéraire sur le Poète Laevius* (Bibliothèque des Universités du Midi, 1900), 76–77.: "Mais un moment vient où la littérature romaine prétend devenire purement alexandrine, où l'imitation d'Homère et de Sophocle cède la place à l'imitation des poètes du Musée. Laevius est le poète de ce moment. Comme Livius Andronicus avait initié la littérature latine à l'hellénisme classique, il l'imitie à son tour à l'alexandrinisme. . . . Inventeur des mots, versificateur rompu à toutes les difficultés d'une métrique savante et compliquée, il est l'élève érudit des Alexandrins du Musée et le premier des Alexandrins de Rome."

[92] Leo, 182: "Unter den durch zufällige Überlieferung uns zugekommenen Resten sind mehr als ein Dutzend Versmasse, darunter die der römischen Dichtung lange geläufigen trochäischen Tetrameter, anapästischen Systeme, auch Hexameter (keine elegischen Distichen und iambischen Trimeter); alle übrigen sind neu aus der griechischen Lyrik übernommen, entweder aus der klassischen Lyrik oder aus dem hellenistischen Formenschatz, der sich die alten Versarten angepasst hatte."

[93] See A. Traglia, "Polimetria e Verba Laeviana," *Studi Classici e Orientali* 6 (1957) 105: "Della poesia drammatica, da cui prendeva lo spunto per molti dei suoi *erotopaegnia*, egli ripeteva schemi metrici ben noti alla tragedia e alla commedia, servendasi soprattutto

and the neoterics owed in their metrical forms to Roman drama. The second group of meters has been discussed by Leo, who finds them derived from early Hellenistic verse. The fragment of the *Phoenix* (22 M.) "war eine Imitation von Simias' 'Erosflügel', das heisst es hat sein Vorbild in den überkünstlichen, metrisch und sprachlich sehr ernst gemeinten Spielen der frühesten hellenistischen Dichtergeneration, noch vor Kallimachos."[94] Leo also discussed the line *omnes sunt denis syllabis versi* (30 M.), decided that it must have stood as an introduction to a poem consisting of lines in different meters but each of ten syllables, and concludes, "Auch die Muster dieser Versspielerei werden in frühhellenistische Zeit gehören."[95] Such indications, and others,[96] show that Laevius' interest lay in early, pre-Callimachean verse, at least as far as metrical technique is concerned; and certainly there is no suggestion of anything Callimachean in the meters of any of the fragments. In addition, Leo observed that "Wir können auch nirgend zeigen, dass er übersetzte": in this Laevius resembles the preneoteric writers of epigram and contrasts with Catullus (and presumably the other neoterics), who translated directly and who speaks occasionally of translation. This point is an important one to observe, since the interest of the New Poets in direct translation marks an interest in poetic technique that goes far beyond mere imitation. Laevius experimented, but even his meters, diverse and original as they are, show no more than a skill in adapting early Hellenistic frivolities; the neoterics' discovery of Alexandrian poetry brought with it an interest in the technical refinements of meter that went far beyond mere adaptation and led them to practise actual translation. Catullus' sources are thus very different from Laevius', just as it is clear that his interest in metrical variety is different from Laevius' experimental profusion: the New Poets were selective, and this selectivity was inspired by their

---

delle monodie e dei *cantica*, secondo il particolare carattere lirico-drammatico delle sue poesie."

[94] Leo, 183–84.

[95] P. 185 and n. 1.

[96] For instance, Laevius' *Centauri* (10 M.) has suggested the mixed meters of Chaeremon's *Centaur*, mentioned by Aristotle (*Poetics* 1447b and 1460a) as a possible source, though the same line may find its way back to Sophocles (see R. Goossens, *Latomus* 10 (1951) 419–24).

Callimachean creed. If Laevius had introduced Alexandrian poetry to Rome, Catullus would have imitated his metrical variety: this, of course, he did not do. Catullus shows no interest in Laevius' Roman dramatic meters, and none in the haphazard experiments Laevius made in adapting the meters of early Hellenistic verse.[97]

Laevius' vocabulary has been studied in detail by de la Ville de Mirmont, and recently by Traglia and Bardon: it will be necessary here only to point out, by a few examples, that although (as Wheeler summarized) diminutives, compounds, and Greek loan-words "are all striking characteristics of Catullus," there are obvious and telling differences in the way such words were formed and used by the two poets which, as was the case in their polymetrics, points to different intentions and attitudes. Traglia has noted that "La lingua di Ennio e di Plauto costituisce, naturalmente, l'eredità più antica, il fondo più ricco del lessico di Levio," and in addition, that contemporary vocabulary must to a certain extent be represented also, "l'elemento satirico, o piuttosto polemico-letterario."[98] With this in mind we may observe that although Laevius used the diminutives *tenellulus* and *tenellus* in much the same way as did Catullus later, we need not agree with Traglia's statement that "Il diminutivo ha in Levio un valore quasi sempre affettivo":[99] Catullus' diminutives, as we have seen, are a marked characteristic of neoteric practice, frequent in both the polymetrics and longer poems but not in the epigrams, always affective, and more often than not obviously a poetic adaptation of elegant colloquial language. Laevius' usage, however, often shows quite clearly that his intentions were of a different order. He uses, for instance, the archaic diminutive form *miserulus* (19 M.) instead of the current *misellus*:[100] Laevius was concerned with experimental novelty, Catullus

[97] One important piece of evidence is frequently overlooked. Porphyrio comments on Hor. *Odes* 3.1.2 (*carmina non prius audita*): "Romanis utique non prius audita, quamvis Laevius lyrica ante Horatium scripserit. Sed videntur illa non Graecorum lege ad lyricum characterem exacta." This clearly indicates that Laevius' experiments were adaptations of Greek metres, not close imitations (*non Graecorum lege*) or translations.

[98] P. 83.

[99] P. 100.

[100] Traglia, 102: "Ma e da notare che Levio usa qui non il tipo del linguaggio familiare 'misellus', ma risale alla forma primitiva 'miserulus', che doveva sapere di arcaizzante ed è comunque attestata per la prima volta qui." Traglia suggests metrical reasons for Laevius'

with a carefully selective expressiveness.[101] In Catullus most Greek loan-words are used in particularly poetic settings, in which they always suggest a Greek tone or source; nothing of the sort can be said for Laevius' use of Greek words, all of which appear to be words either used in a technical sense (as *antipathes, trochiscili*, and *saurae* in the list of *philtra*, 27 M.) or for little else than exotic novelty (as *papyrina stigmata*, 13 M., or *tegmine onychino*, 9 M.). Laevius' compound adjectives are likewise almost all *hapax legomena* and are plainly exotic formations; as has been discussed, Catullus has nothing of the sort in his longer poems (where almost all such compounds are regularly formed and easily paralleled by earlier epic examples), and only sparingly resorts to unusual compounds in his polymetrics (where they are always used for special effects). It is clear, then, that Laevius' vocabulary, though at first sight similar to Catullus' in some important aspects, is entirely different in poetic intention and purpose, and that in his vocabulary and usage Laevius anticipated none of the principles which the neoterics developed.

It cannot be doubted that Catullus and the New Poets must have read Laevius with some interest: there was enough in common between them, though their sources, principles, and purposes were vastly different. Laevius too was interested in the psychology of love and in the details of emotion, but here again there is no real evidence to link this interest specifically with Callimachus and the Alexandrians. Laevius must have read Callimachus, just as the pre-neoteric writers of epigram had; but how much he had read, or absorbed and understood of Callimachus' purpose is questionable. Laevius stands far closer, in many respects, to Roman drama, both comedy and tragedy, than he does to Catullus; and it is not unlikely that the same tendencies in vocabulary and style would appear in the work of Matius and Sueius

---

use of diminutives; such reasons cannot be found for their frequent occurrence in both the polymetrics and longer poems of Catullus.

101 The diminutive nouns in Laevius are similarly of a sort not common in Catullus; all are strange words to begin with, whose effect was one of novelty rather than of expressiveness: *decipula* (29 M.), later used by Mart. Cap. and Apul.; *manciolae* (9 M.), for which de la Ville de Mirmont (p. 89) conjectured *maniculae* (from Plautus); *opsecula* (22 M.); *radicula* (27 M.), which is not to be taken as a literary diminutive but rather as a common term.

(if more existed) and be seen as general characteristics of this generation of poets.[102] That Laevius provides a link with the neoterics cannot be denied, but that Catullus owed more to him than a vague suggestion of certain possibilities is unlikely.[103]

Catullus and the New Poets thus began to write at a time when two possibilities were open for shorter poems. The elegiac couplet, sanctified by its Ennian origin but without the formal restrictions and technical conventions developing rapidly for serious verse, had become well established in a tradition of amateur epigram based loosely on Hellenistic models, and at the same time had been used more and more for occasional invective verses. So widespread and accepted was this tradition that there was little the New Poets could do to change its nature. Difficult though it may be to understand the force of tradition in ancient poetry, it is obvious that the amateur quality of epigram in distichs could not be altered without producing a hybrid so strange as to be unacceptable to sensitive poets and readers; in addition, the unsophisticated quality of epigram had a directness and force of its own. The New Poets thus chose to leave unchanged the basically unpoetic tradition of epigram. On the other hand, the polymetric verse forms initiated by Laevius, being entirely new in Latin, representing the very beginnings of a tradition (if indeed the word tradition can even be applied to these novel experiments of Laevius), left the neoterics free to invent, mold, and develop whatever style their

---

[102] Bardon (194) concludes that Laevius was not the originator of Alexandrianism at Rome; he finds that Matius and Sueius also share in "un érotisme de bon ton, ses délicatesses, son érudition aussi et, dans son style, son besoin de rendre, surtout par des néologismes, de complexes subtilités . . .; à cet égard, [Laevius] représente, avec éclat, un mouvement qui l'absorbe et le dépasse.... Pour les sujets, il hellénise.... Pour le style, il subit l'ascendant d'Ennius, de Plaute...."

[103] It should be noted that Catullus never mentions Laevius, though not much one way or the other should be made of this fact (Catullus never mentions Ennius, to whom he owed a great deal). de la Ville de Mirmont, however, explains this silence by noting that Horace mentions Catullus only once because he thought himself the first to have introduced Aeolic verse to Rome (*Odes* 3.30.10–14) and did not want to admit Catullus' priority; in the same way, de la Ville de Mirmont claims, Catullus did not want to recognize the priority of Laevius. This parallel, however, is a poor one (no one would have questioned Horace's claim in any case), and jealousy will not explain Catullus' refusal to admit the priority of Laevius as a Roman Alexandrian: the notion of a debt to Laevius would never have entered Catullus' mind.

conscious efforts to produce a new serious poetry suggested. Until the time of the New Poets there had been no serious poetry in Rome written in the shorter verse forms, no poetry written (as epic and tragedy, for instance, had been earlier) from a conscious desire to develop in the Latin language a set of principles, a poetic creed, which might produce a native art rivaling the Greek: to do this meant the creation of a poetic vocabulary and technique.

Roman literary history tells only one story: the creation of any new genre at Rome is always the result of a Greek mind stimulating native writers at a particularly auspicious time, after which the development of the genre proceeds only as long as it takes Roman poets to work their language and native literary techniques into the molds supplied by the Greek exemplars of the genre; a new genre is created, developed, and, having become a self-conscious compartment of a new literature, quickly loses its original *élan* and dies. Ennius, himself almost a Greek, created the annalistic epic in hexameters from the Greek hexameter of Homer, using and re-creating native vocabulary and the possibilities of a native verse technique; annalistic epic, as the neoterics and later Virgil (more clearly than anyone else) realized, thereupon became stagnant. Tragedy, beginning with Livius Andronicus, met the same fate; comedy too, after the sudden brilliance of Plautus and others, and the discovery of Greek New Comedy (behind which lie the Greek theatres of Sicily), became dormant. On a smaller scale the story is repeated, as we have seen in some detail, in the tradition of amateur epigram at Rome: Antipater of Sidon and Archias must represent only two of many Greek writers of epigram who came early to Rome and found an occupation in amusing such interested aristocrats as Catulus himself; and after the genre had been developed, after the native elements had been forged and had become rigidly fixed and marked, the genre revived only under new conditions and with new terms for a later generation of poets (in this case, Martial).

Neoteric poetry, then, did not begin in a vacuum. The intrusion of Hellenistic epigram led finally to the discovery of the Alexandrians: Philitas, Aratus, Apollonius, Theocritus, Euphorion, and above all the master and creator of a poetic creed, Callimachus. These poets had been read, at least in some small part, in Rome for several generations, and Callimachus had served as an occasional model for pre-neoteric epigram; yet it is doubtful, if not impossible, that suddenly a new realization of the purpose of Alexandrian poetry could have dawned on Roman poets without a further catalyst. The Greek mind behind the discovery of Callimachus and Alexandrian poetry (and all that it implied) has now been recognized to have been Parthenius of Nicaea, who came to Rome perhaps in 73 B.C.[104] The importance of Parthenius cannot be overestimated: without his timely arrival there could have been no New Poetry, for it is unlikely that Cinna, Calvus, Catullus, and the other neoterics could by themselves have understood or adopted Callimachean poetry, or by themselves have devised the vocabulary and technique necessary for the creation of a new genre, a genre built of Roman elements in a new assemblage especially to satisfy the ideals of Alexandrian verse.[105] Some of the details of the new poetic vocabulary and technique have been discussed above; nor is it necessary, or possible, to restate here the principles held by the Roman Alexandrians.[106] There remain only a few questions concerning Catullus' place in the history of Roman elegy which have never received a satisfactory answer. It is hoped that the present argument can furnish a consistent explanation and provide a resolution for most of the problems long raised about the origins of subjective love-elegy at Rome.

[104] See W. Clausen (above, n. 83) 181–96, for an initial appraisal of the significance of Parthenius. The date of Parthenius' arrival in Rome is presumed from the capture of Nicaea in 73 B.C., at which time Parthenius may have become the prize of Cinna (not further identified by Suidas, s.v. Παρθένιος, but presumably a relative of the poet of the *Zmyrna*; see Clausen, 188). R. Pfeiffer ("A fragment of Parthenius' *Arete*," *CQ* 37 (1943) 30–31) thinks it possible that Parthenius may not have been taken prisoner until the war against Mithridates ended in 65 B.C.; his words of caution do not alter the situation, however, for he notes that "Even if we take the latest possible date for his arrival in the west . . ., this date would be early enough to have enabled him to influence the circle of the *poetae novi* from the very beginning of their career; none of them seems to have started before 65."

[105] It is tempting to find a complimentary reference to Parthenius in the line *Nicaeaeque ager uber aestuosae* (46.5): the rare poetic adjective *aestuosus* is used only once elsewhere by Catullus, in a reference to Callimachus (*oraclum Iovis inter aestuosi / et Batti veteris sacrum sepulcrum*, 7.5–6).

[106] Clausen (above, n. 83) provides the best summary of the important evidence for a definition of the New Poetry; but a complete history of Latin neoteric poetry has not been written.

The question of the origin and ultimate source of Latin love-elegy has been discussed since Leo opened the question in 1895,[107] yet there seems to have been little progress made towards a satisfactory answer. The specter of an Alexandrian prototype has been exorcised: no one today seems to require such a creation, though its usefulness at one time made it popular. In the most complete recent discussion of the problem, A. Day (*The Origins of Latin Love-Elegy*, Oxford 1938) has turned from the search for a single source to the study of many influences, both Greek and Latin, with the result that Leo's original question (it is hoped) has been disposed of forever. But the air remains unclear: diversity of influences has replaced any one supposition of source; the Romans have been given back their own literary creation, but its origin remains uncertain. Catullus' position is as unclear to the moderns as it was to the ancients: is he to be included among writers of elegy (as he is in Prop. 2.34.87, Ovid *Am.* 3.9.62, *Tr.* 2.427–28, in all of which passages he appears admittedly as much in the role of a poet of love as in that of a proper elegist) or not (as in Ovid *Tr.* 4.10.51– 54, *Ars Am.* 3.333–34, Quint. 10.1.93, Suet.-Diomedes 1.484 Keil; where the traditional list of elegists begins with Gallus)? and if he is to be included among the first elegists, just which of his poems are epigrams and which real elegies? Such questions are still far from having an acceptable answer.

The question has long been complicated by two unjustified assumptions. The first is that a distinction can and should be made between objective and subjective elegy. Much of the discussion has centered on defining the exact proportions of the first in Greek elegy and of the second in Latin elegy, and then on determining where Catullus stands in relation to each. How pointless and uncritical such discussions are

---

107 *Plautinische Forschungen*², 140–57. For the basic bibliography of the question, see A. Day, *The Origins of Latin Love-Elegy* (Oxford 1938) 1 nn. 4–7, and his bibliography pp. 141–46, to which may be added G. Provasi, "Il problema dell' origine dell' elegia latina," *Riv FC* 15 (1937) 32–41; A. Guillemin, "Sur les origines de l'élégie latine" and "L'élément humain dans l'élégie latine," *REL* 17 (1939) 282–92, and 18 (1940) 95–111; E. Paludan, "The Development of the Latin Epigram," *ClMed* 4 (1941) 204–29; E. Burck, "Römische Wesenszüge der Augusteischen Liebeselegie," *Hermes* 80 (1952) 163–200.

has been indirectly demonstrated recently by S. Commager,[108] who has suggested the paradox that the essence of Catullus' subjectivity lies in his poetic objectivity. The entire question is one invented solely, it would seem, for scholarly dispute, and, though Latin subjective love-elegy does exist as an historical reality, its existence need not be determined by a pre-existing Greek counterpart, nor need Catullus be placed among or excluded from the originators of elegy by applying any such criterion. The second assumption that has no basis in fact is that a distinction was made by Catullus between elegy and epigram on the grounds of content and expansion. This assumption is partly connected with the first and may be illustrated by a common observation: it is often pointed out that c. 85 is a perfect epigram,[109] that c. 75 is a slightly expanded version, and that c. 76 has been further expanded and is a perfect elegy.[110] Attractive though this supposition may be, there is no indication that Catullus would have considered it valid: why did he (or an early editor) place c. 76 among his epigrams if it properly belonged among the longer elegiac poems 65–68? Much time has been spent hunting down the traces of epigram or epigrammatic themes in the Augustan elegists which might better have been spent considering the literary traditions. The following remarks will take no account either of subjectivity-objectivity or of content in trying to determine Catullus' place as an elegist. It will be argued that the distinction between epigram and elegy was based for Catullus entirely upon technicalities of vocabulary and style, technicalities which reflected the opposing literary traditions in which each group of poems was conceived and composed.

The question may be approached most easily by way of Propertius. Much has been written on the subject of Propertius' acknowledged debt to Callimachus and Philitas: only that part of the discussion which

---

[108] "Notes on Some Poems of Catullus," *HSCP* 70 (1965) 83–110.

[109] See Day, 107, and literature there cited.

[110] Wheeler (*AJP* [1915] 165–66): "This incomparable poem is, therefore, a true elegy of the subjective-erotic type." The idea that elegy developed from epigram is completely hypothetical and without solid evidence (cf. the remarks of Wheeler, *Catullus and the Traditions*, 181: "But as we have just seen, he was the first, so far as we know, to develop such epigrams into elegies. We see him feeling his way from one *genre* into another, a *genre* that is richer in every way . . .").

centers on the question of elements of a subjective elegy in these two Alexandrians need concern us here, and only briefly, because our purpose is to show that the false assumption of a subjective elegy has obscured the real issue. Day has summarized and discussed the evidence and main theories concerning Propertius' (and Ovid's) debt to Callimachus and Philitas; and though he concludes that Propertius need not be understood to have set up the two Alexandrians as his models for a subjective love-elegy, he nevertheless supplies no alternative explanation as to why Propertius acknowledged them so frankly as his models and masters.[111] It is necessary only to examine the passages in which Propertius mentions Philitas or Callimachus to see that evidence for a subjective elegy is lacking: the fact is that there is no mention by Propertius of any debt owed his two models for subject matter or content. A few passages will serve to show what he considered his debt to be:

a) sed neque Phlegraeos Iovis Enceladique tumultus
      intonet angusto pectore Callimachus,
  nec mea conveniunt duro praecordia versu
      Caesaris in Phrygios condere nomen avos. (2.1.39–42)

b) tu satius memorem Musis imitere Philitan
      et non inflati somnia Callimachi. (2.34.31–32, text doubtful)

c) talia Calliope, lymphis a fonte petitis
      ora Philitea nostra rigavit aqua. (3.3.51–52)

d) inter Callimachi sat erit placuisse libellos
      et cecinisse modis, Coe poeta, tuis. (3.9.43–44)

The first observation to be made from these representative passages is that Propertius considered himself a disciple of Callimachus and Philitas in his refusal to write epic. Too often, however, the significance of his *recusatio* has been limited to mere subject matter or content. When Propertius in (a) alludes to Callimachus himself (βροντᾶν οὐκ ἐμόν, ἀλλὰ Διός, *Aetia*, fr. 1.20 Pf.), he implies far more than content. (C) concludes the long testimony of indebtedness that begins with a

111 Day, 14–19 (on Philitas) and 26–36 (on Callimachus). The evidence and the citations from Prop. and Ovid are conveniently collected here. See also Barber's introduction to Butler and Barber, *The Elegies of Propertius* (Oxford 1933) xxxviii–xliv.

reference to Ennius and the fountain from which he drank,[112] and continues with the poet's being held back from the Ennian stream by Apollo and Calliope. (D) is from a *recusatio* addressed to Maecenas, a refusal to enter upon a *scribendi tam vastum aequor* (3.9.3). Far more is implied by these (and other) passages than is at first apparent: had Propertius simply wished to refuse to have anything to do with epic themes and verse, there would have been no need to invoke Philitas and Callimachus—other poets would have served as well; had he wished to acknowledge a debt of subject matter or of precedent for subjective love-elegy, there was no need to confuse the issue by bringing up so insistently the matter of epic; had the question not been one of a poetic doctrine or creed, there was no need to allude repeatedly to the prologue of the *Aetia*.

The terms and images in which Propertius writes all have their origins or parallels in Catullus. Apollo's refusal to let Propertius drink Ennian waters is obviously a reference to annalistic epic, the same sort which became, until Virgil, the only Roman epic, a well-trodden path: Catullus refused it when he paid his vow by burning, in neoteric verse, the *Annales Volusi, cacata carta* (c. 36). In c. 95 Catullus employed the Callimachean image of the two streams, the one muddy, swollen, and turbulent, the other clear:[113] the same image occurs in Propertius' *recusatio* to Maecenas (3.9.3) and elsewhere (as in Apollo's final words in 3.3.24, *medio maxima turba mari est*). For Propertius, Callimachus is *non inflatus* and speaks *angusto pectore*; for Catullus, Antimachus (in whom the many delight, 95[b].2) is *tumidus*; for Callimachus, Antimachus' poem was a παχὺ γράμμα καὶ οὐ τορόν (frg. 398 Pf.). Such terms in such contexts can refer but to one thing: not to content, not to a simple question of epic versus shorter verse, not to a precedent for subjective love-elegy, but to style, a style evolved to meet the demands of a new poetic creed. Only in such a way can the relationship between Propertius (and the other Augustan elegists) and Catullus be seen. The

---

[112] Ennius' well-known dream is itself a reference to and a denial of Callimachus' prologue to the *Aetia*: see Clausen, 185–87.

[113] For the significance of the Satrachus and the Po and their connection with the waters in Call. *Hymn II*, see Clausen, 188–91; the Satrachus is an allusion to Parthenius as well.

New Poets were the first to be introduced to Callimachus and the first
to have accepted his poetic doctrine; the Augustans, separated from the
neoterics by a generation, obviously acknowledged the same masters.
In the intervening generation, however, an evolution of the uses to
which Callimachean principles were put produced poetry as diversified
as Virgil's *Eclogues*, *Georgics*, and *Aeneid*, Horace's *Odes*, and Augustan
elegy; it is a small wonder then that Propertius' poetry differs so from
that of Catullus and that all attempts to find the beginnings of subjective love-elegy in Catullus end in such contradiction and confusion.
The relationship, however, as sketched above, is obvious. The neoterics
and the Augustans stand clearly in the same tradition, the tradition of
Alexandrian and Callimachean poetry at Rome, united and given a
common purpose by the desire to write poetry which was elegant,
polished, urbane, and not for the eyes of the mass; the common effort
was to create a Latin style which, regardless of genre or content, would
be faithful to the principles of Alexandrian verse.[114]

The Roman poets and critics who disagreed and even contradicted
themselves on the question of whether Catullus was an elegist no doubt
did so for a good reason. Catullus, as a neoteric developing a style of
vocabulary and verse technique in accordance with Callimachean
principles, was certainly a major figure in the same tradition in which
Propertius and the other Augustans wrote. This, however, is true only
to a certain extent: it has been demonstrated that Catullus is a neoteric
only in the polymetrics and longer poems, but that neoteric elements,
whether of vocabulary or other technical features, are surprisingly rare
in the epigrams 69–116. A reason and explanation for these observations have been advanced and may explain the doubt felt even by the
ancients of the next generation about Catullus' place in elegy. He
employed the pentameter couplet in two distinct groups of poems: the
neoteric elegies 65–68 are, stylistically, undoubtedly a precedent for
later elegy; the epigrams proper, however, stand at the end of a separate

---

[114] A good idea of the common principles behind neoteric and Augustan poetry can
be had from S. Commager, *The Odes of Horace* (1962) chapter I: "Literary Conventions
and Stylistic Criticism in the Augustan Age," esp. 31–41. A sampling of the key passages
for the importance of the idea λεπτός *-tenuis-gracilis-deductum* versus παχύς *-tumidus-pinguis*
is given in pp. 36–39. The point has been made so often that it need not be labored here.

and opposed tradition and contain little which represents the work of a neoteric poet. C. 76, frequently cited by modern critics as an early example (along with c. 68) of perfected subjective love-elegy, is, on the contrary, perhaps the best example among all the epigrams proper of the pre-neoteric tradition of epigram and for this reason has been cited equally frequently as an example of the stylistic roughness of Catullus' distichs. Day is right when he concludes that "Catullus, then, in various respects anticipated, if he did not occasion, the perfected love-elegy of the Augustans, and he may well have been responsible for the direction in which later elegy was to proceed,"[115] but he is wrong to find the reasons for this in Catullus' themes and in the content of his poetry. Catullus anticipated later elegy in his longer poems, including 65–68, and in his polymetrics, but the anticipation was in style, in vocabulary and verse technique. Only the epigrams proper remained outside this stylistic revolution and looked backwards rather than forwards.

The generation which separates the New Poets from the Augustans also separates the discovery of Callimachus from the full realization of the implications and possibilities of that discovery. The neoterics had made only a start: the epyllion, the masterwork required of every neoteric (Cinna's *Zmyrna*, Calvus' *Io*, Valerius Cato's *Lydia*, Catullus' *Peleus and Thetis*), was afterwards practised only by belated neoterics (by the poets of the *Ciris* and *Culex*) or in a somewhat disguised form (as by Virgil in the Aristaeus episode in G. IV). Callimachean principles were turned to other forms of verse, and language and meter were further refined. The pre-neoteric tradition of epigram was finally abandoned by serious poets and the pentameter couplet devoted solely to the new style. There can be no doubt that Catullus' neoteric elegiacs suggested the direction and showed, somewhat roughly, how the vocabulary and technique developed by the neoterics might be applied to the couplet. There is every reason to believe, as T. Frank suggested,[116] that Gallus, the friend of Virgil and disciple of Parthenius,

---

[115] P. III.

[116] *Catullus and Horace* (New York 1928) 61, though he concludes, "Catullus was of course, though unconsciously, the originator." The main evidence is that Gallus precedes

was responsible for the completed creation of the new genre, but it is certain that he must have used Catullus' neoteric elegiacs, not the epigrams proper (and not c. 76), as his starting point and guide. The line of continuity, however, was unbroken, but this continuity was one of style, not of theme, content, or even of genre. It was by style alone that the Latin poets claimed descent from, and acknowledged indebtedness to, the line of their predecessors and masters.

Prop., Tib., and Ovid in what appears to have become the standard catalogue (Quint. 10.1.93, Diomedes I.484 Keil; also Ovid, *Tr.* 4.10.51–54 and *Ars. Am.* 3.333–34).

POSTSCRIPT

One may ask at this point whether Catullus has not been "simply classi-
fied and labelled like some figure in a literary museum." Vocabulary,
metrical features, and other stylistic criteria have been collected,
described, and arranged; the outlines of a literary history of Republican
poetry have been suggested; but little has been said directly (though I
hope something has been implied) of Catullus the poet, or of his
poems, or of the significance of the neoterics. The purpose of this
study was to present, by means of the analysis of stylistic features alone,
a coherent picture of the sort of poems Catullus wrote, to suggest
explanations for the diversity of his poems, to examine the validity of
the grouping of the poems as we have them, and finally to understand
the poems as Catullus wrote them—that is, to sense the difference, in an
ancient literature in a dead language, between a limerick and a sonnet.

It may be objected, too, that we have once again "split" Catullus. To
this we can answer that it is the poetry rather than the poet that has
been split. The poetic personality remains intact: there is no learned and
mannered Catullus opposed to one passionate and lyric, resulting from
this analysis. At the risk of repetition, we may summarize here what, it
is hoped, has been accomplished in these pages, and suggest how
Catullus may be read and studied as the result.

The great moments in Latin poetry are the result of the combination
of the historical situation (in its widest sense), a fresh source of literary
inspiration, and an individual genius. Virgil and Horace, for instance,
thoroughly (and honestly) reacted to the preceding hundred years of
political horror and to the unreal promise of Augustan peace to produce poetry that was not political, not propaganda, but that cannot be
understood without an awareness of the chaos and promise of their
times. The *pax Augusta* coincided with the re-evaluation of Catullus and
neoteric poetry; it was finally possible for a Roman poet of genius to
turn the subtle possibilities of poetic technique, initiated by Ennius and

refined by the conscious artistic awareness of the neoterics, to the expression of the promise of hope and the horror of chaos: poetry had become Roman.

Of the three elements we have generalized, the least understood is the literary: the nineteenth century, in regarding Virgil and Horace primarily as Augustan propagandists, ignored it completely; current literary criticism too often substitutes its own terms (created by and valid for a very different literature) for the study and recovery of the Roman traditions. To understand the contribution of the neoterics, one need only consider Catullus' epigrams 69–116. The tradition they are a part of is relatively artless, the possibilities for poetic expression limited and confined. J. P. Elder has asked "why Catullus chose to entrust one mood, one set of feelings, one idea, to one metrical form, and others to other forms."[1] It is hoped that this study has provided the basis for an answer. If one considers two invective poems, one polymetric and one epigram, the difference should now be apparent: literary wit, sophistication, and innuendo will characterize the polymetric, while direct and coarse attack will be the natural inheritance of the epigram. Or, for example, consider the difference between such Lesbia poems as c. 75 (*Huc est mens deducta tua mea, Lesbia, culpa*) and c. 8 (*Miser Catulle, desinas ineptire*): the epigram is confined, tight, and focuses on a circumscribed emotion, whereas the polymetric, within an artistically tight form, seems to suggest continually changing and expanding possibilities of mood and expression. I do not wish to suggest that the epigrams are less effective: what they lack in expressiveness they gain by directness.

Two poems, cc. 76 and 11, may be considered briefly. C. 76, as discussed above, is the fullest expression of the natively Roman concept of political alliance, employed by Catullus (and perhaps his alone) as the controlling image, though only in the epigrams, for his affair with

---

[1] *HSCP* 60 (1951) 111; he continues, "The sane starting point in this investigation is surely Wilamowitz' comment that Catullus did not ask whether the "rules" allowed this metre or that one. But is it not a matter that transcends mere metre? Are there any notable artistic differences between the poems written in, say hendecasyllables and those in elegiacs, differences in techniques so marked that one may conclude that, when Catullus intuitively selected this or that metre as the vehicle for his self-expression, he subconsciously selected a number of other technical elements which went automatically along with the metre?"

Lesbia. To this (it is to be remembered that the first five lines of the poem thus speak directly, through the image, of his affair with Lesbia) is added a prayer, forming a second and concluding part to the poem:

> o di, si vestrum est misereri, aut si quibus umquam
> extremam iam ipsa in morte tulistis opem,
> me miserum aspicite et, si vitam puriter egi,
> eripite hanc pestem perniciemque mihi . . .
>
> o di, reddite mi hoc pro pietate mea. (76.17-20, 26)

The prayer follows naturally from the opening insistence on the poet's *pietas*, and yet there is an even greater unity which has never been remarked upon: the plea is essentially Roman and practical, just as is Catullus' concept, and its presentation in this poem, of his love for Lesbia, his *amicitia*. This becomes apparent only when the literary prayer form (essentially a Greek development, from Homer to Hellenistic poetry) in Catullus is compared. The literary form has been discussed above: cult, sites, and epithets are a natural and essential part of this form (natural of course in Greek religion, and essential in any literary development of Greek prayer), but such prayers in Catullus are found only in the polymetrics or longer poems. The prayer in c. 76 calls upon no specific deity, mentions no cult, site, or epithet, and contains only the specific plea based on the reminder (though expressed in the usual Roman conditional clauses) that the request has precedent, is within the gods' power, and that the recipient is worthy (*pro pietate mea*). Many stylistic features of c. 76 have been discussed in the previous pages (e.g., the violation of Hermann's Bridge in the first line, and the numerous elisions); other unpoetical words and phrases can be collected (as the phrases *verum hoc qua lubet efficias, sive id non pote sive pote, quod non potis est*). At every level the poem is Roman, and at every point seems foreign to the literary standards of the succeeding generation (and, we need hardly add, to the standards of Catullus' own polymetrics and longer poems). The poem develops directly, the emotion is concentrated and linear, and in this lies its power. The question of its being an epigram or an elegy can only be answered (if indeed it need now be asked) by consideration of the validity of these terms for

Catullus: it is a part of native, pre-neoteric tradition (stylistically, in the concepts—*amicitia*, the Roman prayer—it employs, and in the concentrated directness of its emotion), a tradition we may label epigram for convenience so long as we use the term to suggest the tradition rather than to classify a form or genre.

C. 11 is an expression of the same emotional situation, yet might easily be the work of a different poet at a different time. Eleven lines of geographical excursus follow the address to *Furi et Aureli, comites Catulli*: the form, however, is an extension of the literary (Greek) prayer (as discussed above). The Indians and the "Eastern wave" are followed by the epic peoples of the distant world and the mention of the Alexandrian Nile (2–8), but then the effect of the purely literary (and, some would say, purely ornamental) is broken by the shift to the Roman world, and the *Caesaris monimenta magni* (9–12) bring the long movement back to Catullus and the *non bona dicta* which occupy the following stanza (17–20)—sudden, harsh, and impetuous, but falling just short of crude invective. The Sapphic image of the final stanza (21–24) is a third miniature movement of quiet and pathetic delicacy.[2] No epigram (even c. 76) can parallel the fluidity, the dramatic and extreme shifts of tone and mood, and the changing suggestiveness of this short poem, all of which was made possible only by the literary moment of Catullus' time and circle: in one poem are united the solidity of early Roman epic, Alexandrian form and technique, neoteric invective, and the capability (finally realized) of writing a Latin stanza with the light delicacy of Greek lyric.

Some of the technical means contributing to this new maturity of Latin poetry have been discussed in detail above. Much more could (and should) be said about the individual genius of Catullus, in order to understand the use to which every poetic possibility was put, for this was his achievement and contribution. We have remarked continually on neoteric elements in certain epigrams, that, particularly to convey a tone of effeminacy or homosexuality, certain Gellius epigrams

[2] The structure of the poem should be compared with c. 58, which reverses the movement: first the lover's repetition of the name and the statement, lyrical in its simplicity, of his love; then the abrupt and shocking *nunc in quadriviis et angiportis / glubit*; then the epic finale *magnanimi Remi nepotes*.

or the long Juventius epigram are experiments in the language and style of the polymetrics; but for the most part Catullus retained the character of pre-neoteric epigram for its own effectiveness, whether for coarse invective, or to give direct and immediate expression to his love, or for the sacral and ritual statement of grief at his brother's death. There are many reasons why Catullus chose the epigrammatic form (and all that the tradition involved) for certain poems, but through style and content he sought in his epigrams the immediacy of a relatively unsophisticated tradition, one which we have (unfortunately, for want of a better word) often called unpoetic.

It was neoteric poetry, however, which offered the individual genius of the poet its widest range of expression, for it was not until the neoterics that poetry was made to afford the means of giving abstract literary expression to the most compelling inner necessities of an individual. It is now recognized that Ariadne is an expression of Catullus' own experience, just as is Laodamia; and I would add, perhaps its fullest expression. I have discussed elsewhere the personal implications of c. 45 and the figures of Septimius and Acme.[3] But the finest example of what neoteric poetry meant for Catullus is again c. 11. Its geographical excursus is far from ornamental, and in itself suggests poetry as a means for escape, the means to forget his love, and, at the same time, as a means to see it most clearly and truly, to give an abstract universality to a personal chaos. The final two stanzas of the poem tell more about Catullus, his love and his poetry, than any amount of paraphrase can ever hope to, and are in themselves the explanation of the preceding four stanzas: first the reality of the situation, direct but explaining nothing, Lesbia *nullum amans vere, sed identidem omnium | ilia rumpens;* and then the poetic abstraction, ancient and therefore suggestive of all experience, the creation of the new poetry especially for the individual of depth and genius:

> nec meum respectet, ut ante, amorem,
> qui illius culpa cecidit velut prati
> ultimi flos, praetereunte postquam
> tactus aratro est.

[3] *CP* 90 (1965) 256–59.

The point, however, has been sufficiently suggested. The neoterics inherited epigram as the only possibility for short personal poems, a tradition of limited and constricting possibilities, however direct and immediate. The fresh source of poetic expression was provided by Parthenius at a time when Roman society had finally found room for a circle of wit and sophisticated elegance with the leisure necessary for poetry to become more than the pastime of aristocratic dilettantes. The historical accident of the survival and discovery of the single Verona manuscript of the poems of Catullus is noticed by almost every scholar. Seldom considered, if ever, is the accident of history, literature, and individual which led to the creation of the poems themselves.

SELECTED BIBLIOGRAPHY

Most, though not all, of the works cited in the text have been included here. Other works are included only when they have been of particular help or are of special importance. Many of these studies contain useful bibliographies, and thus it has not been felt necessary to include more complete references either here or in the notes to the text. Grammars, literary histories, handbooks, etc., are, with a few exceptions, not listed. General studies of Catullus, criticisms, editions and commentaries, etc., are restricted to those of particular relevance; studies of the literary language (such as most of the work of Marouzeau) have been similarly restricted. In addition to Marouzeau's *L'Année Philologique*, important bibliographies for Catullan scholarship of this century are:

Schulze, K. P., "Bericht über die Literatur zu Catullus für die Jahre 1905–1920," *Bursian's Jahresb.* 183 (1920) 1–47.

Braga, D., "Catullo (1938–1948)," *Doxa* 3 (1950) 161–90.

Leon, H. J., "A Quarter Century of Catullan Scholarship (1934–1959)," *CW* 53 (1960) 104–13, 141–48, 173–80, 281–82.

Levens, R. G. C., in M. Platnauer's *Fifty Years of Classical Scholarship* (Oxford 1954) 284–305.

Editions and Commentaries:

The text of Catullus used for this study has been that of R. A. B. Mynors, *C. Valerii Catulli Carmina* (Oxford 1960); quotations of Catullus, however, often depart somewhat from Mynors' text. Other editions and commentaries of particular interest referred to are:

Baehrens, A. (nova editio a K. P. Schulze curata), *Catulli Veronensis Liber* (Lipsiae 1893).

Ellis, R., *Catulli Veronensis Liber*² (Oxford 1878).

——— *A Commentary on Catullus*² (Oxford 1889).

——— *Catulli Carmina* (Oxford 1904).

Fordyce, C. J., *Catullus* (Oxford 1961).

Friedrich, G., *Catulli Veronensis Liber* (Leipzig 1908).

Kroll, W., *C. Valerius Catullus*² (Leipzig 1929).

Merrill, E. T., *Catullus* (Boston 1893).

Munro, H. A. J., *Criticisms and Elucidations of Catullus* (Cambridge 1878).

Riese, A., *Die Gedichte des Catullus* (Leipzig 1884).

Schuster, M., and Eisenhut, W., *Catulli Veronensis Liber* (Lipsiae 1958).

Fragments of early Latin poetry are cited from:

Morel, W., *Fragmenta Poetarum Latinorum* (Lipsiae 1927).

Ribbeck, O., *Tragicorum Romanorum Fragmenta*³ (Lipsiae 1897).

Selected Bibliography

Vahlen, J., *Ennianae Poesis Reliquiae*[2] (Lipsiae 1903).
The editions of other authors cited are noted where necessary.

General:

Alfonsi, L., "Catullo Elegiaco," *Gedenkschrift für Georg Rohde* (Tübingen 1961) 9–21.

ALL = *Archiv für Lateinische Lexikographie und Grammatik*, herausgegeben von E. Wölfflin (Leipzig 1884–1908).

Axelson, B., *Unpoetische Wörter, Ein Beitrag zur Kenntnis der Lateinischen Dichtersprache*, Skrifter Utgivna av Vetenskaps-Societeten i Lund, 29 (1945).

Barber, E. A.: see Butler, H. E.

Bardon, H., *La Littérature Latine Inconnue* I (Paris 1952) [=Bardon].

———— *L'Art de la Composition chez Catulle* (Paris 1943).

———— "Catulle et ses modèles poétiques de la langue latine," *Latomus* 16 (1957) 614–27.

Bayet, J., "Catulle, la Grèce et Rome," in *L'Influence Grecque sur la Poésie Latine de Catulle à Ovide* (Entretiens II 1956, Fondation Hardt) 3–55.

Buecheler, F., "Pompejanisch-Römisch-Alexandrinishes," *RhM* 38 (1883) 474–76.

———— *Carmina Latina Epigraphica* I and II (Lipsiae 1895 and 1897).

Burck, E., "Römische Wesenszüge der Augusteischen Liebeselegie," *Hermes* 80 (1952) 163–200.

Butler, H. E., and Barber, E. A., *The Elegies of Propertius* (Oxford 1933).

Clarke, M. L., "The Hexameter in Greek Elegiacs," *CR* 5 (1955) 18.

Clausen, W., "Callimachus and Latin Poetry," *GRBS* 5 (1964) 181–96.

Clement, W. K., "The Use of *enim* in Plautus and Terence," *AJP* 18 (1897) 402–15.

Commager, S., *The Odes of Horace* (New Haven 1962): chap. I, "Literary Conventions and Stylistic Criticism in the Augustan Age."

———— "Notes on Some Poems of Catullus," *HSCP* 70 (1965) 83–110.

Conrad, C., "Traditional Patterns of Word Order in Latin Epic from Ennius to Vergil," *HSCP* 69 (1965) 195–258.

Cooper, F. T., *Word Formation in the Roman Sermo Plebeius* (Diss., New York 1895).

Coulter, C. C., "Compound Adjectives in Early Latin Poetry," *TAPA* 47 (1916) 153–72.

Day, A. A., *The Origins of Latin Love-Elegy* (Oxford 1938).

Durham, D. B., "Mimnermus and Propertius," *AJP* 37 (1916) 194–205.

Elder, J. P., "Notes on Some Conscious and Subconscious Elements in Catullus' Poetry," *HSCP* 60 (1951) 101–36.

Elmer, H. C., "*Que, et, atque* in the Inscriptions of the Republic, in Terence, and in Cato," *AJP* 8 (1887) 292–328.

Ernout, A., *RevPhil* 21 (1947) 55–70 (review of Axelson, *Unpoetische Wörter*).

Ferrero, L., *Interpretazione di Catullo* (Torino 1955).

Fraenkel, E., "Kallimachos und Catull," *Gnomon* 5 (1929) 265–8.

———— *Elementi Plautini in Plauto* (Firenze 1960).

Frank, T., *Catullus and Horace* (New York 1928).

Glenn, J. C., "Compounds in Augustan Elegy and Epic," *CW* 29 (1936) 65–69, 73–77.

Goold, G. P., "A New Text of Catullus," *Phoenix* 12 (1958) 93–116.

Goossens, R., "Les 'Centaures' de Laevius," *Latomus* 10 (1951) 419–24.

Gow, A. S. F., "Diminutives in Augustan Poetry," *CQ* 26 (1932) 150–57.

—— and Page, D. L., *The Greek Anthology: Hellenistic Epigrams* I and II (Cambridge 1965).

Guillemin, A., "Sur les origines de l'élégie latine," *RevPhil* 17 (1939) 282–92.

—— "L'élément humain dans l'élégie latine," *RevPhil* 18 (1940) 95–111.

Harder, F., "*E* und *Ex* vor Consonanten in den Fragmenten der ältern römischen Poesie," *Fleck. J. Suppl.* 141 (1890) 771–77.

Havelock, E. A., *The Lyric Genius of Catullus* (Oxford 1939).

Herescu, N., *Catullo* (Rome 1943).

Heusch, H., *Das Archaische in der Sprache Catulls* (Bonn 1954).

Hezel, O., *Catull und das Griechische Epigramm*, Tübinger Beiträge zur Altertumswissenschaft 17 (1932).

Highet, G., *Poets in a Landscape* (New York 1957): chap. I, "Catullus."

Hofmann, J. B., *Lateinische Umgangssprache*³ (Heidelberg 1951).

Horváth, I. K., "Catulli Veronensis Liber," *Acta Antiqua* 14 (1966) 141–73.

Housman, A. E., "*ΑΙΟΣ* and *ΕΙΟΣ* in Latin Poetry," *JP* 33 (1914) 54–75.

Jacoby, F., "Zur Entstehung der Römischen Elegie," *RhM* 60 (1905) 38–105.

Kent, R. G.: see Sturtevant, E. H.

Kroll, W., *Studien zum Verständnis der römischen Literatur* (Stuttgart 1924).

—— "Die Sprache des Sallust," *Glotta* 15 (1927) 280–305.

de Labriolle, P., "L'emploi du diminutif chez Catulle," *RevPhil* 29 (1905) 277–88

La Penna, A., "Problemi di Stile Catulliano," *Maia* 8 (1956) 141–60.

La Ville de Mirmont, H. de, *Étude Biographique et Littéraire sur le Poète Laevius* (Bibliothèque des Universités du Midi 1900).

Lease, E. B., "On the Use of *Neque* and *Nec* in Silver Latin," *CR* 16 (1902) 212–14.

—— "Livy's Use of *Neque* and *Neve* with an Imperative or Subjunctive," *CP* 3 (1908) 302–15.

Leo, F., "Die Römische Poesie in der Sullanischen Zeit," *Hermes* 49 (1914) 161–95.

Leumann, M., "Die lateinische Dichtersprache," *MusHelv* 4 (1947) 116–39.

Lieberg, G., "L'ordinamento ed i reciproci rapporti dei carmi maggiori di Catullo," *RivFC* 36 (1958) 23–47.

Lindsay, R. J. M., "The Chronology of Catullus' Life," *CP* 43 (1948) 42–4.

Löfstedt, E., *Philologischer Kommentar zur Peregrinatio Aetheriae* (Uppsala 1936) [=Löfstedt, *PA*].

—— *Syntactica, Studien und Beiträge zur historischen Syntax des Lateins* I² and II (Lund 1942 and 1933).

Maas, P., "The Chronology of the Poems of Catullus," *CQ* 36 (1942) 79–82.

—— *Greek Metre* (Oxford 1962).

Marmorale, E., *L'Ultimo Catullo*² (Napoli 1957).

Marouzeau, J., "Pour mieux comprendre les textes latins," *RevPhil* 45 (1921) 149–93.

―――― "Essai sur la Stylistique du Mot," *REL* 10 (1932) 336–72.

Norden, E., *Aeneis Buch VI*[4] (Stuttgart 1957).

―――― Gercke-Norden, *Einleitung in die Altertumswissenschaft* I, 4.Heft (Leipzig 1923).

Otto, A., *Die Sprichwörter und sprichwörtlichen Redensarten der Römer* (Leipzig 1890).

Paludan, E., "The Development of the Latin Epigram," *ClMed* 4 (1941) 204–29.

Paratore, E., "Osservazioni sui rapporti fra Catullo e gli epigrammisti dell' *Antologia*," *Miscellanea di Studi Alessandrini in memoria di Augusto Rostagni* (Torino 1963) 562–87.

Patzer, H., "Zum Sprachstil des neoterischen Hexameters," *MusHelv* 12 (1955) 77–95.

Pfeiffer, R., "A Fragment of Parthenius' *Arete*," *CQ* 37 (1943) 23–32.

―――― *Callimachus* I and II (Oxford 1949 and 1953).

Platnauer, M., "Elision of *Atque* in Roman Poetry," *CQ* 42 (1948) 91–93.

―――― *Latin Elegiac Verse; a Study of the Metrical Usages of Tibullus, Propertius, and Ovid* (Cambridge 1951).

Platner, S. B., "Diminutives in Catullus," *AJP* 16 (1895) 186–202.

Provasi, G., "Il problema dell' origine dell' elegia latina," *RivFC* 15 (1937) 32–41.

Putnam, M. C. J., "The Art of Catullus 64," *HSCP* 65 (1961) 165–205.

Quinn, K., *The Catullan Revolution* (Melbourne 1959).

Reitzenstein, R., "Epigramm," Pauly-Wissowa *RE* 6 (1909) 71–111.

Richmond, J. A., "A Note on the Elision of final ĕ in certain Particles used by Latin Poets," *Glotta* 43 (1965) 78–101.

Ronconi, A., *Studi Catulliani* (Bari 1953).

Rostagni, A., "Parthenio di Nicea," *Atti di R. Acc. delle Scienze di Torino* 86 (1933) II 497–545.

―――― *Storia della Letteratura Latina* I (Torino 1949).

Rothstein, M., *Die Elegien des Sextus Propertius* (Berlin 1898).

―――― "Catull und Lesbia," *Philologus* 78 (1922) 1–34.

Rudd, W. J. N., "Libertas and Facetus," *Mnemos.* 10 (1957) 319–36.

Salvatore, A., "Rapporti tra nugae e carmina docta nel canzoniere catulliano," *Latomus* 12 (1953) 418–31.

Schnelle, I., "Untersuchungen zu Catulls dichterischer Form," *Philologus* Supplementband 25, Heft 3 (1933).

Schulze, K. P., "Die Sprache Catulls," *Bursian's Jahresb.* 183 (1920) 47–72.

Sedgwick, W. B., "Catullus' Elegiacs," *Mnemos.* 3 (1950) 64–69.

Shackleton Bailey, D. R., *Propertiana* (Cambridge 1956).

Sogliano, A., *Not. d. Scavi* (1883) 52–53.

Sturtevant, E. H., and Kent, R. G., "Elision and Hiatus in Latin Prose and Verse," *TAPA* 46 (1915) 129–55.

Svennung, J., *Catulls Bildersprache I*, Uppsala Universitets Årsskrift 3, 1945.

Selected Bibliography

ThLL = *Thesaurus Linguae Latinae* (Lipsiae 1900–).

Tränkle, H., *Die Sprachkunst des Properz und die Tradition der Lateinischer Dichtersprache*, Hermes Einzeischriften 15 (1960).

Traglia, A., "Polimetria e Verba Laeviana," *Studi Class. e Orient.* 6 (1957) 82–108.

Wagenvoort, H., *Studies in Roman Literature, Culture and Religion* (Leiden, 1956): "Ludus Poeticus," 30–42.

Weinreich, Otto: *Die Distichen des Catulls* (Tübingen 1926).

West, D. A., "The Metre of Catullus' Elegiacs," *CQ* 7 (1957) 98–102.

Whatmough, J., *Poetic, Scientific, and other Forms of Discourse*, Sather Classical Lectures 29 (Berkeley 1956): chap. II, "Pudicus Poeta: Words and Things," 29–55.

Wheeler, A. L., "Erotic Teaching in Roman Elegy," *CP* 5 (1910) 440–50, and 6 (1911) 56–77.

——— "Catullus as an Elegist," *AJP* 36 (1915) 155–84.

——— *Catullus and the Traditions of Ancient Poetry*, Sather Classical Lectures 9 (Berkeley 1934).

Wilamowitz-Moellendorff, U. von, *Sappho und Simonides* (Berlin 1913): "Mimnermos und Properz," 276–304.

——— *Hellenistische Dichtung in der Zeit des Kallimachos* II (Berlin 1924): "Catulls hellenistische Gedichte," 277–310.

Wilkinson, L. P., "The Augustan Rules for Dactylic Verse," *CQ* 34 (1940) 30–43.

Zicàri, M., "Some Metrical and Prosodical Features of Catullus' Poetry," *Phoenix* 18 (1964) 193–205.

INDEX OF PASSAGES

Index of Passages

PLINY

Epist. 5.3:138n56

PROPERTIUS

STATIUS

TIBULLUS

VIRGIL

GENERAL INDEX

A!, 30, 64
A, ab, 47n94, 49n98
Aedituus, *see* Pre-neoteric epigram
Aerius/aereus, 60n131
Aestuosus, 162n105
Amicitia, 83–84, 80–95 *passim*
Anaphora, 97, 98, 99, 153
Antimachus, 166
Antipater of Sidon, 13, 142–143, 161
Apocolocyntosis, 120n13
Archias, 143, 161
-arum (-orum), pronunciation of, 126n29

Basium, 104–105
Bellus, 110–111
Beneficium (benefactum), 86
Benevolentia (bene velle), 86

Caelicola, 20, 21
Callimachus: adapted by Catullus, 150; and Ennius, 139; influence on Latin poetry, 152; influence on New Poets, 161–162, 167; observed Hermann's Bridge, 129; as precedent for Catullus, 67; spondaic lines in, 131; translated by Catullus, 20, 65, 68n158, 101, 152–153
Calvus, 13n19, 51
Catullus, ancient edition of, 7–8
Catulus, circle of, 142–143. *See also* Pre-neoteric epigram
Cicero: *Aratea* of, 134n48; *bene . . . beate* in, 31
Ciris, 13n19, 25n37, 40n78, 79, 102n241, 168
Compounds, in Laevius and Catullus contrasted. 159
Culex, 13n19, 30, 40n78, 102n241, 168
Cuniculosus, 99

Deliciae, 111
Diminutives, in Laevius and Catullus, contrasted, 158–159

Elegy, question of Roman origin of, 163–164
Elision, 118–128; frequency of in the poets, 119–120; frequency of in Catullus, 120–121; in pre-neoteric epigram, 145–146; expressive of emotion, 118–119, 127; at halfway point of pentameter, 123–128; of longs, 121; of long before short, 121, 127, 146, 148; of dactylic word before short, 121–122, 127; of cretics in *-m* before short, 127n31; of *-ē* before *-ĕ*, 119n7, 128n33
Ennius: and Callimachus, 139; distichs of, 116, 117, 137–139; echoed by Catullus, 103, 104; known to Catullus, 30; as source of Catullus, 28–29
Epigram, *see* Pre-neoteric epigram
Epigrams of Catullus: distinct from polymetrics and longer poems, 17, 22, 24, 26, 28, 33, 34, 43, 50–51, 52–53, 59, 63, 65, 67, 70, 72, 78, 79, 91, 94, 96, 100, 102; tradition of, 25, 46, 49, 122, 125, 128, 130, 131, 137, 145, 147, 151, 155, 160, 161, 173–174; neoteric elements in, 48, 58, 63, 103, 105, 110–111, 131, 174

Fides, 85
Foedus, 84–85

Gallus, 52, 163, 168
Genitor, 103
Geography, in Catullus, 21, 29, 79n187, 173, 174; excursus similar to prayer (hymn) form, 97; excursus used for parody, 98–99